Asynchronous Android Programming

Second Edition

Unlock the power of multi-core mobile devices to build responsive and reactive Android applications

Helder Vasconcelos

PUBLISHING

BIRMINGHAM - MUMBAI

Asynchronous Android Programming

Second Edition

First published: July 2016

Production reference: 1260716

Published by Packt Publishing Ltd.
Livery Place
35 Livery Street
Birmingham B3 2PB, UK.

ISBN 978-1-78588-324-8

www.packtpub.com

Credits

Author
Helder Vasconcelos

Reviewer
Gavin Matthews

Commissioning Editor
Edward Gordon

Acquisition Editor
Indrajit Das

Content Development Editor
Siddhesh Salvi

Technical Editor
Danish Shaikh

Copy Editor
Vibha Shukla

Project Coordinator
Nidhi Joshi

Proofreader
Safis Editing

Indexer
Mariammal Chettiyar

Graphics
Disha Haria

Production Coordinator
Arvindkumar Gupta

Cover Work
Arvindkumar Gupta

About the Author

Helder Vasconcelos is a Portuguese Software Engineer based on Dublin, Ireland, with more than 10 years of experience designing and developing real-time/multithreaded Java and C++ applications for the telecommunications and aviation industries. Apart from his day-to-day job, he occupies his spare time building native Android applications for Bearstouch Software and other third-party companies.

He graduated with a degree in Electronic and Telecommunications Engineering from the University of Aveiro in January 2006. During his career, he has worked as a Software Engineer for companies such as PT Inovação (Portugal), Airtel ATN (Dublin, Ireland) and Axway (Dublin, Ireland). You can find Hélder on LinkedIn at (`https://ie.linkedin.com/in/heldervasc/en`) or on his website at (`http://hvasconcelos.github.io`).

I would like to sincerely thanks all technical reviewers, but especially Gavin. I really appreciate your invaluable feedback and commit that shaped the quality of the book. A special thanks to my awesome wife Tania for encourage me when the lack of motivation was killing my productivity. It would not have been possible without your precious support. Thanks also to my parents and family for their awesome effort in my education. Additionally, I would like to thank my friends, colleagues, clients, and teachers for helping me to shape and improve my skills and perspectives during my career.

About the Reviewer

Gavin Matthews is a veteran software engineer specializing in enterprise scale B2B, MFT and EFSS systems.

www.PacktPub.com

eBooks, discount offers, and more

Did you know that Packt offers eBook versions of every book published, with PDF and ePub files available? You can upgrade to the eBook version at www.PacktPub.com and as a print book customer, you are entitled to a discount on the eBook copy. Get in touch with us at customercare@packtpub.com for more details.

At www.PacktPub.com, you can also read a collection of free technical articles, sign up for a range of free newsletters and receive exclusive discounts and offers on Packt books and eBooks.

https://www2.packtpub.com/books/subscription/packtlib

Do you need instant solutions to your IT questions? PacktLib is Packt's online digital book library. Here, you can search, access, and read Packt's entire library of books.

Why subscribe?

- Fully searchable across every book published by Packt
- Copy and paste, print, and bookmark content
- On demand and accessible via a web browser

Table of Contents

Preface

Whether you are Android beginner developer or an Android seasoned programmer, this book will explore how to achieve efficient and reliable multithreaded Android applications.

We'll look at best asynchronous constructs and techniques, commonly used by Android Developer community, to execute computation intensive or blocking tasks off the main thread, keeping the UI responsive, telling the user how things are going, making sure we finish what we started, using those powerful multicore processors, and doing it all without wasting the battery.

By using the right asynchronous construct, much of the complexity is abstracted from the developer, making the application source code more readable and maintainable and less error prone.

Using step-by-step guidelines and code examples, you will learn how manage interactions between several threads and avoid concurrency and synchronization problems that might occur when two or more threads access a shared resource to complete a background job, to update the UI or retrieve the latest application data.

At the end of this journey you will know how build well-behaved applications with smooth, responsive user-interfaces that delight users with speedy results and data that's always fresh.

What this book covers

Chapter 1, *Asynchronous Programming in Android*, gives an overview of the Android process and thread model, and describes some of the challenges and benefits of concurrency in general, before discussing issues specific to Android.

Chapter 2, Performing Work with Looper, Handler and HandlerThread details the fundamental and related topics of `Handler`, `HandlerThread`, and `Looper`, and illustrates how they can be used to schedule tasks on the main thread, and to coordinate and communicate work between cooperating background threads.

Chapter 3, Exploring the AsyncTask, covers the most common concurrent construct of programming in Android. We learn how `AsyncTask` works, how to use it correctly, and how to avoid the common pitfalls that catch out even experienced developers.

Chapter 4, Exploring the Loader, introduces the `Loader` framework and tackles the important task of loading data asynchronously to keep the user interface responsive and glitch free.

Chapter 5, Interacting with Services, we explored the very powerful `Service` Android component, putting it to use to execute long-running background tasks with or without a configurable level of concurrency. This component gives us the means to perform background operations beyond the scope of a single `Activity` lifecycle and to ensure that our work is completed even if the user leaves the application.

Chapter 6, Scheduling Work with AlarmManager, introduces to us a system API that could be used to defer work or create periodic tasks. The scheduled task could wake up the device to complete the work or alert users to new content.

Chapter 7, Exploring the JobScheduler API, covers a job scheduling system API introduced with Android Lollipop that allows us to start background work when a set of device conditions, such as energy or network, are fulfilled.

Chapter 8, Interacting with the Network, we cover in detail `HttpUrlConnection` Android HTTP client. With the `HttpUrlConnection` HTTP client, we will create an asynchronous toolkit that is able to fetch JSON documents, XML or text from a remote server.

Chapter 9, Asynchronous Work on the Native layer, introduces the JNI interface, an Java standard interface that will allow us to execute concurrent tasks on native code (C/C++), interact with the Java code from the native layer or update the UI from the native code.

Chapter 10, Network Interactions with GCM, we will learn how to use the Google GCM to efficiently push and pull efficiently realtime messages from your server and how to schedule work with Google Play Services framework.

Chapter 11, Exploring Bus-based Communications, we will introduce to the reader the publish-subscribe messaging pattern and the Event Bus Library, a publish-subscribe implementation that allow us to deliver asynchronous messages between Android application components.

Chapter 12, *Asynchronous Programing with RxJava*, we will introduce RxJava, a library used to easily compose asynchronous and event-based tasks on Java by using observable data streams.

What you need for this book

To follow along and experiment with the examples, you will need a development computer with a Java 7 (or 8) SE Development Kit and the Android Software Development Kit Version 9 or above (you will need at least Version 21 to try all of the examples).

You will also need Android Studio IDE. The examples have been developed using Google's new Android Studio IDE and use its integrated build system, Gradle.

While you can run the examples using the emulator provided by the Android SDK, it is a poor substitute for the real thing. A physical Android device is a much faster and more pleasurable way to develop and test Android applications!

Many of the examples will work on a device running any version of Android since 2.3, GingerBread. Some examples demonstrate newer APIs and as a result, require a more recent Android version—up to Android 5, Lollipop.

Who this book is for

This book is for Android Developers who want to learn how to build multithreaded and reliable Android applications using high level and advanced asynchronous techniques and concepts.

They want to learn this technology because they want learn how to build efficient applications that are able to interact orderly with internal/external services and frameworks using Android standard constructs and APIs.

No prior knowledge of of concurrent and asynchronous programming is required. This book is also targeted towards Java experts who are new to Android.

Conventions

In this book, you will find a number of text styles that distinguish between different kinds of information. Here are some examples of these styles and an explanation of their meaning.

Code words in text, database table names, folder names, filenames, file extensions, pathnames, dummy URLs, user input, and Twitter handles are shown as follows: "We can include other contexts through the use of the `include` directive."

A block of code is set as follows:

```
[default]
exten => s,1,Dial(Zap/1|30)
exten => s,2,Voicemail(u100)
exten => s,102,Voicemail(b100)
exten => i,1,Voicemail(s0)
```

When we wish to draw your attention to a particular part of a code block, the relevant lines or items are set in bold:

```
[default]
exten => s,1,Dial(Zap/1|30)
exten => s,2,Voicemail(u100)
exten => s,102,Voicemail(b100)
exten => i,1,Voicemail(s0)
```

Any command-line input or output is written as follows:

```
# cp /usr/src/asterisk-addons/configs/cdr_mysql.conf.sample
   /etc/asterisk/cdr_mysql.conf
```

New terms and **important words** are shown in bold. Words that you see on the screen, for example, in menus or dialog boxes, appear in the text like this: "Clicking the **Next** button moves you to the next screen."

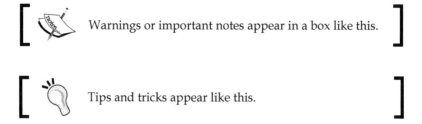

Warnings or important notes appear in a box like this.

Tips and tricks appear like this.

Reader feedback

Feedback from our readers is always welcome. Let us know what you think about this book—what you liked or disliked. Reader feedback is important for us as it helps us develop titles that you will really get the most out of.

To send us general feedback, simply e-mail `feedback@packtpub.com`, and mention the book's title in the subject of your message.

If there is a topic that you have expertise in and you are interested in either writing or contributing to a book, see our author guide at `www.packtpub.com/authors`.

Customer support

Now that you are the proud owner of a Packt book, we have a number of things to help you to get the most from your purchase.

Downloading the example code

You can download the example code files for this book from your account at `http://www.packtpub.com`. If you purchased this book elsewhere, you can visit `http://www.packtpub.com/support` and register to have the files e-mailed directly to you.

You can download the code files by following these steps:

1. Log in or register to our website using your e-mail address and password.
2. Hover the mouse pointer on the **SUPPORT** tab at the top.
3. Click on **Code Downloads & Errata**.
4. Enter the name of the book in the **Search** box.
5. Select the book for which you're looking to download the code files.
6. Choose from the drop-down menu where you purchased this book from.
7. Click on **Code Download**.

You can also download the code files by clicking on the **Code Files** button on the book's webpage at the Packt Publishing website. This page can be accessed by entering the book's name in the **Search** box. Please note that you need to be logged in to your Packt account.

Once the file is downloaded, please make sure that you unzip or extract the folder using the latest version of:

- WinRAR / 7-Zip for Windows
- Zipeg / iZip / UnRarX for Mac
- 7-Zip / PeaZip for Linux

The code bundle for the book is also hosted on GitHub at `https://github.com/PacktPublishing/Asynchronous-Android-Programming`. We also have other code bundles from our rich catalog of books and videos available at `https://github.com/PacktPublishing/`. Check them out!

Errata

Although we have taken every care to ensure the accuracy of our content, mistakes do happen. If you find a mistake in one of our books—maybe a mistake in the text or the code—we would be grateful if you could report this to us. By doing so, you can save other readers from frustration and help us improve subsequent versions of this book. If you find any errata, please report them by visiting `http://www.packtpub.com/submit-errata`, selecting your book, clicking on the **Errata Submission Form** link, and entering the details of your errata. Once your errata are verified, your submission will be accepted and the errata will be uploaded to our website or added to any list of existing errata under the Errata section of that title.

To view the previously submitted errata, go to `https://www.packtpub.com/books/content/support` and enter the name of the book in the search field. The required information will appear under the **Errata** section.

Piracy

Piracy of copyrighted material on the Internet is an ongoing problem across all media. At Packt, we take the protection of our copyright and licenses very seriously. If you come across any illegal copies of our works in any form on the Internet, please provide us with the location address or website name immediately so that we can pursue a remedy.

Please contact us at `copyright@packtpub.com` with a link to the suspected pirated material.

We appreciate your help in protecting our authors and our ability to bring you valuable content.

Questions

If you have a problem with any aspect of this book, you can contact us at `questions@packtpub.com`, and we will do our best to address the problem.

Asynchronous Programming in Android

Asynchronous programming has become an important topic of discussion in the past few years, especially when using the concurrent processing capabilities available on the most recent mobile hardware.

In recent years, the number of independent processing units (cores) available on the CPU have increased, so to benefit from this new processing power, a new programming model called asynchronous programming has appeared to orchestrate the work between the several independent hardware-processing units available on the device. Asynchronous programming comes to the rescue to solve the problems that could arise from this new processing paradigm.

Android applications, since they mostly run on devices with multiple units of processing, should take advantage of asynchronous programming to scale and improve the application performance when blocking operations, and when CPU-intensive tasks are required.

Android is an open source operating system (OS) based on Linux kernel that was devised in 2003 by Andy Rubin, Nick Sears, Chris White, and Rick Miner, and then acquired by Google in July, 2005.

The Android OS, actually maintained by Google and the Open Handset Alliance, was created to provide an open mobile-device platform for devices with limited resources of computation, memory, and energy.

The platform has been incorporating advanced mobile devices standards, such as NFC and Bluetooth LE, and its scope has grown from a pure smartphone platform to a broader software platform for smart watches, TVs, tablets, and consoles.

The maintainers have been regularly updating the platform with great features and some improvements over minor and major releases since the first release.

The following diagram displays the Android versions over time:

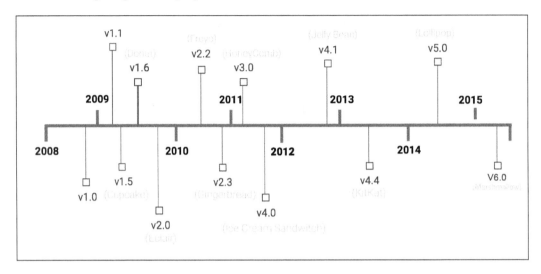

Android software stack

Android software stack (C libraries and Java frameworks), orchestrated by the Android runtime (Dalvik VM, and most recently, ART) was created around the Linux kernel to provide highly interactive user experiences over a well-proven group of technologies.

In each new OS version, a well-defined application interface (API) is provided to the developer in order to create applications around the new features and standards introduced with the release.

The Android application compiled code (bytecode), typically a Java compiled code, runs on a virtual machine based on Dalvik or ART.

Dalvik runtime

The **Dalvik VM (DVM)** runtime, created by **Dan Borstein**, was the first runtime for the platform and is a register-based virtual machine that was created to run the Java code efficiently in a constrained runtime with a limited amount of power processing, RAM, and electric power.

Dalvik's creators claim that the DVM is, on an average, around 30% more efficient than the standard Java VM (Oracle). According to Bornstein, it requires 30% less instructions and 35 % less coding units.

Clearly, Google has gone to great lengths to squeeze every drop of performance out of each mobile device to help developers build responsive applications.

The virtual machine, which runs the Java code compiled and transformed to the dex format over the dx tool, runs on a Linux process with its own memory space and file descriptors. It also manages its own group of threads.

In more advanced architectures, an Android application might run a service in a separate process and communicate over the IPC mechanism, but most of the time, it runs on a single self-contained process.

The dex file and application resources are packed in an **Android application package** (**APK**) by the AAPT and installed over Google Play in the end user devices.

 The application store distribution model has become extremely popular on the mobile platforms since the launch of the Apple iPhone in 2007.

Since Android 2.2 the DVM comes with a trace-based **Just-In-Time** (**JIT**) compilation feature that actively optimizes every time the application runs some short segments of frequently used bytecode called traces.

The generated machine code provides significant performance improvements in the application execution and on the time spent on some intensive CPU tasks, and thereafter, decreases the battery power used.

ART runtime

The ART runtime is a new version of the DVM and was introduced to improve the runtime performance and memory consumption. The new runtime was introduced in Android 4.4 KitKat as an experimental runtime, and since the Android 5.0 Lollipop, it has become the main Android runtime.

This new runtime, making use of the **ahead-of-time** (**AOT**) compilation, brings new app-performance optimizations on startup time and application execution. The AOT, as opposed to DVM JIT (Just in Time), compiles the dex files during the installation time using the device dex2oat tool. The compiled code generated from the dex2oat tool generates system-dependent code for the target device and removes the delay introduced by the JIT compilation during each application execution.

The AOT compiler also reduces the number of processor cycles used by the application as it removes the time spent by the JIT compiler to convert the code into machine code, and then uses less battery power to run the application.

One of the drawbacks of the AOT compilation is the larger memory footprint in comparison with the JIT used by DVM.

With the new runtime, some improvements were also introduced in the memory allocation and on **Garbage Collection (GC)**, resulting in a more responsive UI and better application experience.

Memory sharing and Zygote

Basically, the platform runs an instance of DVM/ART for each application, but large optimization of the platform is brought about by the way a new DVM instance is created and managed.

A special process called the Zygote (first life cell in an animal's reproduction) — the process that all the Android applications are based on — is launched when an Android device initially boots.

The Zygote starts up a virtual machine, preloads the core libraries, and initializes various shared structures. It then waits for instructions by listening on a socket.

When a new Android application is launched, the Zygote receives a command to create a virtual machine to run the application on. It does this by forking its pre-warmed VM process and creating a new child process that shares some memory portions with the parent, using a technique called **copy-on-write (COW)**.

The COW technique, available on most Unix systems, only allocates new memory on the child process when the process tries to change the memory cloned from the parent process.

This technique has some fantastic benefits, as listed in the following:

- First, the virtual machine and core libraries are already loaded into the memory. Not having to read this significant chunk of data from the filesystem to initialize the virtual machine drastically reduces the startup overhead.
- Second, the memory in which these core libraries and common structures reside is shared by the Zygote with all other applications, resulting in saving a lot of memory when the user is running multiple apps.

Android process model

Android is a multiuser, multitasking system that can run multiple applications in parallel, where all the applications attempt to acquire CPU time to execute its job.

Each application runs independently on an isolated Linux process cloned from the Zygote process, and by default, all the Android components run within the same process with the same name as the application package specified in **Android Application Manifest (AAM)**.

The Linux kernel will fairly allocate small amounts of CPU time for application execution called CPU time slices. This time-slicing approach means that even a single-processor device can appear to be actively working in more than one application at the same time, when in fact, each application is taking very short turns on the CPU.

Process ranks

The Android operating system tries to maintain the application running for as long as possible, but when the available memory is low, it will try to free resources in the system by killing the processes with lower importance first.

This is when process ranking comes into the picture; the Android processes are ranked in the next five categories from the higher priority to the lower priorities:

- **Foreground process**: This is a process that hosts an activity or service that the user is currently interacting with: a service started in the foreground or service running its life cycle callbacks

- **Visible process**: This is a process that hosts a paused activity or service bounded to a visible activity

- **Service process**: This is a process that hosts a service not bound to a visible activity

- **Background process**: This is a process that hosts a non-visible activity; all background processes are sorted over a **Least-Recently-Used (LRU)** list, therefore, the most recently used processes are the last killed processes when they have the same rank

- **Empty process**: This is a process used to cache inactive Android components and to improve any component startup time

When the system reaches a point that it needs to release resources, the processes available to be killed will be sorted, taking into account the process rank, last used processes, and components running.

Process sandboxing

The Android application always runs under a unique **Linux user ID (UID)** assigned to the application during the application installation so that the process runs on a sandboxed environment, which by default, isolates your data and code execution from other apps.

In some cases, a user could explicitly be required to share the UID with another application to have access to their data:

```
USER      PID    PPID  VSIZE  RSS  PC  NAME
root             319   1      1537236 31324 S zygote
....
u0_a221   5993   319          1731636 41504 S com.whatsapp
u0_a96    3018   319          1640252 29540 S com.dropbox.android
u0_a255   4892   319          1583828 34552 S com.accuweather.android…
```

The preceding table that results from running the `adb shell ps` command in the computer with Android SDK Table is a list of Android running processes.

The first column shows the **user identifier (UID)** assigned at the time of installation, the second column is the **process ID (PID)**, the third column shows the **parent process ID (PPID)** that for Android applications is the Zygote process, and the last column shows the application package.

From this list, we can assure that the WhatsApp application is running under the user ID `u0_a221` with the process ID `5993` and the parent process is the Zygote process with the PID `319`.

Android thread model

Within an Android process, there may be many threads of execution. Each thread is a separate sequential flow of control within the overall program—it executes its instructions in order, one after the other, and they also share allocated slices of CPU time managed by the operating system task scheduler.

While the application process is started by the system and prevented from directly interfering with data in the memory address space of other processes, the threads may be started by an application code and can communicate and share data with other threads within the same process. Apart from the shared data that all the threads share in the same process, a thread can use its own memory cache to store its data in its own memory space.

The main thread

When the application process starts, apart from DVM housekeeping threads, the system creates a thread of execution called `main`. This thread, as the name explains, plays a crucial role in the application lifetime as it is the thread that interacts with the Android UI components, updating the state and their look on the device screen.

Moreover, by default, all the Android application components (`Activity`, `Service`, `ContentProvider`, and `BroadcastsReceiver`) are also executed over the main thread line of execution. The following image shows the lists of threads running inside an application process with the main thread at the top of the list with a unique **thread ID (TID)** assigned by the system:

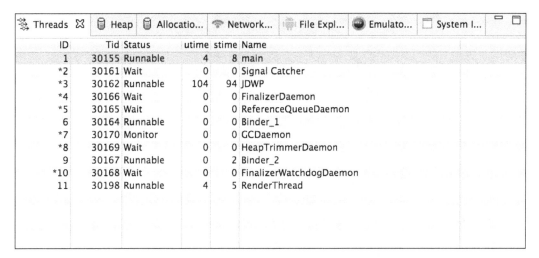

The main thread, also known as UI Thread, is also the thread where your UI event handling occurs, so to keep your application as responsible as possible, you should:

- Avoid any kind of long execution task, such as **input/output (I/O)** that could block the processing for an indefinite amount of time

- Avoid CPU-intensive tasks that could make this thread occupied for a long time

The following diagram displays the main interactions and components involved in the Looper line of execution thread:

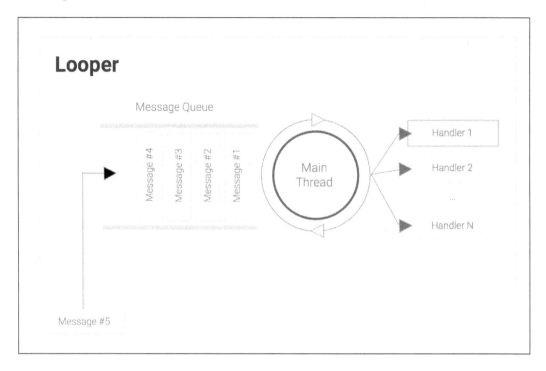

The **UI/Main** thread, which has a Looper facility attached to it, holds a queue of messages (MessageQueue) with some unit of work to be executed sequentially.

When a message is ready to be processed on the queue, the **Looper Thread** pops the message from the queue and forwards it synchronously to the target handler specified on the message.

When the target Handler finishes its work with the current message, the Looper thread will be ready to process the next message available on the queue. Hence, if the Handler spent a noticeable amount of time processing the message, it will prevent Looper from processing other pending messages.

For example, when we write the code in an onCreate() method in the Activity class, it will be executed on the main thread. Likewise, when we attach listeners to user-interface components to handle taps and other user-input gestures, the listener callback executes on the main thread.

For apps that do little I/O or processing, such as applications that don't do complex math calculations, don't use the network to implement features, or don't use filesystem resources, this single thread model is fine. However, if we need to perform CPU-intensive calculations, read or write files from permanent storage, or talk to a web service, any further events that arrive while we're doing this work will be blocked until we're finished.

 Since the Android 5.0 (Lollipop), a new important thread named **RenderThread** was introduced to keep the UI animations smooth even when the main thread is occupied doing stuff.

The Application Not Responding (ANR) dialog

As you can imagine, if the main thread is busy with a heavy calculation or reading data from a network socket, it cannot immediately respond to user input such as a tap or swipe.

An application that doesn't respond quickly to user interaction will feel unresponsive — anything more than a couple of hundred milliseconds delay is noticeable. This is such a pernicious problem that the Android platform protects users from applications that do too much on the main thread.

 If an app does not respond to user input within five seconds, the user will see the **Application Not Responding** (**ANR**) dialog and will be offered the option to quit the application.

The following screenshot shows a typical Android ANR dialog:

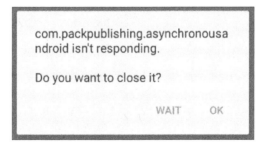

Android works hard to synchronize the user interface redraws with the hardware-refresh rate. This means that it aims to redraw at the rate of 60 frames per second — that's just 16.67 ms per frame. If we do work on the main thread that takes anywhere near 16 ms, we risk affecting the frame rate, resulting in jank — stuttering animations, jerky scrolling, and so on.

Ideally, of course, we don't want to drop a single frame. Jank, unresponsiveness, and especially the ANR, offer a very poor user experience, which translates into bad reviews and unpopular applications. A rule to live by when building Android applications is: do not block the main thread!

 Android provides a helpful strict mode setting in **Developer Options** on each device, which will flash on the screen when applications perform long-running operations on the main thread.

Further protection was added to the platform in Honeycomb (API level 11) with the introduction of a new Exception class, NetworkOnMainThreadException, a subclass of RuntimeException that is thrown if the system detects network activity initiated on the main thread.

Maintaining responsiveness

Ideally then, we may want to offload any long-running operations from the main thread so that they can be handled in the background by another thread, and the main thread can continue to process user-interface updates smoothly and respond in a timely fashion to user interactions.

The typical time-consuming tasks that should be handled on a background thread include the following:

- Network communications
- Input and output file operations on the local filesystem
- Image and video processing
- Complex math calculations
- Text processing
- Data encoding and decoding

For this to be useful, we must be able to coordinate the work and safely pass data between cooperating threads—especially between background threads and the main thread, and it is exactly to solve this problem that asynchronous programming is used.

Let's get started with the synchronous versus asynchronous diagram:

The preceding example graphically shows the main differences between the two models of processing. On the left-hand side, the data download task occurs on the main thread, keeping the thread busy until the download data is finished. So if the user interacts with the UI and generates an event such as a touch event, the application will suffer a lag or will become unresponsive if the download task takes a substantial amount of time to finish.

On the right-hand side, the asynchronous model will hand over the download data task to another background thread, keeping the main thread available to process any event coming from the UI interaction. When the downloaded data is available, the background task could post the result to the main thread if the data handling needs to update any UI state.

When we use an asynchronous model to program our application, the Android OS will also take advantage of additional CPU cores available in the most recent devices to execute multiple background threads at the same time and increase the application's power efficiency.

This simultaneous execution of separate code paths that potentially interact with each other is known as **concurrency**.

The simultaneous execution of subunits of work in parallel to complete one unit of work is known as **parallelism**.

Concurrency in Android

As explained before, in order to achieve a scalable application in a multicore device environment, the Android developer should be capable of creating concurrent lines of execution that combine and aggregate data from multiple resources.

The Android SDK, as it is based on a subset of Java SDK, derived from the Apache Harmony project, provides access to low-level concurrency constructs such as `java.lang.Thread`, `java.lang.Runnable`, and the `synchronized` and `volatile` keywords.

These constructs are the most basic building blocks to achieve concurrency and parallelism, and all the high-level asynchronous constructs are created around these building blocks.

The most basic one, `java.lang.Thread`, is the class that is mostly used and is the construct that creates a new independent line of execution in a Java program:

```
public class MyThread extends Thread {
    public void run() {
        Log.d("Generic", "My Android Thread is running ...");
    }
}
```

In the preceding code, we subclassed `java.lang.Thread` to create our own independent line of execution. When `Thread` is started, the run method will be called automatically and it will print the message on the Android log:

```
MyThread myThread = new MyThread();
myTread.start();
```

At this time, we will create an instance of our `MyThread`, and when we start it in the second line, the system creates a thread inside the process and executes the `run()` method.

Other helpful thread-related methods include the following:

- `Thread.currentThread()`: This retrieves the current running instance of the thread

- `Thread.sleep(time)`: This pauses the current thread from execution for the given period of time

- `Thread.getName()` and `Thread.getId()`: These get the name and TID, respectively so that they can be useful for debugging purposes

- `Thread.isAlive()`: This checks whether the thread is currently running or it has already finished its job

- `Thread.join()`: This blocks the current thread and waits until the accessed thread finishes its execution or dies

The `Runnable` interface, which is another building block that comes from the Java API, is an interface defined to specify and encapsulate code that is intended to be executed by a Java thread instance or any other class that handles this `Runnable`:

```
package java.lang;

public interface Runnable {
    public abstract void run();
}
```

In the following code, we basically created the `Runnable` subclass so that it implements the `run()` method and can be passed and executed by a thread:

```
public class MyRunnable implements Runnable {

    public void run(){
        Log.d("Generic","Running in the Thread " +
                        Thread.currentThread().getId());
    // Do your work here
    ...
    }
}
```

Now our `Runnable` subclass can be passed to `Thread` and is executed independently in the concurrent line of execution:

```
Thread thread = new Thread(new MyRunnable());
thread.start();
```

While starting new threads is easy, concurrency is actually a very difficult thing to do. Concurrent software faces many issues that fall into two broad categories: correctness (producing consistent and correct results) and liveness (making progress towards completion). Thread creation could also cause some performance overhead, and too many threads can reduce the performance, as the OS will have switch between these lines of execution.

Correctness issues in concurrent programs

A common example of a correctness problem occurs when two threads need to modify the value of the same variable based on its current value. Let's consider that we have a myInt integer variable with the current value of 2.

In order to increment myInt, we first need to read its current value and then add 1 to it. In a single-threaded world, the two increments would happen in a strict sequence – we will read the initial value 2, add 1 to it, set the new value back to the variable, and then repeat the sequence. After the two increments, myInt holds the value 4.

In a multithreaded environment, we will run into potential timing issues. It is possible that two threads trying to increment the variable would both read the same initial value 2, add 1 to it, and set the result (in both cases, 3) back to the variable:

```
int myInt = 2;
...
public class MyThread extends Thread {

    public void run() {
            super.run();
            myInt++;
    }
}
...
Thread t1 = new MyThread();
Thread t2 = new MyThread();
t1.start();
t2.start();
```

Both threads behaved correctly in their localized view of the world, but in terms of the overall program, we will clearly have a correctness problem; 2 + 2 should not equal 3! This kind of timing issue is known as a race condition.

A common solution to correctness problems, such as race conditions, is mutual exclusion—preventing multiple threads from accessing certain resources at the same time. Typically, this is achieved by ensuring that threads acquire an exclusive lock before reading or updating shared data.

To achieve this correctness, we can make use of the `synchronized` construct to solve the correctness issue on the following piece of code:

```
Object lock = new Object();
public class MyThread extends Thread {
    public void run() {
        super.run();
        synchronized(lock) {
            myInt++;
        }
    }
}
```

In the preceding code, we used the intrinsic lock available in each Java object to create a mutually exclusive scope of code that will enforce that the increment sentence will work properly and will not suffer from correctness issues as explained previously. When one of the threads gets access to the protected scope, it is said that the thread acquired the lock, and after the thread gets out of the protected scope, it releases the lock that could be acquired by another thread.

Another way to create mutually exclusive scopes is to create a method with a synchronized method:

```
int myInt = 2;
synchronized void increment(){
    myInt++;
}
...
public class IncrementThread extends Thread {
    public void run() {
        super.run();
        increment();
    }
}
```

The synchronized method will use the object-intrinsic lock, where `myInt` is defined to create a mutually exclusive zone so `IncrementThread`, incrementing `myInt` through the `increment()`, will prevent any thread interference and memory consistency errors.

Liveness issues in concurrent programs

Liveness can be thought of as the ability of the application to do useful work and make progress towards goals. Liveness problems tend to be an unfortunate side effect of the solution to the correctness problems.

Both properties should be achieved in a proper concurrent program, notwithstanding the correctness is concerned with making progress in a program preventing a deadlock, livelock, or starvation from happening, and the correctness is concerned with making consistent and correct results.

Deadlock is a situation where two or more threads are unable to proceed because each is waiting for the others to do something. Livelock is a situation where two or more threads continuously change their states in response to the changes in the other threads without doing any useful work.

By locking access to data or system resources, it is possible to create bottlenecks where many threads are contending to access a single lock, leading to potentially significant delays.

Worse, where multiple locks are used, it is possible to create a situation where no thread can make progress because each requires exclusive access to a lock that another thread currently owns — a situation known as a deadlock.

Thread coordination

Thread coordination is an important topic in concurrent programming, especially when we want to perform the following tasks:

- Synchronize access of threads to shared resources or shared memory:
    - Shared database, files, system services, instance/class variables, or queues

- Coordinate work and execution within a group of threads:
    - Parallel execution, pipeline executions, inter-dependent tasks, and so on

When we want to coordinate thread efforts to achieve a goal, we should try to avoid waiting or polling mechanisms that keep the CPU busy while we wait for an event in another thread.

The following example shows us a small loop where we will continuously occupy the CPU while we wait for a certain state change to happen:

```
while(!readyToProcess) {
  // do nothing .. busy waiting wastes processor time.
}
```

To overcome the coordination issue, and to implement our own constructs, we should use some low-level signals or messaging mechanisms to communicate between threads and coordinate the interaction.

In Java, every object has the `wait()`, `notify()`, and `notifyAll()` methods that provide low-level mechanisms to send thread signals between a group of threads and put a thread in a waiting state until a condition is met.

This mechanism, also known as *monitor* or *guard*, is a design pattern commonly used in another languages and it ensures that only one thread can enter a given section of code at any given time with an ability to wait until a condition happens.

This design pattern, in comparison with our previous example, delivers a better and efficient CPU-cycle management while waiting for any particular situation to happen on another thread, and is generally used in situations where we need to coordinate work between different lines of execution.

In the following code example, we are going to explain how to use this construct to create a basic multithreaded `Logger` with 10 threads that will wait in the monitor section until a message is pushed (condition) by any other thread in the application.

The `Logger`, which is responsible for logging on to the output, has a queue with a maximum of 20 positions to store the new logging text messages:

```
public class Logger {
    LinkedList<String> queue = new LinkedList<String>();
    private final int MAX_QUEUE_SIZE = 20;
    private final int MAX_THREAD_COUNT = 10;
```

In the next code, we will create a `Runnable` unit of work that runs indefinitely and retrieves a message from the queue to print the message on the Android log.

After that, we will create and start 10 threads that are going to execute the `Runnable` unit of work `task`:

```
public void start() {
    // Creates the Loop as a Runnable
    Runnable task = new Runnable() {
        @Override
```

```
        public void run() {
            while(true) {
                String message = pullMessage();
                Log.d(Thread.currentThread().
                        getName(),message);
                // Do another processing
            }
        }
    };
    // Create a Group of Threads for processing
    for(int i=0; i< MAX_THREAD_COUNT; i++){
        new Thread(task).start();
    }
}
```

The `pullMessage()`, which is a `synchorized` method, runs a mutual exclusion and puts the thread in the waiting state when it reaches the `wait()` method. All the created threads will stay in this state until another thread calls `notifyAll()`:

```
// Pulls a message from the queue
// Only returns when a new message is retrieves
// from the queue.
private synchronized String pullMessage(){
    while (queue.isEmpty()) {
        try {
            wait();
        } catch (InterruptedException e) { ... }
    }
    return queue.pop();
}
// Push a new message to the tail of the queue if
// the queue has available positions
public synchronized void pushMessage(String logMsg) {
    if ( queue.size()< MAX_QUEUE_SIZE ) {
        queue.push(logMsg);
        notifyAll();
    }
}
```

When any thread is in the waiting state, it releases the lock temporarily and gives a chance to another thread to enter the mutual exclusion to push new messages or enter into the wait state.

In the following snippet, we will first create the `Logger` instance and then we will call the start method to start the working threads and we will push 10 messages into a queue of work to be processed.

When the `pushMessage()` method is invoked, a new logging message is inserted at the end of the queue and `notifiyAll()` is invoked to notify all the available threads.

As the `pullMessage()` method runs in a mutual-exclusion (synchronized) zone, only one thread will wake up and return from the `pull` method. Once `pullMessage()` returns, the logging message is printed:

```
Logger logger =new Logger();
logger.start();
for ( int i=0; i< 10 ; i++) {
    ...
    logger.pushMessage(date+" : "+"Log Message #"+i);
}
```

In the following console output, we have an example of the output that this code will generate and the logging messages are processed by any available threads in an ordered manner:

```
D/Thread-108(23915): <Date>: Log Message #0
D/Thread-109(23915): ...: Log Message #1
D/Thread-110(23915): ...: Log Message #2
D/Thread-111(23915): ...: Log Message #3
```

This kind of low-level construct can also be used to control shared resources (polling) to manage background execution (parallelism) and control thread pools.

Concurrent package constructs

Other Java concurrent constructs provided by `java.util.concurrent`, which are also available on Android SDK are as follows:

- **Lock objects** (`java.util.concurrent`): They implement locking behaviors with a higher level idiom.
- **Executors**: These are high-level APIs to launch and manage a group of thread executions (`ThreadPool`, and so on).
- **Concurrent collections**: These are the collections where the methods that change the collection are protected from synchronization issues.

- **Synchronizers**: These are high-level constructs that coordinate and control thread execution (Semaphore, Cyclic Barrier, and so on).
- **Atomic variables** (`java.util.concurrent.atomic`): These are classes that provide thread-safe operations on single variables. One example of it is `AtomicInteger` that could be used in our example to solve the correctness issue.

Some Android-specific constructs use these classes as basic building blocks to implement their concurrent behavior, although they could be used by a developer to build custom concurrent constructs to solve a specific use case.

Executor framework

The `Executor` framework is another framework available on `java.util.concurrent` that provides an interface to submit `Runnable` tasks, decoupling the task submission from the way the task will run:

```
public interface Executor {
    void execute(Runnable command);
}
```

Each `Executor`, which implements the interface that we defined earlier, can manage the asynchronous resources, such as thread creation destruction and caching, and task queueing in a variety of ways to achieve the perfect behavior to a specific use case.

The `java.util.concurrent` comes with a group of implementations available out of the box that cover most generic use cases, as follows:

- `Executors.newCachedThreadPool()`: This is a thread poll that could grow and reuse previously created threads
- `Executors.newFixedThreadPool(nThreads)`: This is a thread pool with a fixed number of threads and a message queue for store work
- `Executors.newSingleThreadPool()`: This is similar to newFixedThreadPool, but with only one working thread

To run a task on `Executor`, the developer has to invoke `execute()` by passing `Runnable` as an argument:

```
public class MyRunnable implements Runnable {
    public void run() {
        Log.d("Generic", "Running From Thread " +
                Thread.currentThread().getId());
        // Your Long Running Computation Task
```

```
        }
    }
    public void startWorking(){
        Executor executor = Executors.newFixedThreadPool(5);
        for ( int i=0; i < 20; i++ ) {
            executor.execute(new MyRunnable());
        }
    }
}
```

In the preceding code, we created `ThreadPool` over the factory methods with a fixed number of five threads ready to process work.

After the `ExecutorService` instance creation, new `Runnable` tasks are posted for asynchronous processing.

When a new unit of work is submitted, a thread that is free to work is chosen to handle the task; but when all the threads are occupied, `Runnable` will wait in a local queue until a thread is ready to work.

Android primary building blocks

A typical Android application is composed of the following four main building blocks:

- `android.app.Activity`
- `android.app.Service`
- `android.content.BroadcastReceiver`
- `android.content.ContentProvider`

The Activity, Service, and `BroadcastReceiver` are activated explicitly or implicitly over an asynchronous message called `Intent`.

Each of these building blocks have their own life cycle, so they could be exposed to different concurrency issues if an asynchronous architecture is used to offload work from the main thread.

Activity concurrent issues

The Activity building block has a tight connection with a presentation layer because it's the entity that manages the UI view over a defined tree of fragments and views that display information and respond to user interactions.

Android applications are typically composed of one or more subclasses of `android.app.Activity`. An Activity instance has a very well-defined lifecycle that the system manages through the execution of lifecycle method callbacks, all of which are executed on the main thread.

To keep the application responsive and reactive, and the activity transition smooth, the developer should understand the nature of each Activity lifecycle callback.

The most important callbacks on the Activity lifecycle are as follows:

- `onCreate()`: At this state, Activity is not visible, but it is here where all the private Activity resources (views and data) are created. The long and intensive computations should be done asynchronously in order to decrease the time when the users don't get a visual feedback during an Activity transition.

- `onStart()`: This is the callback called when the UI is visible, but not able to interact on the screen. Any lag here could make the user angry as any touch event generated at this stage is going to be missed by the system.

- `onResume()`: This is the callback called when Activity is going to be in the foreground and at an interactable state.

- `onPause()`: This is a callback called when Activity is going to the background and is not visible. Computations should end quickly as the next Activity will not resume until this method ends.

- `onStop()`: This is a callback called when Activity is no longer visible, but can be restarted.

- `onDestroy()`: This is a callback called when the Activity instance is going to be destroyed in the background. All the resources and references that belong to this instance have to be released.

An Activity instance that is completed should be eligible for garbage collection, but background threads that refer to Activity or part of its view hierarchy can prevent garbage collection and create a memory leak.

Similarly, it is easy to waste CPU cycles (and battery life) by continuing to do background work when the result can never be displayed as Activity is completed.

Finally, the Android platform is free at any time to kill processes that are not the user's current focus. This means that if we have long-running operations to complete, we need some way of letting the system know not to kill our process yet.

All of this complicates the do-not-block–the-main-thread rule as we need to worry about canceling background work in a timely fashion or decoupling it from the Activity lifecycle where appropriate.

Manipulating the user interface

The other Android-specific problem lies not in what you can do with the UI thread, but in what you cannot do.

 You cannot manipulate the user interface from any thread other than the main thread.

This is because the user interface toolkit is not thread-safe, that is, accessing it from multiple threads may cause correctness problems. In fact, the user interface toolkit protects itself from potential problems by actively denying access to user interface components from threads other than the one that originally created these components.

If the system detects this, it will instantly notify the application by throwing `CalledFromWrongThreadException`.

The final challenge then lies in safely synchronizing background threads with the main thread so that the main thread can update the user interface with the results of the background work.

If the developer has access to an `Activity` instance, the `runOnUiThread` instance method can be used to update the UI from a background thread.

The method accepts a `Runnable` object like the one used to create an execution task for a thread:

```
public final void runOnUiThread (Runnable)
```

In the following example, we are going to use this facility to publish the result from a synonym search that was processed by a background thread.

To accomplish the goal during the `OnCreate` activity callback, we will set up `onClickListener` to run `searchTask` on a created thread:

```
// Get the Views references
Button search = (Button) findViewById(R.id.searchBut);
final EditText word = (EditText) findViewById(R.id.wordEt);

// When the User clicks on the search button
// it searches for a synonym
search.setOnClickListener(new View.OnClickListener() {
    @Override
    public void onClick(View v) {
```

```
        // Runnable that Searchs for the synonym and
        // and updates the UI.
        Runnable searchTask = new Runnable() {
            @Override
            public void run() {
                // Retrieves the synonym for the word
                String result = searchSynomim(
                    word.getText().toString());
                // Runs the Runnable SetSynonymResult
                // to publish the result on the UI Thread
                runOnUiThread(new SetSynonymResult(result));
            }
        };
        // Executes the search synonym an independent thread
        Thread thread = new Thread(searchTask);
        Thread.start();
    }
});
```

When the user clicks on the **Search** button, we will create a `Runnable` anonymous class that searches for the word typed in `R.id.wordEt` `EditText` and starts the thread to execute `Runnable`.

When the search completes, we will create an instance of `Runnable SetSynonymResult` to publish the result back on the synonym `TextView` over the UI thread:

```
class SetSynonymResult implements Runnable {
    final String synonym;

    SetSynonymResult(String synonym) {
        this.synonym = synonym;
    }
    public void run() {
        TextView tv = (TextView)findViewById(R.id.synonymTv);
        tv.setText(this.synonym);
    }
};
```

This technique is sometime not the most convenient one, especially when we don't have access to an Activity instance; therefore, in the following chapters, we are going to discuss simpler and cleaner techniques to update the UI from a background computing task.

Service concurrent issues

These are the Android entities that run in the background, which usually perform tasks in the `name` application that does not require any user interaction.

`Service`, by default, runs in the main thread of the application process. It does not create its own thread, so if your `Service` is going to do any blocking operation, such as downloading an image, play a video, or access a network API, the user should design a strategy to offload the time of the work from the main thread into another thread.

As `Service` could have its own concurrent strategy, it should also take into account that, like Activity, it should update the UI over the main thread, so a strategy to post back the results from the background into the main loop is imperative.

In the Android services domain, the way the service is started distinguishes the nature of `Service` into the following two groups:

- **Started services**: This is the service that is started by `startService()` that can run definitively even if the component that started it was destroyed. A started service does not interact directly with the component that started it.

- **Bound services**: This service exists while at least one Android component is bounded to it by calling `bindService()`. It provides a two-way (client-server) communication channel for communication between components.

Started services issues

When we implement a started service, any application component is able to start it when it invokes the `startService(Intent)` method. Once the system receives `startService(Intent)` and the service is not yet started, the system calls `onCreate()` and then `onStartCommand()` with the arguments encapsulated on an Intent object. If the `Service` already exists, only `onStartCommand()` is invoked.

The callbacks used by a started service are as follows:

```
// Called every time a component starts the Service
// The service arguments are passed over the intent
int onStartCommand(Intent intent, int flags, int startId)

// Used to initialize your Service resources
void onCreate()

// Used to release your Service resources
void onDestroy()
```

In the `onStartCommand()` callback, once a long computing task is required to handle the service request, a handover to the background threads should be explicitly implemented and coordinated in order to avoid an undesired ANR:

```
int onStartCommand (Intent intent, int flags, int startId){
    // Hand over the request processing to your
    // background tasks
...
}
```

When the service is done, and it needs to publish results to the UI, a proper technique to communicate with the main thread should be used.

Bound services issues

A bound service generally used when a strong interaction between an Android component and a service is required.

When the service runs on the same process, the interaction between the Android component (client) and the bound service (server) is always provided by a `Binder` class returned on `onBind()`. With the `Binder` instance on hand, the client has access to the service's public methods, so when any component invokes the bound service public methods, the component should be aware of the following:

- When a long running operation is expected to take place during the method invocation, the invocation must occur in a separate thread

- If the method is invoked in a separated thread, and the service wants to update the UI, the service must run the update over the main thread:

```
public class MyService extends Service {

    // Binder given to clients
    private final IBinder mBinder = new MyBinder();

     public class MyBinder extends Binder {
         MyService getService() {
             // Return this instance of MyService
             // so clients can call public methods
             return MyService.this;
         }
    }
    @Override

    public IBinder onBind(Intent intent) {
```

```
            return mBinder;
    }

    /** Method for clients */
    public int myPublicMethod() {
        //
    }
    ...
```

Service in a separate process

When an Android service runs on its own process, it runs in an independent process, with its own address space, making the communication with the main process UI thread harder to implement the following:

```
<service
    android:name="SynonymService"
    android:process=":my_synonnym_search_proc"
    android:icon="@drawable/icon"
    android:label="@string/service_name"
    >
</service>
```

To implement a service in a different process, we need to use an **inter-process communication (IPC)** technique to send messages between your application and the service.

 IPC is the activity of sharing data across multiple processes, usually using a well-defined communication protocol. It typically has a process that acts as the client and a process that acts as the server.

There are two technologies available on the Android SDK to implement this, as follows:

- **AIDL (Android Interface Definition Language)**: This allows you to define an interface over a set of primitive types. It allows you create multithreaded processing services, but it adds other levels of complexity to your implementation. This is only recommended to advanced programmers.

- **Messenger**: This is a simple interface that creates a queue of work for you in the service side. This executes all the tasks sequentially on single thread managed by a `Handler`.

We haven't given more details about these techniques yet; however, an example of this construct is going to be presented later in a more advanced chapter where all the concepts involved are more mature.

Broadcast receiver concurrent issues

This building block is a component that subscribes to system and application events and is notified when these events occur on the system. The broadcast receivers are defined statically in the application manifest or dynamically via the `Context.registerReceiver()`.

The broadcast received is activated though the `onReceive()` callback and this method runs on the main thread, blocking another Android component from running if we try to execute time-consuming tasks.

Once `onReceive()` finishes, the system considers the object inactive and can release the resources attached to this instance and recycle the whole object. This behavior has a tremendous impact on what we can do inside, because if we hand over some processing to a concurrent thread, the resources that belong to `BroadcastReceiver` might be recycled and are no longer available, or in an extreme case, the process could be killed if there were no important components running on it.

 Android version 11 introduced the `goAsync()` method on the broadcast receiver to keep the broadcast active after returning from the `onReceive()` function.

Android concurrency constructs

The good news is that the Android platform provides specific constructs to address the concurrency general issues and to solve the specific problems presented by Android.

There are constructs that allow us to defer tasks to run later on the main thread, communicate easily between cooperating threads, and issue work to the managed pools of worker threads and reintegrate the results back in the main thread.

There are solutions to the constraints of the Activity lifecycle, both for medium-term operations that closely involve the user interface and longer-term work that must be completed even if the user leaves the application.

While some of these constructs were only introduced with newer releases of the Android platform, they are available through the support libraries, and with a few exceptions, the examples in this book target devices that run API level 8 (Android 2.2) and higher versions.

Summary

In this chapter, we took a detailed look at the available Android runtimes, Android processes, and thread models.

We then introduced the concurrent issues that we would cope with when we try to implement robust concurrent programs.

Finally, we listed the basic concurrent building blocks available on the SDK to design concurrent programs.

In the next chapter, we'll take a look at some Android-specific low-level building blocks on which the other concurrency mechanisms are built: `Handler`, `Looper`, and `LooperThread`.

2
Performing Work with Looper, Handler, and HandlerThread

In the previous chapter, you were introduced to the most basic concurrent issues that a developer might face while developing a responsive and concurrent Android application. As the most interactable items run on the main thread, it is crucial to coordinate the backgrounds code to handle the work without any UI stuttering that compromises the user experience.

In this chapter, we will meet some of most fundamental constructs used on Android systems to perform tasks and schedule on a main thread or an ordinary background thread created by the developer to perform and schedule tasks long-running operations.

We will cover the following topics:

- Understanding Looper
- Understanding Handler
- Sending work to Looper
- Scheduling work with post
- Using Handler to defer work
- Leaking implicit references
- Leaking explicit references
- Updating the UI with Handler
- Canceling pending messages
- Multithreading with Handler and HandlerThread
- Applications of Handler and HandlerThread

Understanding Looper

Before we can understand `Looper`, we need to understand where it gets its name from.

 A loop is a group of instructions that are repeated continually until a termination condition is met.

Following this definition, Android's `Looper` executes on a thread that has a `MessageQueue`, executes a continuous loop waiting for work, and blocks when there is no work pending. When work is submitted to its queue, it dispatches it to the target `Handler` defined explicitly on the `Message` object.

 A message is a notification object containing a description and arbitrary data object that can be sent to a Handler.

The Looper on Android is an implementation of a common UI programming concept known as an event loop. Later, at the end of this processing sequence, the `Handler` will process the `Message` and execute your domain logic in order to solve an application user problem.

The `Looper` sequence on Android follows these steps:

1. Wait until a Message is retrieved from its MessageQueue
2. If logging is enabled, print dispatch information
3. Dispatch the message to the target Handler
4. Recycle the Message
5. Go to step 1

As mentioned on the previous chapter, the main thread implicitly creates its own `Looper` to sequentially process all that is needed to keep the application running and to manage the interaction between the application components.

To access the main thread's Looper you want access to the main thread's `Looper` instance, use the static method `getMainLooper()`:

```
Looper mainLooper = Looper.getMainLooper();
```

To set up our own `Looper` thread, we need to invoke two static methods of `Looper` — `prepare` and `loop` — from within the thread, and they will handle the continuous loop. Here is a simple example:

```
class SimpleLooper extends Thread {

    public void run() {
      // Attach a Looper to the current Thread
        Looper.prepare();
      // Start the message processing
        Looper.loop();
    }
}
```

In the snippet, when the `SimpleLopper` object is created and started by invoking the `start()` method, a new thread is created in the current application process, and `run()` is automatically called inside the new thread. When the `run()` method is called, we attach a `Looper` to the current thread when we invoke the static `Looper.prepare()` method. Following that, we start processing messages when `loop()` is called. The `prepare()` method is responsible for initializing the `MessageQueue` and attaching the queue as a `ThreadLocal` parameter to the current thread.

When `loop()` is invoked, the `run()` method will block until the looper is interrupted to process new messages be added to the queue.

 `Looper.prepare()` must only be called once from within the same thread; otherwise, a `RuntimeException` will to be thrown that says only one looper may be created per thread.

When we want to stop the continuous `Looper` execution, we can either invoke its member function `quit()` to stop it without processing the remaining messages in its queue or `quitSafely()` to process the remaining work on the queue and stop.

Understanding Handler

Together with `Looper`, the `Handler` class is fundamental to the infrastructure of Android apps. It underpins everything that the main thread does — including the invocation of the `Activity` lifecycle methods.

While `Looper` takes care of dispatching work on its message-loop thread, `Handler` serves two purposes: providing an interface to submit messages to its `Looper` queue, and implementing the callback for processing those messages when they are dispatched by the `Looper`.

It is also import to know that each `Handler` is bound to a single `Looper` and, by extension, to one thread and its looper `MessageQueue`.

To bind to the `Looper` of the current thread, we need to instantiate it over the default `Handler()` constructor after we initialize the `Looper` by calling the `prepare` method. Since we create our handler inside our `SimpleLooper` thread over the default constructor `Handler()`, `myHandler` will be attached to the current thread's `Looper` instead of the main thread's `Looper`:

```
public class SimpleLooper extends Thread{

    private Handler myHandler;

    @Override
    public void run() {
        Looper.prepare();
        myHandler  =  new MyHandler();
        Looper.loop();
    }

    public Handler getHandler(){
        return myHandler;
    }
}
```

Apart from providing an interface to submit work to `Looper` threads, `Handler` also defines the code that process the messages submitted. In the following code, the `MyHandler` class overrides the superclass' (`Handler`) `handleMessage` member method to define our message-handling code:

```
public class MyHandler extends Handler {

    @Override
    public void handleMessage(Message msg) {
```

```
            // Add here your message handling
        // processing
    }
}
```

Once started, the `Looper` thread will wait inside `Looper.loop()` for messages to be added to its queue.

When another thread adds a `Message` to the queue using the `submit` method, the waiting thread will then dispatch the message to our target `MyHandler` by invoking the handler's `handleMessage()` method.

With the `Handler` object reference in hand, we are able to able to send messages to the `Handler` from any thread, and as a consequence, it is always dispatched to the `Looper` thread and handled by the correct `Handler`, as shown in the following diagram:

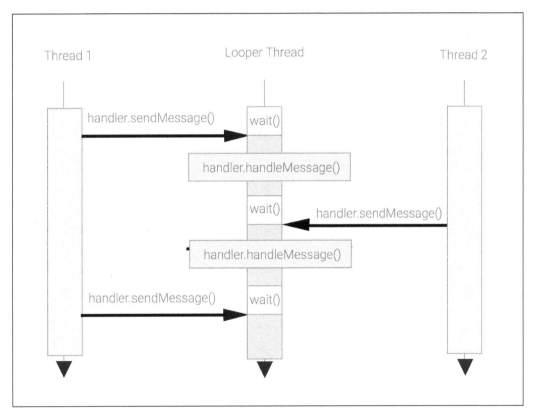

Figure 2.1: Posting work to other Threads

We already saw that we can create our own `Looper` threads, but as detailed and mentioned before, the main thread is in also a `Looper` thread. To make it more clear, we are going to create a `StackTraceHandler` that prints the stack trace of the current thread:

```
public class StackTraceHandler extends Handler {

    @Override
    public void handleMessage(Message msg) {
        // Prints the Stack Trace on the Android Log
        Thread.currentThread().dumpStack();
    }
}
```

Since the activity's `onCreate()` function runs on the main thread, we will create an instance of our handler that implicitly calls the handler's super constructor, which binds the handler to the current thread's `Looper`.

 If the current thread does not have a Looper and we try to create a handler over the super constructor, a runtime exception with the message **Can't create handler inside thread that has not called Looper.prepare()** is thrown.

With the `Handler` instance created, we retrieve a message from its recycled messages pool by calling the handler's `obtainMessage`, and we post an empty message to the main thread's `Looper`. The messages obtained by `obtainMessage` are cached and will also set the handler as the destination's `Handler` object:

```
public void onCreate(Bundle savedInstanceState) {
    super.onCreate(savedInstanceState);
    ...
    Handler handler = new StackTraceHandler();
    Message msg = handler.obtainMessage();
    handler.sendMessage(msg);
}
```

As mentioned before, when our `handleMessage()` gets dispatched it prints active stack frames at the time of the `handleMessage()` execution, as we can see in the following stack trace:

```
.....StackTraceHandler.handleMessage(StackTraceHandler.java:18)
android.os.Handler.dispatchMessage(Handler.java:99)
android.os.Looper.loop(Looper.java:137)
android.app.ActivityThread.main(ActivityThread.java:4424)
java.lang.reflect.Method.invokeNative(Native Method)
java.lang.reflect.Method.invoke(Method.java:511)
```

That's right, `handleMessage()` is running in the `dispatchMessage()` call invoked by the main `Looper`, and it is dispatched to the main thread's line of execution.

Sending work to a Looper

Previously, the `StackTraceHandler` was implicitly bound to the current main thread's `Looper`, so to make it flexible, let's take the next step and make it attachable to any `Looper`.

In the following code, we are going to override the default `Handler` constructor and define a constructor that accepts the `Looper` that is going to the queue, and we will then process and dispatch the message:

```
public class StackTraceHandler extends Handler {

    StackTraceHandler(Looper looper){
        super(looper);
    }
```

Our new constructor basically attaches the Handler to the `Looper` passed as an argument, making the `StackTraceHandler` attachable to any `Looper` instead of the current thread's `Looper`.

Our `SimpleLooper` was also extended to provide a `getter` method to retrieve the `Looper` object associated with its thread:

```
public class SimpleLooper extends Thread{
    // start condition
    boolean started = false;
    Object startMonitor =  new Object();
    Looper threadLooper = null;

    @Override
    public void run() {
        Looper.prepare();
        threadLooper = Looper.myLooper();
        synchronized (startMonitor){
            started = true;
            startMonitor.notifyAll();
        }
        Looper.loop();
    }

    Looper getLooper(){
        return threadLooper;
```

```
        }
        // Threads could wait here for the Looper start
        void waitforStart(){
            synchronized (startMonitor){
                while (!started){
                    try {
                        startMonitor.wait(10);
                    } catch (InterruptedException e) {
                        ...
                    }
                }
            }
        }
    }
```

Now, from the main thread, we start the SimpleLooper and its own thread, and when it starts up, we get the Looper instance to bind our Handler to the SimpleLooper thread and Looper:

```
SimpleLooper looper = new SimpleLooper();
looper.start();
looper.waitforStart();
Handler handler = new StackTraceHandler(looper.getLooper());
```

Now, we are going to send the message, as we did in the previous example, from the activity's onCreate() callback, which runs in the main thread:

```
Message msg = handler.obtainMessage();
handler.sendMessage(msg);
```

As we can see in the following stack trace, the thread stack frame at the bottom points to SimpleLooper.run(), and at the top of the stack trace, we have our Handler callback, StackTraceHandler.handleMessage:

```
at...activity.StackTraceHandler.handleMessage(StackTraceHandler.
java:18)
at android.os.Handler.dispatchMessage(Handler.java:99)
at android.os.Looper.loop(Looper.java:137)
at ...activity.SimpleLooper.run(SimpleLooper.java:23)
```

The interesting thing to realize here is that we can send messages from the main thread to the background thread managed by SimpleLooper (or even from the background thread to the main thread) and, in doing so, hand over work from background threads to the main thread — for example, to have it update the user interface with the results of background processing.

Scheduling work with post

As we discussed in the previous paragraph, we can submit work to the main or background thread by passing a reference to a `Looper` instance into the `Handler` constructor.

Exactly what we mean by work can be described by the subclasses of `java.lang.Runnable` or instances of `android.os.Message`. We can post runnables to a `Handler` instance or send messages to it, and it will add them to the `MessageQueue` belonging to the associated `Looper` instance.

We can post work to a `Handler` quite easily, for example, by creating an anonymous inner runnable:

```
final TextView myTextView = (TextView) findViewById(R.id.myTv);
// Get the main thread Looper by calling the Context
// function getMainLooper
Handler handler = new Handler(getMainLooper());

handler.post(new Runnable(){
    public void run() {
        String result = processSomething();
        myTextView.setText(result);
    }
});
```

The `Looper` instance to which the `Handler` is bound works its way through the queue, executing each `Runnable` as soon as possible. Posting with the `post` method simply adds a new `Runnable` at the end of the queue.

If we want our runnable to take priority over anything currently in the queue, we can post it to the front of the queue, ahead of existing work:

```
handler.postAtFrontOfQueue(new Runnable(){
public void run() {
    . . .
    }
});
```

In a single-threaded app, it might seem as if there isn't a whole lot to be gained from posting work to the main thread like this, but breaking things down into small tasks that can be interleaved and potentially reordered is very useful for maintaining responsiveness.

Moreover, with the encapsulation of work into more fine-grained units of work, we encourage the reuse of components, improve the testability of the code, and increase the aptitude for work composition:

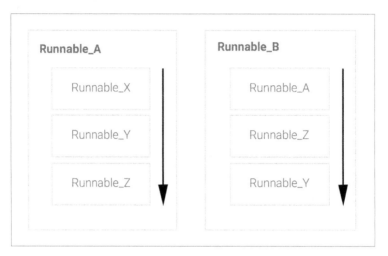

Figure 2.2: Runnable composition

Using Handler to defer work

When we use the normal `post` work function, the work is processed as soon as all the previous units of work are processed on the `Looper` — but what happens if we want to schedule some work in 10 seconds' time?

Using `Thread.sleep` to block the main thread for 10 seconds would mean that we are holding up the main thread from doing other work, and we are guaranteed to get an ANR dialog. The alternative is to use the handler functions that supply us with deferring functionality:

```
public class MyRunnable implements Runnable {

    @Override
    public void run() {
        // do some work
    }
};
// Defer work in the main Thread
// by 10 seconds time
    handler.postDelayed(new MyRunnable(), TimeUnit.SECONDS.
toMillis(10));
```

We can still post additional work for execution in the meantime, and our delayed `Runnable` instance will execute after the specified delay. Note that we're using the `TimeUnit` class from the `java.lang.concurrent` package to convert seconds to milliseconds.

A further scheduling option for posted work is `postAtTime`, which schedules `Runnable` to execute at a particular time relative to the system uptime (how long it has been since the system booted):

```
// Work to be run at a specific time
handler.postAtTime(new MyRunnable(),
                    SystemClock. uptimeMillis() +
                    TimeUnit.SECONDS.toMillis(10));
```

Since `postAtTime()` is implemented in terms of an offset from the `SystemClock` uptime, the scheduling could suffer from some delay issues, especially if the device has recently fallen in some deep-sleep states. Taking this into account, and when timing accuracy is required, it is usually better to use `handler.postDelayed` to defer work.

Leaking implicit references

Deferring work with `Handler` and anonymous or nonstatic nested classes requires care in order to avoid potential resource leakage. In these cases, the object submitted to the handler usually creates a reference to the class where it was defined or created. Since the Looper message queue will keep the `Runnable` object alive until the scheduled time, an indirect reference to the original Android component could prevent an entire component and its objects from being garbage-collected.

Let's look at this issue with the following examples:

```
public class MyActivity extends Activity {
  // non-static inner class
  public class MyRunnable implements Runnable {

    @Override
    public void run() {
      // do some work
    }
  }


    @Override
    public void onCreate(Bundle savedInstanceState) {
```

```
      . . .
    // Post Inner class instance Runnable
    handler.postDelayed(new MyRunnable(),
                     TimeUnit.MINUTES.toMillis(10));

    // Post an Anonymous class instance
    handler.postDelayed(new Runnable() {
     @Override
     public void run() {
     // do some work
     }
    }, TimeUnit.MINUTES.toMillis(20));
    . . .
    }
  }
```

Both objects, the `MyRunnable` object created over his default constructor and the anonymous `Runnable` class created on the second `handler.postDelayed`, hold a reference to the `Activity` object.

By declaring an anonymous inner `Runnable` inside an activity, we have made an implicit reference to that containing `Activity` instance. We've then posted the `Runnable` to a handler and told it to execute in 10 minutes' time.

If the activity finishes before the 10 minutes are up, it cannot yet be garbage-collected because the implicit reference in our runnable means that the activity is still reachable by live objects.

So, although it makes for a concise example, it is not a good idea in practice to post non-static Runnables onto the main thread's `Handler` queue (especially with `postDelayed` or `postAtTime`) unless we're very careful to clean up after ourselves all the references to the inactive Activities.

If the `MyActivity` object is not garbage-collected in 10 minutes, a memory leak with all the activity views and resources will increase your memory consumption until you reach the maximum heap space per application available. Worse, if you create several instances of this activity when the user navigates through the application, the application will run out of memory in a snap.

 The heap size limit available per application varies from device to device. When an application reaches this limit, the system will throw an `OutOfMemoryError`.

One way to minimize this problem is to use static nested classes or top-level classes in their own files (direct member of a package) to remove the reference to the original `Activity` object when we create a deferred `Runnable` work task. This means that references must be explicit, which makes them easier to spot and nullify:

```
public class MyActivity extends Activity {
    // static inner class
    public static class MyRunnable implements Runnable {
```

Leaking explicit references

If we are to interact with the user interface, we'll at least need a reference to an object in the `View` hierarchy, which we might pass into our static or top-level runnable's constructor:

```
static class MyRunnable implements Runnable {
        private View view;
        public MyRunnable(View view) {
            this.view = view;
        }
        public void run() {
            // ... do something with the view.
        }
    }
```

However, by keeping a strong reference to the `View`, we are again subject to potential memory leaks if our `Runnable` outlives the `View`; for example, if some other part of our code removes this `View` from the display before our `Runnable` executes.

One solution to this is to use a weak reference and check for `null` before using the referenced `View`:

```
static class MyRunnable implements Runnable {

    private WeakReference<View> view;

  public MyRunnable(View view) {
    this.view = new WeakReference<View>(view);
  }
  public void run() {
   View v = view.get(); // might return null
   if (v != null) {
     // ... do something with the view.
    }
  }
}
```

If you haven't used `WeakReference` before, what it gives us is a way to refer to an object only for as long as some other live object has a stronger reference to it (for example, a normal property reference).

When all strong references are garbage-collected, our `WeakReference` will also lose its reference to the `View`, `get()` will return `null`, and the `View` will be garbage-collected.

This fixes the resource leakage problem, but we must always check for `null` before using the returned object in order to avoid potential `NullPointerException` instances.

If we're sending messages to our `Handler` and expecting it to update the user interface, it will also need a reference to the view hierarchy. A nice way to manage this is to attach and detach the `Handler` from `onResume` and `onPause`:

```
private static class MyHandler extends Handler {
    private TextView view;
    public void attach(TextView view) {
        this.view = view;
    }
    public void detach() {
        view = null;
    }
    @Override
    public void handleMessage(Message msg) {
      // handle message
    }
}

@Override
protected void onResume() {
  super.onResume();
  myHandler.attach(myTextView);
}

@Override
  protected void onPause() {
    super.onPause();
    myHandler.detach();
}
```

Updating the UI with Handler

Since we instantiated our handler in the main thread, all work submitted to it executes on the main thread. This means that we must not submit long-running operations to this particular handler, but we can safely interact with the user interface:

```
handler.post(new Runnable(){
  public void run() {
    TextView text = (TextView) findViewById(R.id.text);
    text.setText("updated on the UI thread");
  }
});
```

This applies regardless of which thread posts the `Runnable`, which makes `Handler` an ideal way to send the results of work performed by other threads to the main thread:

```
public void onCreate(Bundle savedInstanceState) {
    ...
    // Handler bound to the main Thread
    final Handler handler = new Handler();

    // Creates an assync line of execution
    Thread thread = new Thread() {
        public void run() {
            final String result = searchSynomym("build");
            handler.post(new Runnable() {
                public void run() {
                    TextView text = (TextView)
                        findViewById(R.id.text);
                    text.setText(result);
                }
            });
        }
    };
    // Start the background thread with a lower priority
    thread.setPriority(Thread.MIN_PRIORITY);
    thread.start();
```

> If you start your own threads for background work, make sure to set the priority to `Thread.MIN_PRIORITY` to avoid starving the main thread of CPU time. The system CPU scheduler will give more CPU cycle times to threads with higher priority.

`Handler` is so fundamental that its API is integrated right into the `View` class's member functions:

- `View.post(Runnable).`
- `View.postDelayed(action,delayMillis).`

So, we can rewrite the previous example as follows:

```
final TextView text = (TextView) findViewById(R.id.text);
Thread thread = new Thread(){
  public void run(){
    final String result = searchSynonym("build");
    // Using the view post capabilities
    text.post(new Runnable(){
      public void run() {
        text.setText(result);
        }
      });
    }
  };
thread.setPriority(Thread.MIN_PRIORITY);
thread.start();
```

When writing code in an `Activity` class, there is an alternative way to submit a `Runnable` on the main thread using the `runOnUiThread(Runnable)` method of `Activity`, as explained in the previous chapter. If the current thread is the UI thread, then the action is executed immediately. If the current thread is not the UI thread, the action is posted to the event queue of the main UI thread.

Canceling a pending Runnable

During your application execution, you could have a situation where you want to cancel a posted `Runnable`, for instance, when you submit a deferred task on your activity's `onCreate()` and you want to cancel it when you are executing `onDestroy()` because the activity is going to be destroyed. The `Handler` function `removeCallbacks()` can cancel a pending operation by removing a posted `Runnable` task from the queue of work:

```
final Runnable runnable = new Runnable(){
  public void run() {
    // ... do some work
  }
};
handler.postDelayed(runnable, TimeUnit.SECONDS.toMillis(10));
Button cancel = (Button) findViewById(R.id.cancel);
```

```
cancel.setOnClickListener(new OnClickListener(){
  public void onClick(View v) {
  handler.removeCallbacks(runnable);
  }
});
```

Notice that in order to be able to specify what to remove, we must keep a reference to the `Runnable` instance, and that cancelation applies only to pending tasks—it does not attempt to stop a `Runnable` that is already mid-execution.

 Keep in mind that if you post the same object more than one time, `removeCallbacks()` will remove all the non-running entries that reference that object.

Scheduling work with send

When we post a `Runnable`, we can—as seen in the previous examples—define the work at the local or member scope with an anonymous `Runnable`. As such, the `Handler` does not know in advance what kind of work it might be asked to perform.

If we often need to perform the same work from different scopes, we could define a static or top-level `Runnable` class that we can instantiate from anywhere in our application's lifecycle.

Alternatively, we can turn the approach on its head by sending messages to a `Handler` and defining the `Handler` to react appropriately to different messages.

Taking a simple example, let's say we want our `Handler` to display `hello` or `goodbye`, depending on the type of message it receives. To do that, we'll extend `Handler` and override its `handleMessage()` method:

```
public static class SpeakHandler extends Handler {

    public static final int SAY_HELLO = 0;
    public static final int SAY_BYE = 1;

    @Override
    public void handleMessage(Message msg) {
        switch (msg.what) {
            case SAY_HELLO:
                sayWord("hello");
                break;
            case SAY_BYE:
                sayWord("goodbye");
```

```
                    break;
                default:
                    super.handleMessage(msg);
            }
        }
        private void sayWord(String word) {
            // Say word
        }
    }
```

Here, we've implemented the `handleMessage()` method to expect messages with two different `what` values and react accordingly. Apart from the `what` property, which is used to identify what the message is about, the message object provides three extra integer fields, `arg`, `arg2`, and `obj`, which can be used to identify and specify your message.

 If you look carefully at the `Speak` handler class example explained earlier, you'll notice that we defined it as a static class. Subclasses of `Handler` should always be declared as top-level or static inner classes to avoid inadvertent memory leaks!

To bind an instance of our `Handler` to the main thread, we simply instantiate it from any method that runs on the main thread, such as the `Activity onCreate()` callback:

```
private Handler handler;
protected void onCreate(Bundle savedInstanceState) {
    super.onCreate(savedInstanceState);
    handler = new SpeakHandler();
    ...
}
```

Remember that we can send messages to this `Handler` from any thread, and they will be processed by the main thread. We send messages to our `Handler`, as shown here:

```
handler.sendEmptyMessage(SpeakHandler.SAY_HELLO);
...
handler.sendEmptyMessage(SpeakHandler.SAY_BYE);
```

When we post a message over the previous method, the `Handler` will create a message for us, fill in the message's `what` property with the integer passed in, and post the message to the handler's `Looper` queue. This construct could be extremely useful when we need to send basic commands to a handler, although when we need more complex messages, we need to use other message properties, such as `arg1`, `arg2`, and `obj`, to carry more information about our request.

As messages may carry an object payload as the context for the execution of a message, let's extend our example to allow our `Handler` to say any word that the message sender wants:

```java
public static class SpeakHandler extends Handler {
    public static final int SAY_HELLO = 0;
    public static final int SAY_BYE = 1;
    public static final int SAY_WORD = 2;
    @Override
    public void handleMessage(Message msg) {
        switch(msg.what) {
            case SAY_HELLO:
                sayWord("hello"); break;
            case SAY_BYE:
                sayWord("goodbye"); break;
            case SAY_WORD:
                // Get an Object
                sayWord((String)msg.obj); break;
            default:
                super.handleMessage(msg);
        }
    }
    private void sayWord(String word) { ... }
}
```

Within our `handleMessage` method, we can access the payload of the message directly by accessing the public `obj` property. The `Message` payload can be set easily via alternative static `obtain` methods:

```java
Message msg =  Message.obtain(handler,
                SpeakHandler.SAY_WORD, "Welcome!");
handler.sendMessage(msg);
```

In the previous example, we basically create a message that the `what` property is SAY_WORD and the `obj` property is `Welcome!`.

While it should be quite clear what this code is doing, you might be wondering why we didn't create a new instance of `Message` by invoking its constructor and instead invoked its static method, `obtain`.

The reason is efficiency. Messages are used only briefly — we instantiate, dispatch, handle, and then discard them. So, if we create new instances each time, we are creating work for the garbage collector.

Garbage collection is expensive, and the Android platform goes out of its way to minimize object allocation whenever it can. While we can instantiate a new `Message` object if we wish, the recommended approach is to obtain one that reuses `Message` instances from a pool and cuts down on garbage collection overhead. By reducing the memory footprint, fewer objects are recycled, leading to faster and less frequent garbage collection.

 In cases where you can build your messages over low-cost integer arguments, you should use them instead of complex arguments such as `obj` or `data`, which always create extra work for the GC.

Just as we can schedule runnables with variants of the `post` method, we can schedule messages with variants of `send`:

```
handler.sendMessageAtFrontOfQueue(msg);
handler.sendMessageAtTime(msg, time);
handler.sendMessageDelayed(msg, delay);
```

There are also empty-message variants for convenience, when we don't have a payload:

```
handler.sendEmptyMessageAtTime(what, time);
handler.sendEmptyMessageDelayed(what, delay);
```

Cancelling pending messages

Canceling sent messages is also possible and actually easier than canceling posted runnables because we don't have to keep a reference to the messages that we might want to cancel—instead, we can just cancel messages by their `what` values or by the `what` value and object reference:

```
String myWord = "Do it now!";
handler.removeMessages(SpeakHandler.SAY_BYE);
handler.removeMessages(SpeakHandler.SAY_WORD, myWord);
```

Note that just as with posted runnables, message cancellation only removes pending operations from the queue—it does not attempt to stop an operation already being executed.

Besides the canceling functionality, the handler also provides functions to verify whether there are any pending messages in the queue. With the handler object in hand, we can query the handler by the message's what value, hasMessages(what), and by the hasMethods(what,object) message object value. Let's put some examples together with our previous examples:

```
handler.hasMessages(SpeakHandler.SAY_BYE)
handler.hasMessages(SpeakHandler.SAY_WORD, myWord)
```

The first example will verify whether there is any message whose what code is SAY_BYE, and the second will verify whether there is any message whose what code is SAY_WORD and whose object points to the same reference as myWord.

It is really important to remember that the removeMessages and hasMessages methods with an object argument will search the queue, comparing the object by the == reference comparison and not a comparison of object values such as (equals()). Here is a simple example to explain the situation:

```
String stringRef1 = new String("Welcome!");
String stringRef2 = new String("Welcome Home!");
Message msg1 =  Message.obtain(handler,
                    SpeakHandler.SAY_WORD,stringRef1);
Message msg2 =  Message.obtain(handler,
                    SpeakHandler.SAY_WORD, stringRef2);

// Enqueue the messages to be processed later
handler.sendMessageDelayed(msg1,600000);
handler.sendMessageDelayed(msg2,600000);

// try to remove the messages
handler.removeMessages(SpeakHandler.SAY_WORD,
                    stringRef1);
handler.removeMessages(SpeakHandler.SAY_WORD,
                    new String("Welcome Home!"));
// Create a Print Writer to Process StandardOutput
PrintWriterPrinter out =
    new PrintWriterPrinter(new PrintWriter(System.out,true));

// Dump the Looper State
handler.getLooper().dump(out,">> Looper Dump ");
```

As explained before, the second remove invocation will not remove the message added previously, because the stringRef1 reference is different from the new reference passed in, despite the string content being the same.

Here is the output from the looper dump, with the message that was not canceled successfully:

```
>> Looper Dump Looper (main, tid 1) {a15844a}
>> Looper Dump Message 0: { when=+10m0s0ms
        what=2
        obj=Welcome Home! target=...SpeakHandler }
>> Looper Dump (Total messages: 1,
        polling=false, quitting=false)
```

Composition versus inheritance

So far, we've subclassed `Handler` to override its `handleMessage` method, but that isn't our only option. We can favor composition over inheritance by passing an instance of `Handler.Callback` during handler construction:

```
boolean handleMessage(Message msg)
```

Let's suppose we want to extend our speaker without changing the original `Handler`, and we want to add new actions over a `Handler.Callback` class:

```
public class Speaker implements Handler.Callback {

    public static final int SAY_WELCOME = 2;
    public static final int SAY_YES = 3;
    public static final int SAY_NO = 4;

    @Override
    public boolean handleMessage(Message msg) {
        switch(msg.what) {
            case SAY_WELCOME:
                sayWord("welcome"); break;
            case SAY_YES:
                sayWord("yes"); break;
            case SAY_NO:
                sayWord("no"); break;
            default:
                return false;
        }
        return true;
    }
    private void sayWord(String word) {  }
}
```

Notice that the signature of `handleMessage` is slightly different here—we must return a `boolean` value indicating whether or not the `Message` was handled. To create a `Handler` that uses our extension, we simply pass the `Handler.Callback` implementation during handler construction:

```
Handler handler = new SpeakHandler(new Speaker());
```

If we return `false` from the `handleMessage` method of our callback, the Handler will invoke its own `handleMessage` method, so we could choose to use a combination of inheritance and composition to implement the default behavior in a `Handler` subclass and then mix in special behavior by passing in an instance of `Handler.Callback`.

In the aforementioned code, we use the composition to process the `SAY_HELLO` message and the inheritance to process the `SAY_YES` message:

```
// will be handled by SpeakHandler Handler
handler.sendEmptyMessage(SAY_HELLO);
// will be handled by Speaker Handler.Callback
handler.sendEmptyMessage(SAY_YES);
```

> **Inheritance** should only be used when the relationship between a subclass and the superclass is permanent and strong and can't be decoupled. On the other hand, **composition** offers more flexibility for enhancements and testing.

Multithreading with Handler and ThreadHandler

In a typical Android asynchronous application, the UI thread hands over long computing operations to a background thread, which in turn executes the task and posts back the results to the main thread.

So far, we have just used the `Handler` to send messages to the main thread, so the next natural step is to design a multithreaded scenario where the `interthread` communication is managed by the `Handler` construct.

Let's extend our previous examples and create a weather forecast retriever.

Imagine this scenario: when we click on a UI button, the main thread will ask for our background thread to retrieve the weather forecast and, when the weather forecast response is received, the background thread will ask the main thread to present the weather forecast received.

We will start by creating the WeatherRetriever that is responsible for receiving the weather forecast requests and then retrieve the forecast sentence and post back the result to the mainHandler object.

During the scenario assembly, the WeatherRetriever handler is attached to a background Looper over the first constructor argument in order to execute in a separate line of execution away from the main thread. The second constructor argument is used to set the handler to post the results.

On the handleMessage method, the handler is able to process the current day's forecast message requests (GET_TODAY_FORECAST) or the next day's requests (GET_TOMORROW_FORECAST), eventually calling the long-computing getForecast() operation.

The long-computing getForecast() could block the thread execution for a long time, but this is not a problem anymore, since we are going to run it in a background thread with lower priority, which does not block the UI from being rendered in time, and hence prevents an ANR error from occurring and makes the application more responsive to user interactions:

```java
public class WeatherRetriever extends Handler {

    private final Handler mainHandler;

    public static final int GET_TODAY_FORECAST = 1;

    public WeatherRetriever(Looper looper, Handler mainHandler) {
        super(looper);
        this.mainHandler = mainHandler;
    }
    // Long Computing Operation
    String getForecast() { ... }

    @Override
    public void handleMessage(Message msg) {
        switch(msg.what) {
            case GET_TODAY_FORECAST:
                ...
                final String sentence = getForecast();
                Message resultMsg =
                    mainHandler.obtainMessage(
                        WeatherPresenter.TODAY_FORECAST, sentence);
```

```
        this.mainHandler.sendMessage(resultMsg);
        break;
      }
    }
  };
```

Secondly, we will build the `WeatherPresenter`, which will handle the forecast results coming from the background operation, presenting it to the user on the main thread:

```
public class WeatherPresenter extends Handler {
  public static final int TODAY_FORECAST = 1;

  @Override
  public void handleMessage(Message msg) {
    switch(msg.what) {
    case TODAY_FORECAST:
      readTodayWeather((String) msg.obj); break;
      ...
    }
  }
  private void readTodayWeather(String word) {
    // Present the weather forecast on the UI
    ...
  }
};
```

We described one way of setting up a `Looper` thread with the `SimpleLooper` class, detailed earlier in this chapter, but there's an easier way, using a class provided by the SDK for exactly this purpose: `android.os.HandlerThread`.

When we create a `HandlerThread`, we specify two things: a name for the thread, which can be helpful when debugging, and its priority, which must be selected from the set of static values in the `android.os.Process` class:

```
HandlerThread thread = new HandlerThread("background",    Process.
THREAD_PRIORITY_BACKGROUND);
```

Thread priorities in Android are mapped into Linux nice levels, which govern how often a thread gets to run. A niceness of -20 is the highest priority, and 19 is the lowest priority. The default nice level is 0. In addition to prioritization, Android limits CPU resources using Linux cgroups. Threads that are of background priority are moved into the bg_non_interactive cgroup, which is limited to 5 percent of available CPU if threads in other groups are busy.

Adding THREAD_PRIORITY_MORE_FAVORABLE to THREAD_PRIORITY_BACKGROUND when configuring your HandlerThread moves the thread into the default cgroup, but always consider whether it is really necessary — it often isn't!

In the the next table, the mapping from Android thread priority to Linux nice levels is detailed; however, the use of nice levels lower than **-2** in regular applications is not recommended:

Java priority	Thread priority	Nice level
	THREAD_PRIORITY_URGENT_AUDIO	-19
	THREAD_PRIORITY_AUDIO	-16
MAX_PRIORITY	THREAD_PRIORITY_URGENT_DISPLAY	-8
	THREAD_PRIORITY_DISPLAY	-4
	THREAD_PRIORITY_FOREGROUND	-2
NORM_PRIORITY	THREAD_PRIORITY_DEFAULT	0
	THREAD_PRIORITY_BACKGROUND	10
MIN_PRIORITY	THREAD_PRIORITY_LOWEST	19

HandlerThread extends java.lang.Thread, and we must start it with start() before it actually begins processing its queue:

```
thread.start();
```

Now, from an Activity callback, we are going to detail how to lift up our scenario, building all the instances and objects required to submit and process requests:

```
// Background Thread
private HandlerThread thread;

protected void onCreate(Bundle savedInstanceState) {
    ...
```

```
WeatherPresenter presHandler = new WeatherPresenter();

// Creates a Thread with a looper attached
handlerThread = new HandlerThread("background",
        Process.THREAD_PRIORITY_BACKGROUND);
// start The Thread and waits for work
handlerThread.start();

// Creates the Handler to submit requests
final WeatherRetriever retHandler =
    new WeatherRetriever(handlerThread.getLooper(),presHandler);
```

As we saw previously, the retriever handler is using the `HandlerThread`'s `Looper` instead of the main thread's `Looper`, so it processes the forecast requests on a background thread, allowing us to run long-computing operations on the `WeatherRetriever`.

With a `WeatherRetriever` object (`retHandler`) reference in our hands, we are able to enqueue a new forecast request to the background thread by sending a message with the `WeatherRetriever` handler. In the next example, we listen for taps on the UI's `today` button in order to initiate a forecast request:

```
todayBut.setOnClickListener(new View.OnClickListener() {
  @Override
  public void onClick(View v) {
    retHandler.sendEmptyMessage(WeatherRetriever.
                        GET_TODAY_FORECAST);
  }
}
```

When the forecast is processed by the background thread on the `WeatherRetriever` callback, a message is dispatched to the main `Looper` through the `WeatherPresenter` reference, and `readTodayWeather(String)` is invoked on the main thread in order to present the forecast to the user.

As you can see in the following trace output, the forecast retriever runs on the low-priority background thread with TID 120, and the forecast result is presented on the main UI thread, which has a TID of 1:

```
I/MTHandler(17666): Retrieving Today Forecast at
Thread[background,120]
I/MTHandler(17666): Presenting Today Forecast at Thread[main,1]
```

If we create a `HandlerThread` to do background work for a specific `Activity`, we will want to tie the `HandlerThread` instance's life cycle closely to that of the activity's to prevent resource leaks.

A `HandlerThread` can be shut down by invoking `quit()`, which will stop the `HandlerThread` from processing any more work from its queue. A `quitSafely` method was added at API level 18, which causes the `HandlerThread` to process all remaining tasks before shutting down. Once a `HandlerThread` has been told to shut down, it will not accept any further tasks:

```
protected void onPause() {
   super.onPause();
   if (( handlerThread != null) && (isFinishing()))
     handlerThread.quit();
}
```

Looper message dispatching debugging

When you want to follow the dispatching and processing of your messages, it could be handy to print a message in the Android logs when any of your messages get routed by the `Looper` and when the handler finishes the processing. The `Looper` object supplies us with a method to set a printer facility for the message-dispatching debugging, so, from our `HandlerThread`, we are able to set it and enable the extra logging required to follow our requests:

```
   . . .
// Creates a Print writer to standard output
PrintWriterPrinter out= new PrintWriterPrinter(
   new PrintWriter(System.out,true)
);
handlerThread.getLooper().setMessageLogging(out);
   . . .
reqHandler.sendEmptyMessageDelayed (
   WeatherRetriever.GET_TODAY_FORECAST,
   10000
);
```

Here is an example of debugging messages printed when our forecast request gets processed by the `Looper`:

```
>>>>> Dispatching to Handler (...WeatherRetriever) {a15844a} null: 1
<<<<< Finished to Handler (...WeatherRetriever) {a15844a} null
```

The format for the dispatching debug message is (`<Target_Handler>`) `{Callback_Obj}` : `<what>`.

In our simple example, we print the messages for the process's standard output stream (`java.io.OutputStream`), but in more advanced cases, we can print to any kind of `OutputStream` subclass (file, network, and so on).

Sending messages versus posting runnables

It is worth spending a few moments to consider the difference between posting runnables and sending messages.

The runtime difference mostly comes down to efficiency. Creating new instances of `Runnable` each time we want our handler to do something adds garbage-collection overhead, while sending messages reuses `Message` instances, which are sourced from an application-wide pool.

For prototyping and small one-offs, posting runnables is quick and easy, while the advantages of sending messages tend to grow with the size of the application.

It should be said that message-sending is more *the Android way* and is used throughout the platform to keep garbage to a minimum and apps running smoothly.

Applications of Handler and HandlerThread

The `Handler` class is incredibly versatile, which makes its range of applications very broad.

So far, we've looked at `Handler` and `HandlerThread` in the context of the `Activity` lifecycle, which constrains the sort of applications where this construct might be used—ideally, we do not want to perform long-running operations (more than a second or so) at all in this context.

With that constraint in mind, good candidate uses include performing calculations, string processing, reading and writing small files on the file system, and reading or writing to local databases using a background `HandlerThread`.

Summary

In this chapter, we learned how to use `Handler` to queue work for the main thread and how to use `Looper` to build up a queueing infrastructure for our own `Thread`.

We saw the different ways in which we can define work with `Handler`: arbitrary work defined at the call site with `Runnable` or predefined work implemented in the `Handler` itself and triggered by message-sending.

In the meantime, we learned how to defer work properly without leaking memory on the way.

We learned how to use `Handler` in a multithreaded application to pass work and results back and forth between cooperating threads, performing blocking operations on an ordinary background thread and communicating the results back to the main thread to update the user interface.

In the next chapter, we'll start to build responsive applications by applying the `AsyncTask` instance to execute work in the background using pools of threads and returning progress updates and results to the main thread.

3
Exploring the AsyncTask

In *Chapter 2, Performing Work with Looper, Handler and HandlerThread*, we familiarized ourselves with the most basic asynchronous and concurrency constructs available on the Android platform: `Handler` and `Looper`. Those constructs underpin most of the evented and sequential processing used by the main thread to render the UI and to run the Android components life cycle.

In this chapter, we are going to explore `android.os.AsyncTask`, a higher level construct that provides us with a neat and lean interface to perform background work and publish results back to the main thread without having to manage the thread creation and the handler manipulation.

In this chapter we will cover the following topics:

- Introducing AsyncTask
- Declaring AsyncTask types
- Executing AsyncTasks
- Providing indeterministic progress feedback
- Providing deterministic progress feedback
- Canceling an AsyncTask
- Handling exceptions
- Controlling the level of concurrency
- Common AsyncTask issues
- Applications of AsyncTask

Introducing AsyncTask

`AsyncTask` was introduced on the Android platform with Android Cupcake (API Level 3), with the express purpose of helping developers to avoid blocking the main thread. The Async part of the name of this class comes from the word asynchronous, which literally means that the blocking task is not occurring at the same time we call it.

The `AsyncTask` encloses the creation of the background thread, the synchronization with the main thread, and the publishing of the progress of the execution in a single construct.

In contrast to the `Handler` and `Looper` constructs, the `AsyncTask` exempts the developer from the management of low level components, thread creation, and synchronization.

`AsyncTask` is an abstract class, and as such, must be subclassed for use. At the minimum, our subclass must provide an implementation for the abstract `doInBackground` method, which defines the work that we want to get done off the main thread.

```
protected Result doInBackground(Params... params)
```

The `doInBackground` is going to be executed in the current process in a parallel thread with the priority `THREAD_PRIORITY_BACKGROUND` (Nice level 10) and with the name following the next form `AsyncTask #<N>`.

Apart from the method `doInBackground` the construct offers distinct methods which the developer might implement in the subclass to set up the task, publish progress, and post the final result into the main thread.

There are five other methods of `AsyncTask` which we may choose to override:

```
protected void onPreExecute()
protected void onProgressUpdate(Progress... values)
protected void onPostExecute(Result result)
protected void onCancelled(Result result)
protected void onCancelled()
```

Although we could override one or more of these five methods, we will not invoke them directly from our own code. These are callback methods, meaning that they will be invoked for us (called back) at the appropriate time throughout the `AsyncTask` lifecycle.

The key difference between `doInBackground()` and the other four methods is the thread on which they execute.

Before any background work begins, `onPreExecute()` will be invoked and will run synchronously to completion on the main thread when we call the execute (Params...) method.

In the `onPreExecute()` method, we could set up the task or any progress dialog on the UI to indicate to the user that your task has just begun.

Once `onPreExecute()` completes, `doInBackground()` will be scheduled and will start work on a background thread.

During the background work, the developer can publish progress updates from `doInBackground()`, which trigger the main thread to execute `onProgressUpdate` with the progress values we provide. Internally, the `AsyncTask` makes use of a `Handler` bound to the main Thread `Looper` to publish results on the main Thread as explained in *Chapter 2, Performing Work with Looper, Handler and HandlerThread*.

By invoking this on the main thread, `AsyncTask` makes it easy for us to update the user interface to show progress (remember that we can only update the user interface from the main thread).

When the background work completes successfully, doInBackground() may return a result. This result is passed to onPostExecute(), which is invoked for us on the main thread. With the result received on the onPostExecute(), we can update the user interface with the results of our background processing:

This pattern of passing data from one thread to another is very important, because it allows us to run intensive and long tasks away from the crucial main thread. This construct simplifies the communication in the main thread and provides a high level API for executing asynchronous work on background threads.

Our AsyncTask could manipulate fields of the enclosing Activity class, but then we would have to take extra precautions, such as adding synchronization to prevent race conditions and ensure visibility of updates.

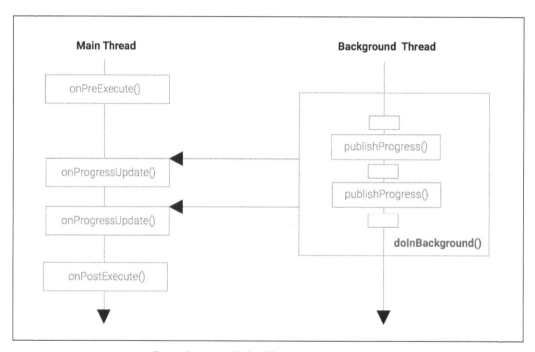

Figure 3.1: AsyncTask callback execution function

The preceding figure displays a sequence of method calls executed by AsyncTask, illustrating which methods run on the main thread versus the AsyncTask background thread.

Since `onPreExecute()`, `onProgressUpdate()`, `onPostExecute()`, and `onCancelled()` methods are invoked on the main thread, we must not perform long-running/blocking operations in these methods.

With the `AsyncTask` reference invoking the `cancel` method before `doInBackground()` completes, `onPostExecute()` will not be called. Instead, the alternative `onCancelled()` callback method is invoked on the UI thread so that we can implement different behavior for a successful versus cancelled completion:

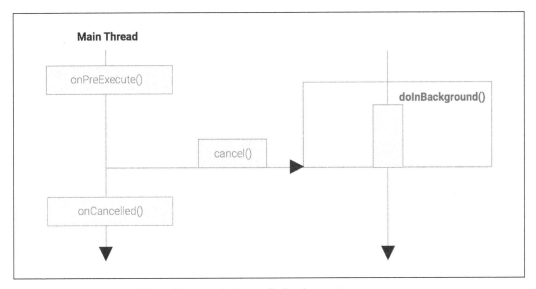

Figure 3.2: AsyncTask cancelled task execution sequence

The preceding figure displays the sequence of method calls when a task is cancelled before the `doInBackground()` finishes. Like we have shown in the previous figure, the `cancel()` might be called by the main thread or from any other thread with access to the `AsyncTask` object reference.

Declaring AsyncTask types

`AsyncTask` is a generically typed class that exposes three generic type parameters:

```
abstract class AsyncTask<Params, Progress, Result>
```

In order to use a generic type, we must provide one type argument per type parameter that was declared for the generic type.

 The generic type class provides a way to re-use the same generic algorithms for different input types. A generic type could have one or more type parameters.

When we declare an `AsyncTask` subclass, we'll specify the types for Params, Progress, and Result; for example, if we want to pass a `String` parameter to `doInBackground`, report progress as a `Float`, and return a `Boolean` result, we would declare our `AsyncTask` subclass as follows:

```
public class MyTask extends AsyncTask<String, Float, Boolean>
```

If we don't need to pass any parameters, or don't want to report progress, a good type to use for those parameters is `java.lang.Void`, which signals our intent clearly, because `Void` is an uninstantiable class representing the void keyword.

Only reference types can be used as type arguments of a generic type. This includes classes, interfaces, enum types, nested and inner types, and array types. Primitive types are not allowed to be used as a type argument. The next declaration is considered illegal on a generic type class definition:

```
// Error
public class MyTask extends AsyncTask<String, float, boolean>
```

Let's take a look at our first example, performing an expensive image download in the background and reporting the result into the current UI:

```
public class DownloadImageTask
   extends AsyncTask<URL, Integer, Bitmap> {

   // Weak reference to the UI View to update
   private final WeakReference<ImageView> imageViewRef;

   public DownloadImageTask(ImageView imageView) {
     this.imageViewRef = new WeakReference<ImageView>(imageView);
   }

   // Retrieves the image from a URL
   private Bitmap downloadBitmap(URL url) {
     // elided for brevity ...
     ...
   }

   @Override
```

```
protected Bitmap doInBackground(URL... params) {
  URL url = params[0];
  // The IO operation invoked will take a significant ammount
  // to complete
  return downloadBitmap(url);
}
...


@Override
protected void onPostExecute(Bitmap bitmap) {
  ImageView imageView = this.imageViewRef.get();
  if (imageView != null) {
    imageView.setImageBitmap(bitmap);
  }
 }
}
```

Here, `DownloadImageTask` extends `AsyncTask`, specifying the Params type as a URL so that we can retrieve an image based on its url, Progress as Integer, and the Result type as Bitmap.

We pass `ImageView` to the constructor so that `DownloadImageTask` has a weak reference to the user interface that it should update upon completion.

We've implemented `doInBackground` to download the image in the background, where url is a URL parameter with the image resource location.

In `onPostExecute`, when the view weak reference is not null, we simply load the bitmap into the view that we stored in the constructor.

The `WeakReference` does not prevent the view from being garbage collected when the activity where the view was created is no longer active.

Executing AsyncTasks

Having implemented `doInBackground` and `onPostExecute`, we want to get our task running. There are two methods we can use for this, each offering different levels of control over the degree of concurrency with which our tasks are executed. Let's look at the simpler of the two methods first:

```
public final AsyncTask<Params, Progress, Result> execute(Params...
params)
```

The return type is the type of our `AsyncTask` subclass, which is simply for convenience so that we can use method chaining to instantiate and start a task in a single line and still record a reference to the instance:

```
class MyTask implements AsyncTask<String,Void,String>{ ... }
MyTask task = new MyTask().execute("hello");
```

The `Params... params` argument is the same Params type we used in our class declaration, because the values we supply to the execute method are later passed to our `doInBackground` method as its Params... params arguments. Notice that it is a varargs (variable number of parameters) parameter, meaning that we can pass any number of parameters of that type (including none).

Each instance of AsyncTask is a single-use object—once we have started an AsyncTask, it can never be started again, even if we cancel it or wait for it to complete first.

This is a safety feature, designed to protect us from concurrency issues such as the race condition.

Executing `DownloadImageTask` is straightforward—we need `Activity`, which constructs an instance of `DownloadImageTask` with a view to update, and then we invoke the `execute` method with a suitable value for the URL:

```
public class ShowMyPuppyActivity extends Activity {

    @Override
public void onCreate(Bundle savedInstanceState) {
super.onCreate(savedInstanceState);
setContentView(R.layout.show_my_puppy);

// Get the show button reference
Button showBut = (Button) findViewById(R.id.showImageBut);
showBut.setOnClickListener(new View.OnClickListener() {

    @Override
    public void onClick(View v) {
      ...
      // My Puppie Image URL
      URL url = new URL("http://img.allw.mn/" +
                  "content/www/2009/03/april1.jpg");
      // Get the Reference to Photo UI Image View
      ImageView iv = (ImageView) findViewById(R.id.photo);
        // Download the Image in background and
```

```
          // load the image on the view
          new DownloadImageTask(iv).execute(url);
          ...
      }
  });
}
```

Once we click on the UI show button, a new `DownloadAsyncTask` is created and attached to an `imageView` and we call the `execute()` method to start the async task in the background. When we call the `execute()` method on the task, this will result in a call to the `onPreExecute()` method followed by a call to the `doInBackground()` method.

Like we explained before, once the download is finished, the `onPostExecute()` is called to load the image downloaded (`Bitmap`) on the image view.

 You can download the example code files for all Packt Publishing books you have purchased from your account at http://www.packtpub.com. If you purchased this book elsewhere, you can visit http://www.packtpub.com/support and register to have the files e-mailed directly to you.

Providing indeterministic progress feedback

Having started what we know to be a potentially long-running task, we probably want to let the user know that something is happening. There are a lot of ways of doing this, but a common approach is to present a dialog displaying a relevant message.

A good place to present our dialog is from the `onPreExecute()` method of `AsyncTask` which executes on the main thread so it is allowed to interact with the user interface.

The modified `DownloadImageTask` will need a reference to a Context, so that it can prepare a `ProgressDialog`, which it will show and dismiss in `onPreExecute()` and `onPostExecute()` respectively. As `doInBackground()` has not changed, it is not shown in the following code, for brevity:

```
public class DownloadImageTask
    extends AsyncTask<URL, Integer, Bitmap> {
    ...
    private final WeakReference<Context> ctx;
```

```
    private ProgressDialog progress;
    ...
    public DownloadImageTask(Context ctx, ImageView imageView) {
      this.imageView = new WeakReference<ImageView>(imageView);
      this.ctx = new WeakReference<Context>(ctx);
    }

    @Override
    protected void onPreExecute() {
      if ( ctx !=null && ctx.get()!= null ) {
        progress = new ProgressDialog(ctx.get());
        progress.setTitle(R.string.downloading_image);
                   progress.setIndeterminate(true);
        progress.setCancelable(false);
        progress.show();
      }
    }


    // ... doInBackground elided for brevity ...
    @Override
    protected void onPostExecute(Bitmap bitmap) {
      ...
      if ( progress != null ) { progress.dismiss(); }
      ...
    }
  }
```

All that remains is to pass a Context to the constructor of our modified
DownloadImageTask. As Activity is a subclass of Context, we can simply
pass a reference to the host Activity:

```
showBut.setOnClickListener(new View.OnClickListener() {

  @Override
  public void onClick(View v) {
      ...
      // Pass in the Context and the image view to load
      // the image
      new DownloadImageTask(
        ShowMyPuppyActivity.this, iv).execute(url);
        ...
  }
});
```

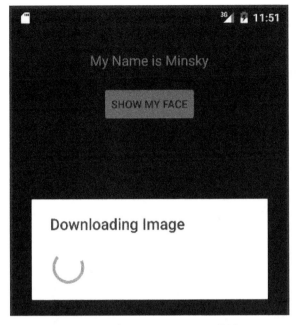

Figure 3.3 : Indeterministic Progress Dialog

Once the async task is started, the `onPreExecute()` callback will create an indeterministic progress dialog and display it as shown in Figure 3.3. The non-cancelable dialog will be placed over the UI screen in an opaque layer with the title defined. By indeterministic, we mean that beforehand, we can't estimate how much longer we have to wait for the task to complete.

Until the download finishes, and the dialog gets dismissed on `onPostExecute()`, the user is not able to interact with the application and the dialog will remain in the foreground.

When any long computation is required before you are able to present your content in your application UI, you must present an indication that something is happening in the background while the user is waiting.

Providing deterministic progress feedback

Knowing that something is happening is a great relief to our users, but they might be getting impatient and wondering how much longer they need to wait. Let's show them how we're getting on by adding a progress bar to our dialog.

Remember that we aren't allowed to update the user interface directly from `doInBackground()`, because we aren't on the main thread. How, then, can we tell the main thread to make these updates for us?

`AsyncTask` comes with a handy callback method for this, whose signature we saw at the beginning of the chapter:

```
protected void onProgressUpdate(Progress... values)
```

We can override `onProgressUpdate()` to update the user interface from the main thread, but when does it get called and where does it get its `Progress... values` from? The glue between `doInBackground()` and `onProgressUpdate()` is another of AsyncTask's methods:

```
protected final void publishProgress(Progress... values)
```

To update the user interface with our progress, we simply publish progress updates from the background thread by invoking `publishProgress()` from within `doInBackground()`. Each time we call `publishProgress()`, the main thread will be scheduled to invoke `onProgressUpdate()` for us with these progress values.

The modifications to our running example to show a deterministic progress bar are quite simple. Since we have already defined the `DownloadImageTask` Progress type as Integer, now, we must change the setting progress values in the range 0 (`setProgress`) to 100 (`setMax`) and set the style and the bounds of the progress bar. We can do that with the following additions to `onPreExecute()`:

```
@Override
protected void onPreExecute() {
    ...
    // Sets the progress bar style
    progress.setProgressStyle(
        ProgressDialog.STYLE_HORIZONTAL);
    progress.setIndeterminate(false);
    progress.setProgress(0);
    progress.setMax(100);
    progress.setCancelable(false);
    progress.show();
}
```

We also need to implement the `onProgressUpdate` callback to update the progress bar from the main thread:

```
@Override
protected void onProgressUpdate(Integer... values) {
  progress.setProgress(values[0]);
  }
```

The final modification is to calculate the progress at each iteration of the `for` loop, and invoke `publishProgress()` so that the main thread knows to call back `onProgressUpdate()`:

```
private Bitmap downloadBitmap(URL url) {
  InputStream is = null;
  ...
  // Before Download starts
  publishProgress(0);
  downloadedBytes = 0;
  // Creates a Connection to the image URL
  HttpURLConnection conn = (HttpURLConnection) url.
                          openConnection();

  ...
  // Retrieves the image total length
  totalBytes = conn.getContentLength();
    ...

  BufferedInputStream bif = new BufferedInputStream(is) {

    int progress = 0;

      public int read(byte[] buffer, int byteOffset,
                  int byteCount) throws IOException {
        // The number of bytes read in each stream read
      int readBytes = super.read(buffer, byteOffset,
                          byteCount);

        ..
      // Actual number of bytes read from the file
      downloadedBytes += readBytes;
      // Percent of work done
      int percent = (int)((downloadedBytes * 100f) /
                  totalBytes);
      // Publish the progress to the main thread
      if (percent > progress) {
        publishProgress(percent);
        progress = percent;
      }
    ...
  }
```

It is important to understand that invoking `publishProgress()` does not directly invoke the main thread, but adds a task to the main thread's queue, which will be processed at some time in the near future by the main thread.

Notice that we're being careful to publish progress only when the percentage actually changes, avoiding any unnecessary overhead:

> Is important to know that every time you invoke `publishProgress()` on the background thread, in `downloadBitmat()`, a new Handler message is sent automatically internally to push the progress to the main thread.

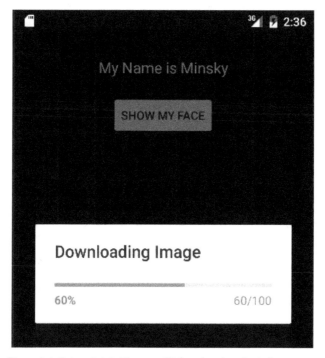

Figure 3.4: Deterministic Progress Dialog showing the task progress

As can be seen in Figure 3.4, the deterministic dialog created in `onPreExecute()` is updated continuously in `doInBackground()` with the current progress of the task. The progress is calculated as a ratio, as in the following division:

The delay between publishing the progress and seeing the user interface update will be extremely short for this example and for any application that doesn't have too much UI work to process. The progress bar will update smoothly following the golden rule of not blocking the main thread for any of our code, since we only dispatch a progress update when the percentage changes.

Canceling an AsyncTask

Another nice usability touch we can provide for our users is the ability to cancel a task before it completes — for example, if after starting the execution, the user is no longer interested in the operation result. AsyncTask provides support for cancellation with the cancel method.

```
public final boolean cancel(boolean mayInterruptIfRunning)
```

The mayInterruptIfRunning parameter allows us to specify whether an AsyncTask thread that is in an interruptible state, may actually be interrupted — for example, if our doInBackground code is performing a blocking interruptible function, such as Object.wait(). When we set the mayInterruptIfRunning as false, the AsyncTask won't interrupt the current interruptible blocking operation and the AsyncTask background processing will only finish once the blocking operation terminates.

> In well behaved interruptible blocking functions, such as Thread.sleep(), Thread.join(), or Object.wait(), the execution is stopped immediately when the thread is interrupted with Thread.interrupt() and it throws an InterruptedException. The InterruptedException should be properly handled and swallowed only if you know the background thread is about to exit.

Simply invoking cancel is not sufficient to cause our task to finish early. We need to actively support cancellation by periodically checking the value returned from isCancelled and reacting appropriately in doInBackground.

First, let's set up our ProgressDialog to trigger the AsyncTask's cancel method by adding a few lines to onPreExecute:

```
@Override
protected void onPreExecute() {
  ...
  progress.setCancelable(true);
  progress.setOnCancelListener(
    new DialogInterface.OnCancelListener() {
      public void onCancel(DialogInterface dialog) {
        DownloadImageTask.this.cancel(false);
      }
    });
  ...
}
```

Now we can trigger cancel by touching outside the progress dialog, or pressing the device's back button while the dialog is visible.

We'll invoke `cancel` with `false`, as we don't want to immediately suspend the current IO operation during a network read or check the return value of the `Thread.interrupted()` function. We still need to check for the cancellation in `doInBackground`, so we will modify it as follows:

```
private Bitmap downloadBitmap(URL url) {
  Bitmap bitmap = null;
  BufferedInputStream bif = new BufferedInputStream(is) {
    ...

    public int read(byte[] buffer, int byteOffset,
                    int byteCount) throws IOException {

      // Read the bytes from the Connection
      int readBytes = super.read(buffer, byteOffset, byteCount);

      // Verify if the download was cancelled
      if ( isCancelled() ) {
        // Returning -1 means that there is
        // no more data and the stream has just ended
        return -1;
      }
      ...
    }
  }
  // If the download is cancelled the Bitmap is null
  if ( !isCancelled() ) {
    bitmap = BitmapFactory.decodeStream(bif);
  }
  return bitmap;
}
```

In the code above, in our Anonymous subclass of `BufferInputStream` we are able to intercept each read that happens on the connection. When that is in place, and once we cancel the AsyncTask, we are able to stop the data stream by simple returning a -1(End of stream) as the result of the read invoke. As soon as the `BitmapFactory.decodeStream` receives the end of the stream, it returns immediately and we return null as the result of the `downloadBitmap` invoke.

The cancelled `AsyncTask` does not receive the `onPostExecute` callback. Instead, we have the opportunity to implement different behavior for a cancelled execution by implementing `onCancelled`. There are two variants of this callback method:

```
protected void onCancelled(Result result);
protected void onCancelled();
```

The default implementation of the parameterized `onCancelled`(Result result) method delegates to the `onCancelled()` method after it finishes.

If AsyncTask cannot provide either a partial result (such as a partial image data) or nothing, then we will probably want to override the zero argument `onCancelled()` method.

On the other hand, if we are performing an incremental computation in `syncTask`, we might choose to override the `onCancelled(Result result)` version when the partial result has some meaning to your application.

In both cases, since `onPostExecute()` does not get called on a canceled `AsyncTask`, we will want to make sure that our `onCancelled()` callbacks update the user interface appropriately—in our example, this entails dismissing the progress dialog we opened in `onPreExecute()`, and updating the image view with a default image available as drawable on the application package.

In our example, when the task is cancelled, the result from `doInBackground()` is a null object so we will override the no-argument `onCancelled()` function to add the behavior described previously:

```
@Override
protected void onCancelled() {
   if ( imageView !=null && imageView.get() != null &&
        ctx !=null && ctx.get() != null ) {

     // Load the Bitmap from the application resources
     Bitmap bitmap = BitmapFactory.decodeResource(
                      ctx.get().getResources(),
                      R.drawable.default_photo
                  );
     // Set the image bitmap on the image view
     this.imageView.get().setImageBitmap(bitmap);
   }
   // Remove the dialog from the screen
   progress.dismiss();
}
```

Another situation to be aware of occurs when we cancel an AsyncTask that has not yet begun its `doInBackground()` method. If this happens, `doInBackground()` will never be invoked, though `onCancelled()` will still be called on the main thread.

AsyncTask Execution State

The `execute()` method, could finish in a cancelled state or in a completed state, however if the user tries to call `execute()` a second time, the task will fail and throw an IllegalStateException exception saying:

Cannot execute task, a task can be executed only once/the task is already running

With a reference to an `AsyncTask` object in hand, we can ascertain the status of your task over the `getStatus()` method, and react according to the status result. Let's take a look at the next snippet:

```
// Create a download task object
DownloadImageTask task  = new DownloadImageTask(
                         ShowMyPuppyActivity.this, iv);
...
if ( task.getStatus() == AsyncTask.Status.PENDING ) {
  // DownloadImageTask has not started yet so
  // we can can invoke execute()
} else if (task.getStatus() == AsyncTask.Status.RUNNING) {
  // DownloadImageTask is currently running in
  // doInBackground()
} else if (task.getStatus() == AsyncTask.Status.FINISHED
          && task.isCancelled()) {
  // DownloadImageTask is done OnCancelled was called
} else {
  // DownloadImageTask is done onPostExecute was called
}
```

Using the `getStatus()` instance method provided by `AsyncTask` we can keep up with the execution of the background task and know exactly what the current status of your background work is.

 If you want to repeat your background you have to instantiate a new task and call the `execute()` method again.

Handling exceptions

The callback methods defined by AsyncTask dictate that we cannot throw checked exceptions, so we must wrap any code that throws checked exceptions with try/catch blocks. Unchecked exceptions that propagate out of AsyncTask's methods will crash our application, so we must test carefully and handle these if necessary.

For the callback methods that run on the main thread — onPreExecute(), onProgressUpdate(), onPostExecute(), and onCancelled() — we can catch exceptions in the method and directly update the user interface to alert the user.

Of course, exceptions are likely to arise in our doInBackground() method too, as this is where the bulk of the work of AsyncTask is done, but unfortunately, we can't update the user interface from doInBackground(). A simple solution is to have doInBackground() return an object that may contain either the result or an exception. First we are going to create a generic class for storing the result of an operation and a member to store an exception:

```
public class Result<T> {
    public T result;
    public Throwable error;
}
```

In the next step we will create a new download AsyncTask, called SafeDownloadImageTask, that takes care of the exception handling and has a result of type Result<Bitmap> instead of the Bitmap:

```
public class SafeDownloadImageTask extends
    AsyncTask<URL, Integer, Result<Bitmap>> {

    // Method executed on the Background Thread
    protected Result<Bitmap> doInBackground(URL... params) {
        Result<Bitmap> result = new Result<Bitmap>();
        try {
            // elided for brevity ...
            ...
            result.result = bitmap;
        } catch (Throwable e) {
            result.error = e;
        } ...
    }
    return result;
}
```

Now we can check in `onPostExecute` for the presence of an `Exception` in the `Result` object. If there is one, we can deal with it, perhaps by alerting the user; otherwise, we just use the actual result as normal and use the bitmap from the result:

```
@Override
protected final void onPostExecute(Result<Bitmap> result) {
    ...
  if ( result.error!= null) {
    // ... alert the user ...
    ...
    Log.e("SafeDownloadImageTask",
          "Failed to download image ",result.exception);
    loadDefaultImage(imageView);
  } else {
    // ... success, continue as normal ...
    imageView.setImageBitmap(result.actual);
  }
}
```

With a safe implementation like the one above, any error thrown on the background thread is safely forwarded to the main thread and does not affect the normal lifecycle of the `AsyncTask`. Let's try to retrieve an image that does not exist and see if the exception is handled properly:

```
URL url = new URL("http://img.allw.mn" +
                  "/content/www/2009/03/notfound.jpg");
new SafeDownloadImageTask(ShowMyPuppyActivity.this, iv)
.execute(url);
```

As expected, the error was caught, wrapped in a `Result` object, and printed in the Android log with a stack trace pointing to the `SafeDownloadImageTask. doInBrackground` method:

```
...downloadBitmap(SafeDownloadImageTask.java:85)
...doInBackground(SafeDownloadImageTask.java:60)
...

84: if (responseCode != HttpURLConnection.HTTP_OK){
85:     throw new Exception(...);
86: }
```

Controlling the level of concurrency

So far, we've carefully avoided being too specific about what exactly happens when we invoke the `AsyncTask` execute method. We know that `doInBackground()` will execute off the main thread, but what exactly does that mean?

The original goal of `AsyncTask` was created to help developers avoid blocking the main thread. In its initial form at API level 3, `AsyncTasks` were queued and executed serially (that is, one after the other) on a single background thread, guaranteeing that they would complete in the order they were started.

This changed in API level 4 to use a pool of up to 128 threads to execute multiple `AsyncTasks` concurrently with each other—a level of concurrency of up to 128. At first glance, this seems like a good thing, since a common use case for `AsyncTask` is to perform blocking I/O, where the thread spends much of its time idly waiting for data.

However, as we saw in *Chapter 1, Building Responsive Android Applications*, there are many issues that commonly arise in concurrent programming, and indeed, the Android team realized that by executing `AsyncTasks` concurrently by default, they were exposing developers to potential programming problems (for example, when executed concurrently, there are no guarantees that `AsyncTasks` will complete in the same order they were started).

As a result, a further change was made at API level 11, switching back to serial execution by default, and introducing a new method that gives concurrency control back to the app developer:

```
public final AsyncTask<Params, Progress, Result>
    executeOnExecutor(Executor exec, Params... params)
```

From API level 11 onwards, we can start AsyncTasks with `executeOnExecutor`, and in doing so, choose the level of concurrency for ourselves by supplying an Executor object.

Executor is an interface from the `java.util.concurrent` package of the JDK, as described in more detail in *Chapter 1, Building Responsive Android Applications*. Its purpose is to present a way to submit tasks for execution without spelling out precisely how or when the execution will be carried out. Implementations of `Executor` may run tasks sequentially using a single thread, use a limited pool of threads to control the level of concurrency, or even directly create a new thread for each task.

The `AsyncTask` class provides two Executor instances that allow you to choose between the concurrency levels described earlier in this section:

- `SERIAL_EXECUTOR`: This Executor queues tasks and makes sure that the tasks are executed by the AsyncTask ThreadPool sequentially, in the order they were submitted.

- `THREAD_POOL_EXECUTOR`: This `Executor` runs tasks using a pool of threads for efficiency (starting a new thread comes with some overhead cost that can be avoided through pooling and reuse). `THREAD_POOL_EXECUTOR` is an instance of the JDK class `ThreadPoolExecutor`, which uses a pool of threads that grows and shrinks with demand. In the case of `AsyncTask`, the pool is configured to maintain at least five threads, and expands up to 128 threads. In Android Lollipop 5.0 (API Level 21), the maximum number of threads was reduced to the number of CPU cores * 2 + 1 and the `ThreadPool` global enqueuing capacity was increased.

To execute `AsyncTask` using a specific executor, we invoke the `executeOnExecutor` method, supplying a reference to the executor we want to use, for example:

```
task.executeOnExecutor(AsyncTask.THREAD_POOL_EXECUTOR,
                       params);
```

As the default behavior of execute since API level 11 is to run AsyncTasks serially on a single background thread, the following two statements are equivalent:

```
task.execute(params);
task.executeOnExecutor(AsyncTask.SERIAL_EXECUTOR, params);
```

In the next image we will show the differences between the serial executor and thread pool when either executors process a group of `AsyncTask` that were enqueued sequentially:

```
new SleepAsyncTask(1).execute(1000);
...
new SleepAsyncTask(4).execute(1000);
```

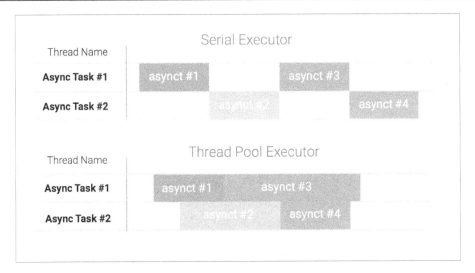

As shown in the preceding image, the serial executor uses the threads available in the `AsyncTask` Thread Pool, however they will only process the next `AsyncTask` when the previous `AsyncTask` finishes. Alternatively, `ThreadPoolExecutor` will start processing the next task as soon as it has a thread available to do the job without guaranteeing that they would complete in the order they were started:

> It is important to mention that all the `AsyncTasks` from the system will share the same static executor `AsyncTask.THREAD_POOL_EXECUTOR`. For the `SerialExecutor` the situation is worse because if an `AsyncTask` is occupying the single executor for a long period of time the next tasks will wait on a queue to get processed.

Besides the default executors provided by `AsyncTask` and the ones that are available on the `java.util.concurrent`, we can choose to create our own. For example, we might want to allow some concurrency by operating off a small pool of threads, and allow many tasks to be queued if all threads are currently busy.

This is easily achieved by configuring our own instance of `ThreadPoolExecutor` as a static member of one of our own classes — for example, our `Activity` class. Here's how we might configure an executor with a pool of four to eight threads and an effectively infinite queue:

```
private static final Queue<Runnable> QUEUE =
    new LinkedBlockingQueue<Runnable>();
public static final Executor MY_EXECUTOR =
    new ThreadPoolExecutor(4, 8, 1, TimeUnit.MINUTES, QUEUE);
```

The parameters to the constructor indicate the core pool size (4), the maximum pool size (8), the time for which idle additional threads may live in the pool before being removed (1), the unit of time (minutes), and the queue to append work when the pool threads are occupied.

Using our own Executor is then as simple as invoking our `AsyncTask` as follows:

```
task.executeOnExecutor(MY_EXECUTOR, params);
```

Common AsyncTask issues

As with any powerful programming abstraction, `AsyncTask` is not entirely free from issues and compromises. In the next sections we are going to list some of the pitfalls that we could face when we want to make use of this construct in our applications.

Fragmentation issues

In the Controlling the level of concurrency section, we saw how `AsyncTask` has evolved with new releases of the Android platform, resulting in behavior that varies with the platform of the device running the task, which is a part of the wider issue of fragmentation.

The simple fact is that if we target a broad range of API levels, the execution characteristics of our `AsyncTask`s — and therefore, the behavior of our apps — can vary considerably on different devices. So what can we do to reduce the likelihood of encountering AsyncTask issues due to fragmentation?

The most obvious approach is to deliberately target devices running at least Honeycomb, by setting a `minSdkVersion` of 11 in the Android Manifest file. This neatly puts us in the category of devices, which, by default, execute `AsyncTasks` serially, and therefore, much more predictably.

At the time of writing in October 2015, only 4% of Android devices run a version of Android in the danger zone between API Levels 4 and 10, and therefore targeting your application to Level 11 would not reduce your market reach significantly.

When the `ThreadPoolExecutor` is used as the executor, the changes introduced in Lollipop (API Level 21) could also bring behavior drifts in relation to older versions (API Level >10). The modern `AsyncTask`'s `ThreadPoolExecutor` is limited to the device's CPU cores * 2 + 1 concurrent threads, with an additional queue of 128 tasks to queue up work.

A second option is to design our code carefully and test exhaustively on a range of devices—always commendable practices of course, but as we've seen, concurrent programming is hard enough without the added complexity of fragmentation, and invariably, subtle bugs will remain.

A third solution that has been suggested by the Android development community is to reimplement AsyncTask in a package within your own project, then extend your own AsyncTask class instead of the SDK version. In this way, you are no longer at the mercy of the user's device platform, and can regain control of your AsyncTasks. Since the source code for AsyncTask is readily available, this is not difficult to do.

Memory leaks

In cases where we keep a reference to an Activity or a View, we could prevent an entire tree of objects from being garbage collected when the activity is destroyed. The developer needs to make sure that it cancels the task and removes the reference to the destroyed activity or view.

Activity lifecycle issues

Having deliberately moved any long-running tasks off the main thread, we've made our applications nice and responsive—the main thread is free to respond very quickly to any user interaction.

Unfortunately, we have also created a potential problem for ourselves, because the main thread is able to finish the Activity before our background tasks complete. The Activity might finish for many reasons, including configuration changes caused by the user rotating the device (the Activity is destroyed and created again with a new address in the memory), the user connecting the device to a docking station, or any other kind of context change.

If we continue processing a background task after the Activity has finished, we are probably doing unnecessary work, and therefore wasting CPU and other resources (including battery life), which could be put to better use.

On occasions after a device rotation, the AsyncTask continues to be meaningful and has valid content to deliver, however, it has reference to an activity or a view that was destroyed and therefore is no longer able to update the UI and finish its work and deliver its result.

Also, any object references held by the `AsyncTask` will not be eligible for garbage collection until the task explicitly nulls those references or completes and is itself eligible for **GC (garbage collection)**. Since our `AsyncTask` probably references the Activity or parts of the View hierarchy, we can easily leak a significant amount of memory in this way.

A common usage of `AsyncTask` is to declare it as an anonymous inner class of the host Activity, which creates an implicit reference to the Activity and an even bigger memory leak.

There are two approaches for preventing these resource wastage problems.

Handling lifecycle issues with early cancellation

First and foremost, we can synchronize our `AsyncTask` lifecycle with that of the Activity by canceling running tasks when our Activity is finishing.

When an `Activity` finishes, its lifecycle callback methods are invoked on the main thread. We can check to see why the lifecycle method is being called, and if the `Activity` is finishing, cancel the background tasks. The most appropriate `Activity` lifecycle method for this is `onPause`, which is guaranteed to be called before the `Activity` finishes:

```
protected void onPause() {
    super.onPause();
    if ((task != null) && (isFinishing()))
        task.cancel(false);
}
```

If the `Activity` is not finishing — say, because it has started another `Activity` and is still on the back stack — we might simply allow our background task to continue to completion.

This solution is straightforward and clean but far from ideal because you might waste precious resources by starting over the background work again unaware that you might already have a valid result or that your `AsyncTask` is still running.

Beyond that, when you start multiple `AsyncTasks` and start them again when the device rotation happens, the waste grows substantially since we have to cancel and fire up the same number of tasks again.

Handling lifecycle issues with retained headless fragments

If the Activity is finishing because of a configuration change, it may still be useful to use the results of the background task and display them in the restarted Activity. One pattern for achieving this is through the use of retained Fragments.

Fragments were introduced to Android at API level 11, but are available through a support library to applications targeting earlier API Levels. All of the downloadable examples use the support library, and target API Levels 7 through 23. To use Fragment, our Activity must extend the FragmentActivity class.

The Fragment lifecycle is closely bound to that of the host Activity, and a fragment will normally be disposed when the activity restarts. However, we can explicitly prevent this by invoking setRetainInstance(true) on our Fragment so that it survives across Activity restarts.

Typically, a Fragment will be responsible for creating and managing at least a portion of the user interface of an Activity, but this is not mandatory. A Fragment that does not manage a view of its own is known as a headless Fragment. Since they do not have a UI related to them, they do not have to be destroyed and recreated again when the user rotates the device, for example.

Isolating our AsyncTask in a retained headless Fragment makes it less likely that we will accidentally leak references to objects such as the View hierarchy, because the AsyncTask will no longer directly interact with the user interface. To demonstrate this, we'll start by defining an interface that our Activity will implement:

```
public interface AsyncListener {
    void onPreExecute();
    void onProgressUpdate(Integer... progress);
    void onPostExecute(Bitmap result);
    void onCancelled(Bitmap result);
}
```

Next, we'll create a retained headless Fragment, which wraps our AsyncTask. For brevity, doInBackground is omitted, as it is unchanged from the previous examples — see the downloadable samples for the complete code.

```
public class DownloadImageHeadlessFragment extends Fragment {

    // Reference to the activity that receives the
    // async task callbacks
    private AsyncListener listener;
```

```java
    private DownloadImageTask task;

    // Function to create new instances
    public static DownloadImageHeadlessFragment
      newInstance(String url) {
      DownloadImageHeadlessFragment myFragment = new
                    DownloadImageHeadlessFragment();
      Bundle args = new Bundle();
      args.putString("url", url);
      myFragment.setArguments(args);
      return myFragment;
    }
    // Called to do initial creation of fragment
    public void onCreate(Bundle savedInstanceState) {
      super.onCreate(savedInstanceState);
      setRetainInstance(true);
      task = new DownloadImageTask();
      url = new URL(getArguments().getString("url"));
      task.execute(url);
    }
    // Called when an activity is attached
    public void onAttach(Activity activity) {
      super.onAttach(activity);
    listener = (AsyncListener)activity;
}

public void onDetach() {
    super.onDetach();
    listener = null;
}
// Cancel the download
public void cancel() {
  if (task != null) {
      task.cancel(false);
  }
}

private class DownloadImageTask extends AsyncTask<URL, Integer,
Bitmap> {

    // ... doInBackground elided for brevity ...          }


}
```

As you might know, a fragment has its lifecycle tied to its own `Activity`, and therefore the callbacks are invoked in an orderly fashion following the current activity lifecycle events. For example, when the activity is stopped, all the fragments attached to it will be detached and notified of the `Activity` state change.

In our example, we're using the `Fragment` lifecycle methods (`onAttach` and `onDetach`) to save or remove the current `Activity` reference in our retained fragment.

When the `Activity` gets attached to our fragment, the `onCreate` method is invoked to create the private `DownloadImageTask` object and thereafter, the execute method is invoked to start the download in the background.

The `newInstance` static method is used to initialize and setup a new fragment, without having to call its constructor and a URL setter. As soon as we create the fragment object instance, we save the image URL in the bundle object stored by the fragment arguments member, using the `setArguments` function. If the Android system restores our fragment, it calls the default constructor with no arguments, and moreover it could make use of the old bundle to recreate the fragment.

Whenever the activity gets destroyed and recreated during a configuration change, the `setRetainInstance(true)` forces the fragment to survive during the activity recycling transition. As you can perceive, this technique could be extremely useful in situations where we don't want to reconstruct objects that are expensive to recreate again or objects that have an independent lifecycle when an Activity is destroyed through a configuration change.

It is important to know that the `retainInstance()` can only be used with fragments that are not in the back stack. On retained fragments, `onCreate()` and `onDestroy()` are not called when the activity is re-attached to a new Activity.

Next, our `Fragment` has to manage and execute a `DownloadImageTask`, that proxies progress updates and results back to the `Activity` via the `AsyncListener` interface:

```
private class DownloadImageTask extends AsyncTask<URL, Integer,
Bitmap> {
  ...
  protected void onPreExecute() {
    if (listener != null)
      listener.onPreExecute();
  }
  protected void onProgressUpdate(Integer... values) {
    if (listener != null)
      listener.onProgressUpdate(values);
```

```
    }
    protected void onPostExecute(Bitmap result) {
      if (listener != null)
        listener.onPostExecute(result);
    }
    protected void onCancelled(Bitmap result) {
      if (listener != null)
        listener.onCancelled(result);
    }
  }
}
```

As described previously, the `AsyncListener`, is the entity that is responsible for updating the UI with the result that will come from our background task.

Now, all we need is the host Activity that implements `AsyncListener` and uses `DownloadImageHeadlessFragment` to implement its long-running task. The full source code is available to download from the Packt Publishing website, so we'll just take a look at the highlights:

```
public class ShowMyPuppyHeadlessActivity
    extends FragmentActivity implements
    DownloadImageHeadlessFragment.AsyncListener {

  private static final String DOWNLOAD_PHOTO_FRAG =
                    "download_photo_as_fragment";
    . .
  @Override
  protected void onCreate(Bundle savedInstanceState) {
    . . .
    FragmentManager fm = getSupportFragmentManager();
    downloadFragment = (DownloadImageHeadlessFragment)
      fm.findFragmentByTag(DOWNLOAD_PHOTO_FRAG);

    // If the Fragment is non-null, then it is currently being
    // retained across a configuration change.
    if (downloadFragment == null) {
     downloadFragment = DownloadImageHeadlessFragment.
        newInstance("http://img.allw.mn/content" +
                  "/www/2009/03/april1.jpg");
          fm.beginTransaction().add(downloadFragment,
      DOWNLOAD_PHOTO_FRAG).
    commit();
    }
  }
```

First, when the activity is created in the `onCreate` callback, we check if the fragment already exists in `FragmentManager`, and we only create the instance if it is missing.

When the fragment is created, we build a fragment instance over the `newInstance` method and then we push the fragment to `FragmentManager`, the entity that will store and make the transition.

If our `Activity` has been restarted, it will need to re-display the progress dialog when a progress update callback is received, so we check and show it if necessary, before updating the progress bar:

```
@Override
public void onProgressUpdate(Integer... value) {
  if (progress == null)
    prepareProgressDialog();

  progress.setProgress(value[0]);
}
```

Finally, `Activity` will need to implement the `onPostExecute` and `onCancelled` callbacks defined by `AsyncListener`. The `onPostExecute` will update the `resultView` as in the previous examples, and both will do a little cleanup— dismissing the dialog and removing Fragment as its work is now done:

```
@Override
public void onPostExecute(Bitmap result) {
  if (result != null) {
    ImageView iv = (ImageView) findViewById(
                      R.id.downloadedImage);
    iv.setImageBitmap(result);
  }
  cleanUp();
}

// When the task is cancelled the dialog is dimissed
@Override
public void onCancelled(Bitmap result) {
  cleanUp();
}

// Dismiss the progress dialog and remove the
// the fragment from the fragment manager
private void cleanUp() {
```

```
    if (progress != null) {
      progress.dismiss();
      progress = null;
    }
    FragmentManager fm = getSupportFragmentManager();
    Fragment frag = fm.findFragmentByTag(DOWNLOAD_PHOTO_FRAG);
    fm.beginTransaction().remove(frag).commit();
  }
```

This technique, well known in the Android development community as a headless `Fragment`, is simple and consistent, since it attaches the recreated activity to the headless `Fragment` each time a configuration change happens. An activity reference is maintained, on the fragment, and updated when the fragment gets attached (Activity creation) and gets detached (Activity destroyed).

Taking advantage of this pattern, the `AsyncTask` never has to follow the unpredictable occurrence of configuration changes or worry about UI updates when it finishes its work because it forwards the lifecycle callbacks to the current `Activity`.

Applications of AsyncTask

Now that we have seen how to use `AsyncTask`, we might ask ourselves when we should use it.

Good candidate applications for `AsyncTask` tend to be relatively short-lived operations (at most, for a second or two), which pertain directly to a specific `Fragment` or `Activity` and need to update its user interface.

`AsyncTask` is ideal for running short, CPU-intensive tasks, such as number crunching or searching for words in large text strings, moving them off the main thread so that it can remain responsive to input and maintain high frame rates.

Blocking I/O operations such as reading and writing text files, or loading images from local files with `BitmapFactory` are also good use cases for `AsyncTask`.

Of course, there are use cases for which `AsyncTask` is not ideally suited. For anything that requires more than a second or two, we should weigh the cost of performing this operation repeatedly if the user rotates the device, or switches between apps or activities, or whatever else may be going on that we cannot control.

Taking these things into account, and the rate at which complexity increases as we try to deal with them (for example, retained headless fragments!), `AsyncTask` starts to lose its shine for longer operations.

AsyncTask is often used to fetch data from remote web servers, but this can fall foul of the Activity lifecycle issues we looked at earlier. End users may be working with a flaky 3G or HSDPA connection, where network latencies and bandwidth can vary widely, and a complete HTTP request-response cycle can easily span many seconds. This is especially important when we are uploading a significant amount of data, such as an image, as the available bandwidth is often asymmetric.

While we must perform network I/O off the main thread, AsyncTask is not necessarily the ideal option—as we'll see later; there are more appropriate constructs available for offloading this kind of work from the main thread.

When we want to compose or chain background processing over AsyncTasks, we could end up in situation where it is extremely difficult to manage the callbacks and coordinate the work so AsyncTask will not help you here.

Other techniques will be introduced and detailed in the next chapters for handling these kinds of problems in a clear way.

Summary

In this chapter, we've taken a detailed look at AsyncTask and how to use it to write responsive applications that perform operations without blocking the main thread.

We saw how to keep users informed of the progress, and even allow them to cancel operations early. We also learned how to deal with issues that can arise when the Activity lifecycle conspires against our background tasks.

Finally, we considered when to use AsyncTask, and when it might not be appropriate.

In the next chapter we'll learn about Loader—a construct designed to streamline the asynchronous loading of data on the Android platform.

4
Exploring the Loader

In the previous chapter we familiarized ourselves with the simplest and high level, Android-specific, asynchronous construct; the `android.os.AsyncTask`. The `AsyncTask` is a lean construct used to create background work that offers a simple interface to publish results and send progress to the main thread. In this chapter we are going to move our focus to `android.content.Loader`, a high level Android-specific pattern used to load content asynchronously from content providers or data sources over a worker thread with content change capabilities and component lifecycle awareness.

In this chapter we will cover the the following topics:

- Introducing loaders
- Loader API
- Loader lifecycle
- Loading data with Loader
- Building responsive apps with AsyncTaskLoader
- Building responsive apps with CursorLoader
- Combining loaders
- Applications of loaders

Introducing Loaders

As the name suggests, the job of Loader is to load data on behalf of other parts of the application, and to make that data available across activities and fragments within the same process. The Loaders framework was created to solve a couple of issues related to asynchronous loading in Activities and Fragments:

- **Background processing**: The heavy lifting is automatically performed on a background thread, and the results are safely introduced to the main thread on completion.

- **Result caching**: Loaded data can be cached and redelivered on repeat calls for speed and efficiency.

- **Lifecycle awareness**: The framework gives us control over when a Loader instance is destroyed, and allows Loaders to live outside the Activity lifecycle, making their data available across the application and across Activity restarts.

- **Data change management**: Loaders monitor their underlying data source, and reload their data in the background when necessary. The framework includes lifecycle callbacks that allow us to properly dispose of any expensive resources held by our Loaders.

Loader API

The Loader API was introduced to the Android platform at API level 11, but are available for backwards compatibility through the support libraries. The examples in this chapter use the support library to target API levels 7 through 23.

The framework defines interfaces, abstract classes, and loader implementations to create first class Android data loaders for your application.

The Loaders are able to monitor the content and deliver new changes, and will survive across an Activity transition or across a replaced Activity triggered by a configuration change. The API classes and interfaces delivered by this framework are:

- `android.content.Loader<DataType>`: Nonfunctional (abstract) base class that defines the base methods

- `android.app.LoaderManager`: Manages loaders in Activities and Fragments

- `android.app.LoaderManager.LoaderCallbacks`: Callbacks used to listen for Loader events

- `android.content.AsyncTaskLoader<DataType>`: Loader subclass that executes the loading over an `AsyncTask`
- `android.content.CursorLoader`: Loader implementation used to deal with Android internal databases and content providers' data sources

The last two classes are non-abstract subclasses that we will go into detail with examples in the next sections of this chapter.

Loader

`Loader` is a generic type class that, by itself, does not implement any asynchronous behavior and exposes one generic type argument:

```
public class Loader<DataType>
```

The `<DataType>` generic type defines the result type that your `Loader` is going to deliver and should be defined by any subclass that implements a domain specific `Loader`.

When you create your own loader there are five methods of `Loader` which we must implement to create a fully functional Loader:

```
protected void onStartLoading()
protected void onStopLoading()
protected void onForceLoad()
protected void onReset()
protected void onCancelLoad()
```

The `onStartLoading()` method is the method that subclass must implement to start loading data, the `onStopLoading()` is a method used to implement behavior when a loader stop was requested because the activity or fragment associated is stopped. At this state, the `Loader` may carry on processing but shouldn't deliver updates to the `Activity` until `onStartLoading()` is invoked again.

The `onForceLoad()` is a method that you should implement to ignore a previously loaded data set and load a new one, like clearing a cache, and the `onReset()` method is a method called for you automatically by LoaderManager to free any loader's resources if your loader is not invoked again.

The `onCancelLoad()` is a method invoked on the main thread used to implement behavior when the load is canceled after invoking the `Loader.cancelLoad()`.

Although we can extend `Loader` directly, it is more common to use one of the two provided subclasses, `AsyncTaskLoader` or `CursorLoader`, depending on our requirements.

AsyncTaskLoader is a general-purpose Loader, which we can subclass when we want to load just about any kind of data from just about any kind of source, and do so off the main thread.

CursorLoader extends AsyncTaskLoader, specializing it to efficiently source data from a local database and manage the associated database Cursor correctly.

Loader Manager

When we use Loaders, we will not do so in isolation, because they form part of a small framework. Loaders are managed objects, and are looked after by a LoaderManager, which takes care of coordinating Loader lifecycle events with the Fragment and Activity lifecycles, and makes the Loader instances available to the client code throughout an application. The LoaderManager abstract class defined in android.support.v4.content.LoaderManager and android.app. LoaderManager is accessible in all the Activities and Fragments through the member function getLoaderManager:

```
LoaderManager getLoaderManager()
// android.support.v4
LoaderManager getSupportLoaderManager();
```

The LoaderManager provides an API that could be used by the client (Activity or Fragment) to set up, initialize, restart, and destroy loaders without being bound to the client lifecycle. The Loader Manager's most relevant methods that are accessible when you retrieve the client-managed LoaderManager instance are:

```
Loader<D> initLoader(int id, Bundle args,
                     LoaderManager.LoaderCallbacks<D> callback)

Loader<D> restartLoader(int id, Bundle args,
                        LoaderManager.LoaderCallbacks<D> callback)
Loader<D> getLoader(int id);
void destroyLoader(int id);
```

The id argument in all the methods defined by the LoaderManager identifies the Loader on the client context, and moreover, is used in all the LoaderManager APIs to trigger any action in a specific Loader.

The `initLoader` method is used to initialize a certain loader but it does not create a new Loader if a Loader with the same ID already exists on the `LoaderManager`.

The `restartLoader` method starts or restarts a loader, however if a Loader associated with the ID passed in already exists, the old loader will be destroyed when it completes its work.

The `destroyLoader` method stops and removes the `Loader` with the ID specified by the argument `id` explicitly from the `LoaderManager`.

LoaderManager.LoaderCallbacks

To interact with the `LoaderManager`, the client needs to implement the `LoaderCallbacks<D>` interface and receive events to create a new `Loader` for a given ID, to receive the Loader results, or reset a Loader respectively:

```
Loader<D> onCreateLoader(int id, Bundle args)
void onLoadFinished(Loader<D> loader, D data)
void onLoaderReset(Loader<D> loader)
```

Like we detailed before, the D generic type specifies the data type that the Loader returns and these callbacks are called by the LoaderManager when a particular state is reached on the Loader lifecycle:

- `onCreateLoader`: This is a creational method that bootstraps a Loader for a specified ID and with a given Bundle object. The Bundle object is used to pass arguments for the Loader creation. This method gets invoked when the client calls `initLoader` and no Loader with that ID exists on LoaderManager.

- `onLoadFinished`: This is the method called when the Loader gets its results; the callback is called with the results and with a reference for the loader that retrieved the result. When the Loader detects a content change on the data requested it will report back the new results, therefore this method could be called several times. This method is typically used to update the UI with the loaded data.

- `onLoaderReset`: This is the method invoked when the Loader for a given ID is going to be destroyed. This is the best place to release some resources and references attached to one specified ID.

Loader lifecycle

Any Loader object managed by a `LoaderManager` can be in six different flags that defines the Loader state:

- **Reset**: This is the flag that sets your loader when you create a Loaders instance. The flag would end up here if the `reset()` method is invoked. The `onReset()` is called when the reset is moving to this state, and the developer must use this method to release the resources allocated on the Loader and to reset any cache result.

- **Started**: This is the flag set when your loader `startLoading()` is invoked. After your loader enters into this state, the `onStartLoading` method gets invoked to setup your loading resources. If the Loader has already delivered results you can call the `forceLoad()` to restart a new loading. Your loader should only deliver results when this flag is on.

- **Stopped**: This is the flag set when the loader is stopped and is not able to deliver new results or delivery of content changes. In this state, the loader could store results to deliver when the loader is restarted. To implement behavior when the loader has this on, the developer must implement the `onStopLoading` and release any resources allocated to load the results.

- **Abandoned**: This is an optional intermediate flag used to pinpoint whether the `Loader` was abandoned. Like the other methods, subclasses must implement the `onAbandon()` to implement behavior when the client is no longer interested in new data updates from the loader. At this state, prior to Reset, the Loader must not report any fresh updates but it can keep results to deliver when the loader is restarted.

- **ContentChanged**: This is a flag used to notify that the Loader content has changed. The `onContentChanged` is callback invoked when a content change is detected on the Load.

- **ProcessingChange**: This is a flag used to notify that the Loader content is processing a change on its content. The following functions `takeContentChanged()`, `commitContentChanged()`, and `rollbackContentChanged()` are used to manage the data content changes and its processing state.

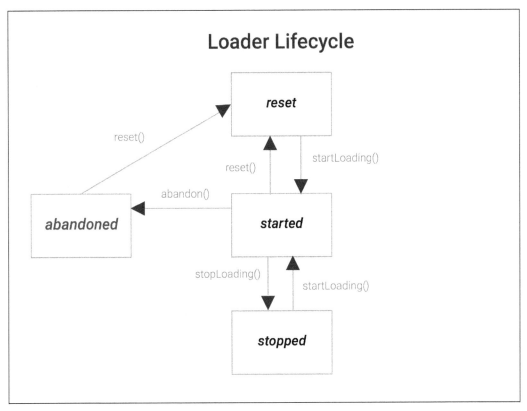

Figure 4.1: Loader Lifecycle

Loading data with Loader

So far, we have only described theoretical entities and the classes available on the API so now is the right time to show these concepts with a simple example.

In our example we will show you how to use LoaderManager, LoaderCallback, and a Loader to present an Activity that lists the name of users that are currently online for a chat application.

First, we are going to create an Activity that will act as a client to the LoaderManager and will have three buttons, **INIT**, **RESTART**, and **DESTROY**; to initialize the loader, to restart, and to destroy the loader respectively. The Activity will receive the LoaderCallbacks callback directly since it implements that interface as member functions:

```java
public class WhoIsOnlineActivity extends FragmentActivity
  implements LoaderCallbacks<List<String>> {
  public static final int WHO_IS_ONLINE_LOADER_ID = 1;

  @Override
  protected void onCreate(Bundle savedInstanceState) {
    ...
    final LoaderManager lm =  getSupportLoaderManager();
    final Bundle bundle =new Bundle();
    bundle.putString("chatRoom", "Developers");
    initButton.setOnClickListener(new View.OnClickListener() {
      @Override
      public void onClick(View v) {
        lm.initLoader(WHO_IS_ONLINE_LOADER_ID, bundle,
                    WhoIsOnlineActivity.this);
      }
    });
    restartButton.setOnClickListener(new View.OnClickListener() {
      @Override
      public void onClick(View v) {
        lm.restartLoader(WHO_IS_ONLINE_LOADER_ID, bundle,
                    WhoIsOnlineActivity.this);
      }
    });
    destroyButton.setOnClickListener(new View.OnClickListener() {
      @Override
      public void onClick(View v) {
        lm.destroyLoader(WHO_IS_ONLINE_LOADER_ID);
      }
    });
  }
}
```

Clicking on the **INIT** button will initialize the Loader with the ID specified and with a bundle object that we use to pass arguments to the Loader, and as said before the **RESTART** button will destroy a previous loader if it already exists and create a new one and the **DESTROY** button will destroy the loader with the given ID if it already exists in the LoaderManager. These buttons are used here only to help us to explain the interaction and flow between the LoaderManager and the Loaders.

In this specific use case we are going to load the list of online users for the chat room developers.

Now let's take a look at the LoaderCallback functions and implement the interface on our Activity.

Starting with onCreateLoader, this LoaderCallback callback gets called only if the loader does not previously exist or when the loader is restarted by calling LoaderManager.restartLoader().

When we initialize WhosOnlineLoader via the LoaderManager initLoader method, it will either return an existing Loader with the given ID (LOADER_ID) or, if it doesn't yet have a Loader with that ID, it will invoke the first of the LoaderCallbacks methods — onCreateLoader.

This means this method will not be called on for a configuration change because a previous loader with this ID is already available and initialized.

```
@Override
public Loader<List<String>> onCreateLoader(int id, Bundle args) {
  Loader res = null;
  switch (id) {
    case WHO_IS_ONLINE_LOADER_ID:
      res = new WhosOnlineLoader(this,
                                 args.getString("chatRoom"));
      break;
  }
  return res;
}
```

This method creates the Loader instance calling the WhosOnlineLoader constructor and passing the chat group name that we are trying to load.

The next `LoaderCallback` function callback implemented is `onLoadFinished`; this callback gets called when the loader gets new results, when the data changes, or could be called when a configuration changes a `Loader` that already exists in the `LoaderManager`.

```
@Override
public void onLoadFinished(Loader<List<String>> loader,
                    List<String> users) {
    switch (loader.getId()) {
      case WHO_IS_ONLINE_LOADER_ID:
      ListView listView = (ListView) findViewById(R.id.list);
      ArrayAdapter<String> adapter = new ArrayAdapter<String>(this,
        android.R.layout.simple_list_item_1,
        android.R.id.text1,
        users);
      listView.setAdapter(adapter);
      break;
    }
}
```

In our example, when the `onLoadFinished` gets called, we update the `ListView` adapter with the list of users received from the loader.

The `OnLoaderReset`, our last `LoaderCallback` function callback, gets called when the loader is destroyed, and in our example it simply cleans up the list view data in its adapter:

```
@Override
public void onLoaderReset(Loader<List<String>> loader) {
    ...
    ListView listView = (ListView)findViewById(R.id.list);
    listView.setAdapter(null);
}
```

The loader reset is called when the `LoaderManager.destroyLoader(id)` is called or when the `Activity` gets destroyed. The Loader reset, as described earlier, will not destroy the loader but tell the Loader not to publish further updates. Hence, it can span multiple Activities.

The last piece of this cake is our custom Loader, the `WhosOnlineLoader`, used to retrieve the list of online users. Our `WhosOnlineLoader` is not going to load any asynchronous results, since a `Loader` subclass does not manage a background thread to load the results. Hence, this Loader should only be used for example purposes and to explain the `LoaderManager` and custom Loader interaction idiosyncrasies.

For debugging purposes, the methods `onStartLoading`, `onStopLoading`, `onReset`, and `onForceLoad` have a log message printed every time they enter on a function. The `deliverResult()`, the Loader function that delivers the result of the load to the registered listener, will also print a message to the Android Log with the users online.

```java
public class WhosOnlineLoader extends Loader<List<String>> {

    private final String mChatRoom;
    private List<String> mResult = null;

    public WhosOnlineLoader(Context context, String chatRoom) {
        super(context);
        this.mChatRoom = chatRoom;
    }
    @Override
    protected void onStartLoading() {
        Log.i("WhoIsOnlineLoader", "onStarting WhoIsOnlineLoader ["
            + Integer.toHexString(hashCode()) + "]");
        ...
        forceLoad();
    }
    // Elided for brevity
    @Override
    public void deliverResult(List<String> data) {
        Log.i("WhoIsOnlineLoader", "DeliverResult WhoIsOnlineLoader ["
            + Integer.toHexString(hashCode()) + "]");
        ...
        super.deliverResult(data);
    }
    @Override
    protected void onReset() {
        Log.i("WhoIsOnlineLoader", "onReset WhoIsOnlineLoader ["
            + Integer.toHexString(hashCode()) + "]");
        onStopLoading();
        ...
    }

}
```

The `WhosOnlineLoader` code is partially omitted on purpose, although the `WhosOnlineLoader` source code is available to download from the Packt Publishing website.

With everything in place, if we start the Activity, the user online list will be empty, although clicking on the **INIT** button will result in a `LoaderManager.init` call.

Since we have some trace messages at the beginning of each `Loader` lifecycle, we can follow the loader callback calls:

```
I ... LoaderManager.init [1]
I ... LoaderCallbacks.onCreateLoader[1]
I ... Loader.new[ee07113]
I ... Loader.onStarting[ee07113]
I ... Loader.onForceload[ee07113]
I ... Loader.deliverResult[ee07113]
I ... LoaderCallbacks.onLoadFinished[1]
```

As shown in the log output, a new `Loader` object instance with the `hashCode` `ee07113` is created when we invoke the `LoaderManager.init` function and the `onCreateLoader` gets called in the meantime. Afterwards, the loader is started and the results are loaded on the `onLoadFinished` callback, delivering the list of users.

Since the `Loader` with the ID now exists on the `LoaderManager`, lets check what happens when we click on the **restart** button:

```
I ... LoaderManager.restart [1]
I ... LoaderCallbacks.onCreateLoader[1]
I ... Loader.new[fb61f50]
I ... Loader.onStarting[fb61f50]
I ... Loader.onForceload[fb61f50]
I ... Loader.deliverResult[fb61f50]
I ... LoaderCallbacks.onLoadFinished[1]
I ... Loader.onReset[ee07113]
I ... Loader.onStopping[ee07113]
```

Since the `Loader` `ee07113` was created previously, it will be stopped and reset, and a new loader instance will be created and started like it did on the `init`.

Now we are going to click on the **DESTROY** button and check the results:

```
I ... LoaderManager.destroy [1]
I ... LoaderCallbacks.onLoaderReset[1]
I ... Loader.onAbandon[fb61f50]
I ... Loader.onReset[fb61f50]
I ... Loader.onStopping[fb61f50]
```

As expected, the `LoaderManager.destroy` gets called, and after that the `onAbandon`, `onReset`, and the `onStopping Loader` member methods were called to stop delivering results, release the loader resources, and to stop loading data. When the Loader is stopped we must cancel any loading but it can still monitor the data source for changes.

Another situation that is really important to explain is the configuration change. In this situation, the `LoaderManager` will continue to receive the results and keep them in a local cache. Once the new activity becomes visible, the cache results are delivered over the method `LoaderCallbacks.onLoadFinished`.

In a typical `Activity` transition where there is no configuration change involved, `LoaderManager` automatically resets the `Loader` resulting in calls to the loader stop and reset functions.

Given that now we understand how to use the `LoaderManager` to manage the loaders in activities, now we can focus our attention on how to use the subclasses `AsyncTaskLoader` and `LoaderCursor` to create asynchronous Loaders.

Building responsive apps with AsyncTaskLoader

`AsyncTaskLoader` is a Loader implementation that uses `AsyncTasks` to perform its background work, though this is largely hidden from us when we implement our own subclasses.

We don't need to trouble ourselves with the `AsyncTasks` — they are completely hidden by `AsyncTaskLoader` — but with what we learned earlier about `AsyncTask`, it is interesting to note that tasks are, by default, executed using `AsyncTask.executeOnExecutor(AsyncTask.THREAD_POOL_EXECUTOR)` to ensure a high degree of concurrency when multiple Loaders are in use.

The `AsyncTaskLoader` in the compatibility package (`android.support.v4.content`) does not rely on the public `AsyncTask` in the platform. Instead, the compatibility package uses an internal `ModernAsyncTask` implementation to avoid Android fragmentation. The `ModernAsyncTask` creates threads with the name `ModernAsyncTask #<N>`.

In the next section we will use `AsyncTaskLoader` to load in the background, a currency to Bitcoin exchange rate, and display an updated exchange rate in our `BitcoinExchangeRateActivity` making use of the `LoaderManager`.

The exchange rate will be refreshed continuously using the onContentChanged() Loader method, used in this case to force a new exchange rate update in background.

Loader is generically typed so when we implement it, we need to specify the type of object that it will load — in our case Double:

```
public class BitcoinExchangeRateLoader extends
  AsyncTaskLoader<Double> {
  // ...
}
```

The Loader abstract class requires a Context passed to its constructor, so we must pass a Context up the chain. We'll also need to know which currency exchange rate to retrieve, and the refresh time interval, so we'll also pass a string to identify the currency and an integer for the interval (milliseconds):

```
private Double      mExchangeRate = null;
private final long   mRefreshinterval;
private final String mCurrency;

BitcoinExchangeRateLoader(Context ctx,
                          String currency,
                          int refreshinterval) {
  super(ctx);
  this.mRefreshinterval = refreshinterval;
  this.mCurrency = currency;
}
```

We don't need to keep our own reference to the Context object — Loader exposes a getContext() method which we can call from anywhere in our class where we might need a Context.

 We can safely pass a reference to an Activity instance as the Context parameter, but we should not expect getContext() to return the same object! Loaders potentially live much longer than a single Activity, so the Loader superclass only keeps a reference to the application Context, a context tied to an application, to prevent memory leaks.

There are several methods we will need to override which we'll work through one at a time. The most important is loadInBackground — the workhorse of our AsyncTaskLoader, and the only method which does not run on the main thread:

```
@Override
public Double loadInBackground() {
  //...
}
```

The `AsyncTaskLoader` is a Loader subclass based on `AsyncTask`. Under the hood, it calls the `loadInBackground` function in an AsyncTask's background thread.

We're going to fetch the real-time bitcoin exchange rate from Internet, more precisely from the blockchain.info website, to delays to establish the connection, to transmit the data between the device and the remote endpoint and to some latency exposed by the access network. Since the delays can range from milliseconds to seconds, this task is a good candidate to perform off the main thread.

The following diagram displays the `Loader` lifecycle, showing callbacks invoked by `LoaderManager` and a typical `AsyncTaskLoader` implementation:

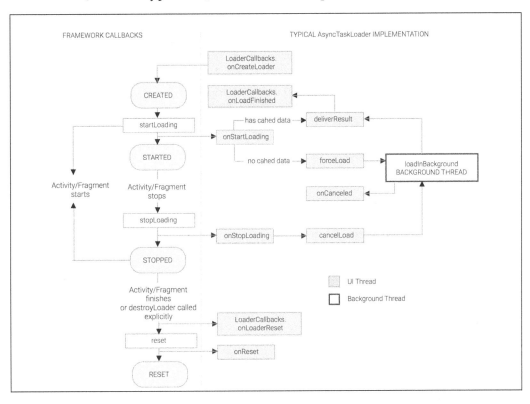

Given that loading the exchange rate from the network entails some delay due to blocking I/O reading from the network, and it is also possible that the remote website does not yet have enough resources to send the response back, we, as conscious developers who don't want to generate annoying Android ANRs, have to transfer these kinds of operations to the `AsyncTaskLoader.loadInBackground` method that is executed by the background thread in the system.

After we receive the response with the exchange rate, we need to decode the JSON response that comes in the HTTP response so this is also an operation we definitely want to perform off the main thread!

```java
public Double loadInBackground() {
    Double result = null;
    StringBuilder builder = new StringBuilder();
    URL url = new URL("https://blockchain.info/ticker");

    // Create a Connection to the remote Website
    HttpURLConnection conn = (HttpURLConnection)
                            url.openConnection();
    ...
    conn.setRequestMethod("GET");
    conn.setDoInput(true);
    conn.connect();
    // ! Read the response with the exchange rate to a String
    ...
    // Decode the Response Received by Blockchain Website
    JSONObject obj = new JSONObject(builder.toString());
    result = obj.getJSONObject(mCurrency)
                    .getDouble("last");
    return result;
}
```

In the preceding code, we execute the blocking operations suggested previously and as a result we return the exchange rate for the currency specified in the `Loader` construct.

We'll want to cache a reference to the Double object that we're delivering, so that any future calls can just return the same Double immediately. We'll do this by overriding `deliverResult` invoked on the main thread:

```java
@Override
public void deliverResult(Double result) {
    this.mExchangeRate = result;
    super.deliverResult(result);
}
```

To make our `Loader` actually work, we still need to override a handful of lifecycle methods that are defined by the `Loader` base class. First and foremost is `onStartLoading`:

```
@Override
protected void onStartLoading() {

   if (mExchangeRate != null) {
     // If we currently have a result available, deliver it
     // immediately.
     deliverResult(mExchangeRate);
   }
   if (takeContentChanged() || mExchangeRate == null) {
     // If the exchange rate has changed since the last time
     // it was  loaded or is not currently available, start a load.
     forceLoad();
   }
}
```

Here, we check our cache (`mExchangeRate`) to see if we have a previously loaded result that we can deliver immediately via `deliverResult`. If the content data has changed recently, `contentChanged` flag is true, and we don't have a cached result, we force a background load to occur — we must do this otherwise our Loader won't ever load anything. As described before this callback runs on the main thread and the load will fire off a new load throughout `loadInBackground()` on the background thread.

We now have a minimal working `Loader` implementation, but there is some housekeeping required if we want our `Loader` to play well with the framework.

First of all, we need to make sure that we clean up the exchange rate when our `Loader` is discarded. Loader provides a callback intended for that exact purpose — `onReset`.

```
@Override
protected void onReset() {
   // Ensure the loader is stopped
   onStopLoading();
   mExchangeRate = null;
}
```

The framework will ensure that `onReset` is called when `Loader` is being discarded, which will happen when the app exits or when the `Loader` instance is explicitly discarded via `LoaderManager`.

There are two more lifecycle methods, which are important to implement correctly if we want our app to be as responsive as possible: `onStopLoading` and `onCanceled` (be careful of the spelling of `onCanceled` here versus `onCancelled` in most places).

The framework will tell us when it doesn't want us to waste cycles loading data by invoking the `onStopLoading` callback. It may still need the data we have already loaded though, and it may tell us to start loading again, so we should not clean up resources yet. In `AsyncTaskLoader` we'll want to cancel the background work if possible, so we'll just call the superclass `cancelLoad` method:

```
@Override
protected void onStopLoading() {
   // Attempt to cancel the current load task.
   cancelLoad();
}
```

When the `Loader` is cancelled we don't stop the current rate loading; in spite of this, in other kinds of use cases, we might have a cancelling behavior on the `loadInBackground()` to stop the current loading by checking the `isAbandoned()` member function.

Finally, we need to implement `onCancelled` to clean up any data that might be loaded in the background after a cancellation has been issued:

```
@Override
public void onCanceled(Double data) {
    // For our data there is nothing to release, at this method
    // we should release the resources associated with 'data'.
}
```

Depending on the kind of data Loader produces, we may not need to worry about cleaning up the result of canceled work—ordinary Java objects will be cleaned up by the garbage collector when they are no longer referenced.

So far, we have implemented the asynchronous exchange rate loading, now we have to implement the refresh feature to continuously fetch the value from the blockchain. info website. To load a new value for the current exchange rate we shall coerce the loader to run the `loadInBackground` again and retrieve the current value for the exchange rate. The `Loader` abstract class offers us the method `onContentChanged()`, that will force a new load if the `Loader` is at the started state.

In our example, once the loader is started with startLoading(), we must continuously call onContentChanged to mimic a value change and force a new load. We will achieve this by using a handler and by posting a Runnable that simply calls the onContentChange on our Loader.

1. First we are going to create the Runnable and create the handler in our loader:

```
public class BitcoinExchangeRateLoader extends
                AsyncTaskLoader<Double> {

  private Handler mHandler;

  // Use to force a exchange rate value change
  private final Runnable refreshRunnable = new Runnable() {
    @Override
    public void run() { onContentChanged(); }
  };

  BitcoinExchangeRateLoader(Context ctx,
                            String currency,
                            int refreshinterval) {
    . . .
    this.mHandler = new Handler();
  }
}
```

2. Second, we need to submit a delayed task to force the next reload, each time the forceLoad() is called. When the Loader is reset we don't submit the next reload:

```
@Override
protected void onForceLoad() {
  mHandler.removeCallbacks(refreshRunnable);

  if (!isReset())
    mHandler.postDelayed(refreshRunnable, mRefreshinterval);
}
```

3. Third, to force a new reload when the loader is cancelled and the task is restarted afterwards, `onCanceled()` sets the `ContentChange` flag on by calling `onContentChanged()`:

```
@Override
  public void onCanceled(Double data) {
    ...
      onContentChanged();
  }
```

4. To finish, we must cancel the next reload if the loader is stopped or cancelled:

```
@Override
protected void onReset() {
  ...
  mHandler.removeCallbacks(refreshRunnable);
}
```

So far so good — we have a `Loader`. Now we need to connect it to a client Activity or Fragment. Since in our previous example we attached our Loader to an Activity, this time we are going to use a different `LoaderManager` client and connect the loader to a Fragment object.

Our `Fragment`, loaded by `BitcoinExchangeRateActivity`, is going to initialize our Loader and display the loader result on the fragment UI. Let's get these easy bits out of the way first:

```
public class BitcoinExchangeRateFragment extends Fragment
implements LoaderManager.LoaderCallbacks<Double> {


  @Override
  public void onActivityCreated(Bundle savedInstanceState) {
    super.onActivityCreated(savedInstanceState);
    LoaderManager lm = getActivity().getSupportLoaderManager();
    Bundle bundle = new Bundle();
    bundle.putString(CURRENNCY_KEY, "EUR");
    bundle.putInt(REFRESH_INTERNAL, 5000);
    lm.initLoader(BITCOIN_EXRATE_LOADER_ID, bundle,
                BitcoinExchangeRateFragment.this);
  }
  ...
}
```

In the preceding code, we mainly load the UI layout used to present the exchange rate on the screen and we implement our loader initialization on the onActivityCreated member function. The onActivityCreated member class callback is either called when the activity has been created or when the Activity is recreated, after a configuration change.

As we explained in previous sections, we call the initLoader passing an int identifier as the first argument, a Bundle of values – the second parameter – to configure the currency exchange rate that we want present on the screen, and a refresh rate interval between onContextChange calls. The third parameter is an object that implements LoaderCallbacks, which, in this case, is our BitcoinExchangeRateFragment instance, where we implement the loader callbacks directly on the fragment.

The onCreateLoader callback method that we implement on our Fragment is similar to the method that we create on the previous WhoIsOnlineActivity Loader, so it basically creates a new BitcoinExchangeRateLoader instance using the arguments passed on to the Bundle object.

```
public Loader<Double> onCreateLoader(int id, Bundle args) {
  Loader res = null;
  switch (id) {
  case BITCOIN_EXRATE_LOADER_ID:
    res = new BitcoinExchangeRateLoader(getActivity(),
          args.getString(CURRENNCY_KEY),
          args.getInt(REFRESH_INTERNAL));
    break;
  }
  return res;
}
```

The implementation of onLoadFdinished must take the loaded exchange rate and display it in the TextView:

```
@Override
public void onLoadFinished(Loader<Double> loader, Double data) {
  switch (loader.getId()) {
  case BITCOIN_EXRATE_LOADER_ID:
    TextView tv  = (TextView) getView().
                   findViewById(R.id.temperature);
    tv.setText(data.toString());
    break;
  }
}
```

For brevity, we omitted the `LoaderCallbacks.onLoaderReset` since the method body is empty. This method should be used to release any resources used that are directly bound to the Loader lifecycle.

 The full source code, with the Activity and `android.xml` layout is available on the Packt Publishing website.

When compared with `AsyncTask`, things here are more complicated — we've had to write more code and deal with more classes, but the payoff is that the data is cached for use across `Activity` restarts and can be used from other Fragments or Activities.

In our `BitcoinExchangeRateLoader`, the successive exchange rate updates are controlled by our refresh rate internal; however, in other kinds of `AsyncTaskLoaders` the rate where a content change happens could result in lots of `onLoadFinished` invocations, and hence potentially dominate the UI thread execution with UI updates and degrade the UI responsiveness.

To overcome this issue, the `AsyncTaskLoader` supplies a member function, called `setUpdateThrottle`, to control the minimum internal between successive data deliveries and as a result adjusts the interval between consecutive `onLoadFinished` invocations:

```
public void setUpdateThrottle(long delayMS)
```

This method must be called when you feel that your loader content change-rate might overload the UI and affect your application smoothness. If a higher update frequency is not required in your data, the developer can make use of this function to reduce the Loader content change deliver frequency.

In the next section we will get a detailed overview on the last Loader subclass type that comes out of box with Android SDK, the `CursorLoader`.

Building responsive apps with CursorLoader

`CursorLoader` is a specialized subclass of `AsyncTaskLoader` that uses its lifecycle methods to correctly manage the resources associated with a database `Cursor`.

A database `Cursor` is a little like an Iterator, in that it allows you to scroll through a dataset without having to worry where exactly the dataset is coming from or what data structure it is a part of.

We're going to use `CursorLoader` to query the Android device for a list of music albums available. Because `CursorLoader` is already implemented to correctly handle all of the details of working with a `Cursor`, we don't need to subclass it. We can simply instantiate it, passing in the information it needs in order to open the `Cursor` it should manage for us. We can do this in the `onCreateLoader` callback:

```
@Override
public Loader<Cursor> onCreateLoader(int id, Bundle args) {
  String[] columns = new String[] {
    MediaStore.Audio.Albums._ID,
    MediaStore.Audio.Albums.ARTIST,
    MediaStore.Audio.Albums.ALBUM
  };
  return new CursorLoader(this,
    MediaStore.Audio.Albums.EXTERNAL_CONTENT_URI,
    columns, // projection
    null, // selection
    null, // selectionArgs
    null // sortOrder
  );
}
```

Just as with the previous example, we'll implement the callbacks in our `Activity` subclass. We're going to use `GridView` to display our album list, so we'll implement an `Adapter` interface to supply views for its cells, and we'll connect the `Adapter` to the `Cursor` created by our `Loader`:

```
public class AlbumListActivitySimple extends FragmentActivity
  implements LoaderCallbacks<Cursor> {

  public static final int ALBUM_LIST_LOADER = "album_list".
                                             hashCode();
  private SimpleCursorAdapter mAdapter;

  @Override
  protected void onCreate(Bundle savedInstanceState) {
    super.onCreate(savedInstanceState);
    setContentView(R.layout.phone_list_layout);
    GridView grid = (GridView) findViewById(R.id.album_grid);
    mAdapter = new AlbumCursorAdapter(getApplicationContext());
    grid.setAdapter(mAdapter);

    // Prepare the loader.
    // Either re-connect with an existing one, or start a new one.
```

```
        getSupportLoaderManager().
          initLoader(ALBUM_LIST_LOADER,
                      null,
                      AlbumListActivitySimple.this);
    }

    @Override
    public void onLoadFinished(Loader<Cursor> loader, Cursor data) {
        // Swap the new cursor in.   (The framework will take
        //  care of closing the old cursor once we return.)
        mAdapter.changeCursor(data);
    }

    @Override
    public void onLoaderReset(Loader<Cursor> loader) {
        // This is called when the last Cursor provided to
        // onLoadFinished() above is about to be closed.
        //  We need to make sure we are no longer using it.
        mAdapter.changeCursor(null);
    }
}
```

Have a look at the parts in bold in the preceding code. We create an
`AlbumCursorAdapter`, and pass it to the `GridView`, we then initialize our
`CursorLoader`. When loading is completed, we pass the loaded Cursor to the
Adapter, and we're done.

The remaining piece to implement is `AlbumCursorAdapter`, which is going to start
out as a very simple class. The job of our `CursorAdapter` is simply to map rows of
data from the `Cursor` to each `View` in the individual row `View`.

The Android SDK provides the very handy `SimpleCursorAdapter` class, which does
just what we need; mapping a database data row into an Album Item View. So for
now we'll just subclass it and instruct it via constructor parameters which layout the
inflation for each cell and the `Cursor` fields to map to each `View` within that layout:

```
    public static class AlbumCursorAdapter extends SimpleCursorAdapter {
      private static String[] FIELDS = new String[] {
        MediaStore.Audio.Albums.ARTIST,
        MediaStore.Audio.Albums.ALBUM
      };
      private static int[] VIEWS = new int[] {
```

```
      R.id.album_artist, R.id.album_name
    };

    public AlbumCursorAdapter(Context context) {
      super(context, R.layout.album_item,
          null, FIELDS, VIEWS, 0);
    }
  }
```

The layout files and source code are available on the accompanying website. When you run this `Activity`, you'll see a grid list where each cell contains album artwork, the album artist, and the album name for each album.

Scroll to somewhere in the middle of the list and rotate your device, and you'll notice that the Activity restarts and redisplays the grid immediately, without losing its place — this is because the `CursorLoader` survived the restart, and still holds the `Cursor` object with the same rows loaded.

This is technically all very interesting, but it isn't much to look at. In the next section we'll combine our two `Loaders` to implement a scrollable grid displaying the album art for each album.

Combining Loaders

In the preceding sections we developed a `CursorLoader` that loads a list of all available music albums on the system and an `AsynTaskLoader` that does a blocking IO operation in the background. Now we are going to use our previous `CursorLoader` together with `AsyncTaskLoader` which loads a thumbnail from the album ID to create an application that tiles the artwork of all the music albums on the device in a scrollable grid, performing all loading in the background.

Thanks to our `CursorLoader`, we already have access to the IDs of the albums we need to load — we're displaying only the album name and album artist — so we just need to pass those IDs to our `AlbumArtworkLoader` for it to asynchronously load the image for us.

Our `AlbumArtworkLoader` could receive the album ID either on the constructor or later, to load an image for a particular `albumId`:

```
    public class AlbumArtworkLoader extends AsyncTaskLoader<Bitmap> {

    private int mAlbumId = -1; // The album Identifier
```

```
Bitmap mData = null;

public AlbumArtworkLoader(Context context, int albumId) {
   super(context);
   this.mAlbumId = albumId;
}
```

We'll enable `AlbumArtworkLoader` to load a new image instead of its current one, by setting a new `albumId`. Since the bitmap is cached (`mData`), just setting a new ID won't suffice — we also need to trigger a reload by using the `Loader.onContentChanged`:

```
public void setAlbumId(int newAlbumId) {

   if (  isDifferentMedia(newAlbumId) || mData == null ) {

      // Album Id change will force the artwork reload
      this.mAlbumId = newAlbumId;
      onContentChanged();

   } else if (!isDifferentMedia(newAlbumId) ) {
      // we already have the Bitmap for this album
      deliverResult(mData);
   }
}
```

The `onContentChanged`, as explained before, is a method of the abstract `Loader` superclass which will force a background load to occur if our `Loader` is currently in the started state. If we're currently stopped, a flag will be set and a background load will be triggered next time the `Loader` is started. Either way, when the background load completes, `onLoadFinished` will be triggered with the new data.

We need to implement the `onStartLoading` method to correctly handle the case where we were `stopped` when `onContentChanged` was invoked. Let's remind ourselves of what it used to look like:

```
@Override
protected void onStartLoading() {

   if (mData != null) {
      deliverResult(mData);
   }
   if (takeContentChanged() || mData == null) {
      forceLoad();
   }
}
```

The onStartLoading method again delivers its data immediately — if it has any.

It then calls takeContentChanged to see if we need to discard our cached Bitmap and load a new one. If takeContentChanged returns true, we invoke forceLoad to trigger a background load and redelivery.

Now we can cause our AlbumArtworkLoader to load and cache a different image, but a single AlbumArtworkLoader can only load and cache one image at a time, so we're going to need more than one active instance.

Let's walk through the process of modifying AlbumCursorAdapter to initialize a AlbumCursorAdapter for each cell in the GridView, and to use those Loaders to asynchronously load the album artwork and display them:

```
public class AlbumCursorAdapter extends CursorAdapter {

    Context ctx;
    private LayoutInflater inf;
    private LoaderManager mgr;
    private List<Integer> ids;
    private int count;

    public AlbumCursorAdapter(Context ctx, LoaderManager mgr) {
        super(ctx.getApplicationContext(), null, true);
        this.ctx = ctx;
        this.mgr = mgr;
        inf = (LayoutInflater) ctx.
                getSystemService(Context.LAYOUT_INFLATER_SERVICE);
        ids = new ArrayList<Integer>();
    }

    @Override
    public View newView(Context context, Cursor cursor, ViewGroup
parent) {
        ..
    }

    @Override
    public void bindView(View view, Context context, Cursor cursor) {
        ...
    }
```

We have two methods to implement—newView and bindView. GridView will invoke newView until it has enough View objects to fill all of its visible cells, and from then on it will recycle these same View objects by passing them to bindView to be repopulated with data for a different cell as the grid scrolls. As a view scrolls out of sight, it becomes available for rebinding.

What this means for us is that we have a convenient method in which to initialize our AlbumArtworkLoaders—newView, and another convenient method in which to retask Loader to load a new thumbnail—bindView.

newView first inflates the album item layout for the row and gives to the parent view, a unique ID based on the ID generated by the adapter class hashcode() method and based on the current number of Loaders.

Later, the unique ID and the imageView is passed to a ArtworkLoaderCallbacks class, which we'll meet in a moment. ArtworkLoaderCallbacks is in turn used to initialize a new Loader, which shares the ID of the parent View. In this way we are initializing a new Loader for each visible row in the grid:

```
@Override
public View newView(Context context, Cursor cursor,
                    ViewGroup parent) {

    View view = (View) inf.inflate(R.layout.album_item,
                                   parent, false);
    ImageView imageView = (ImageView) view.
                              findViewById(R.id.album_art);
        . . .
    int viewId = AlbumCursorAdapter.class.hashCode() + count++;
    view.setId(viewId);
    mgr.initLoader(viewId, null,
                new ArtworkLoaderCallbacks(ctx, imageView));
    ids.add(viewId);
    return view;
}
```

In bindView, we are recycling each existing View to update the image, album name, and album artist that are being displayed by that View. So the first thing we do is clear out the old Bitmap.

Next we look up the correct `Loader` by ID, extract the ID of the next image to load from the `Cursor`, and load it by passing the ID to the method of `AlbumArtworkLoader` — `setAlbumId`:

```
@Override
public void bindView(View view, Context context, Cursor cursor) {
  ImageView imageView = (ImageView) view.
                        findViewById(R.id.album_art);
  imageView.setImageBitmap(null);

  Loader<?> loader = mgr.getLoader(view.getId());
  AlbumArtworkLoader artworkLoader = (AlbumArtworkLoader) loader;
  int albumId = cursor.getInt(
    cursor.getColumnIndex(MediaStore.Audio.Albums._ID));
  ...
  // Sets the album id bound to this imageView,
  // this could force the loader to retrieve a new image
  artworkLoader.setAlbumId(albumId);

}
```

We need to add one more method to our `Adapter` so that we can clean up `AlbumArtworkLoaders` when we no longer need them. We'll call these ourselves when we no longer need these `Loaders` — for example, when our `Activity` is finishing:

```
public void destroyLoaders() {
  for (Integer id : ids) {
    mgr.destroyLoader(id);
  }
}
```

That's our completed `Adapter`. Next, let's look at `ArtworkLoaderCallbacks` which, as you probably guessed, is just an implementation of `LoaderCallbacks`:

```
public static class ArtworkLoaderCallbacks implements
  LoaderManager.LoaderCallbacks<Bitmap> {

  private Context context;
  private ImageView image;

  public ArtworkLoaderCallbacks(Context context,
                                ImageView image) {
```

```
        this.context = context.getApplicationContext();
        this.image = image;
    }

    @Override
    public Loader<Bitmap> onCreateLoader(int i, Bundle bundle) {
        return new AlbumArtworkLoader(context);
    }

    @Override
    public void onLoadFinished(Loader<Bitmap> loader, Bitmap b) {
        image.setImageBitmap(b);
    }

    @Override
    public void onLoaderReset(Loader<Bitmap> loader) {}
}
```

The only interesting thing `ArtworkLoaderCallbacks` does is create an instance of `AlbumArtworkLoader`, and set a loaded Bitmap to its `ImageView`.

Our `Activity` is almost unchanged—we need to pass an extra parameter when instantiating `AlbumCursorAdapter` and, to avoid leaking the Loaders it creates, we need to invoke the `destroyLoaders` method of `AlbumCursorAdapter` in `onPause` or `onStop`, if the Activity is finishing:

```
    @Override
    protected void onStop() {
        super.onStop();
        if (isFinishing()) {
            // Destroy the main album list Loader
            getSupportLoaderManager().destroyLoader(ALBUM_LIST_LOADER);
            // Destroy album artwork loaders
            mAdapter.destroyLoaders();
        }
    }
```

The full source code is available from the Packt Publishing website. Take a look at the complete source code to appreciate how little there actually is, and run it on a device to get a feel for just how much functionality `Loaders` give you for relatively little effort!

Applications of Loader

The obvious applications include reading any kind of data from files or databases local to the device, or Android content providers, as we've done in the examples in this chapter.

One strong advantage of `Loaders` over direct use of `AsyncTask` is that their lifecycle is very flexible with respect to the `Activity` and `Fragment` lifecycles. Without any extra effort we can handle configuration changes such as an orientation change.

We can even start loading in one `Activity`, navigate through the app, and collect the result in a completely separate `Activity`, if that makes sense for our app.

In some ways, this decoupling from the Activity lifecycle makes `Loader` a better candidate than `AsyncTask` to perform network transfers such as HTTP downloads; however, they require more code and still aren't a perfect fit.

The framework is very powerful for managing asynchronous data loading; however, it does not provide a mechanism to show the loading progress, as we have on the `AsyncTask` framework and there is no error handling callback function to manage loading errors or exceptions.

To overcome these issues, the developer must extend the basic Loader framework classes and implement these patterns to match his needs.

Summary

The `Loader` framework in Android does a wonderful job of making it easy to load data in the background and deliver it to the main thread when it is ready.

In this chapter we learned about the essential characteristics of all Loaders— background loading, caching of loaded data, and a managed lifecycle.

We took a detailed look at `AsyncTaskLoader` as a means to perform arbitrary background loading, and `CursorLoader` for asynchronous loading from local database Cursors.

We saw that `Loader` can free us from some of the constraints imposed by the `Activity` lifecycle, and took advantage of that to continue to work in the background even across `Activity` restarts.

In the next chapter we'll free ourselves completely from the constraints of the `Activity` lifecycle and perform background operations with `Service`, even when our app is no longer in the foreground.

5

Interacting with Services

In the previous chapters we focused our attention on the basic, high-level, Android-specific constructs to load data asynchronously on an independent line of execution (background thread); `android.os.AsyncTask` and `android.content.Loader`.

What if we want to provide a common set of operations that implement any kind of business logic over a centralized single entity that could be re-used by different clients and has a lifecycle that is not bound to the client lifecycle? By clients, in Android, we mean any kind of UI entity, such as an `Activity` or `Fragment` object, a `BroadcastReceiver`, or any kind of object that wants to exercise business logic.

The solution for this pattern in Android is available in the form of `android.app. Service`.

In Android, the Service programming pattern, well-known in enterprise architectures, does not necessarily mean background work, so to avoid any kind of responsiveness degradation in the UI we should try keep the main Thread execution of the Service as lean as possible.

Therefore, we have to use asynchronous techniques to coordinate the `Service` work between the main thread and other threads that help to accomplish the `Service` goal, to either keep the responsiveness at quite a decent level and provide results to the Service request.

In this chapter we will cover the following topics:

- Introducing Service
- Started Service
- Building responsive apps with IntentService
- Posting results with pending intents
- Reporting progress on the notification drawer

- Applications of IntentService
- Bound service
- Communicating with a local service
- Broadcasting results with intents
- Applications of services

Introducing Service

A `Service` in Android, as referred to before, is an entity that runs without a user interface that could be used to execute any kind of business logic which the application requires during the execution.

If the basic unit of a visible application is `Activity`, its equivalent unit for non-visible components is `Service`. Just like activities, services must be declared in the AndroidManifest file so that the system is aware of them and can manage them for us:

```
<service android:name=".MyService"/>
```

Service has lifecycle callback methods, similar to those of Activity, that are always invoked on the application's main thread. Here are the most important callbacks that the user must define when it creates a service by extending the Service base class:

```
void onCreate();
void onDestroy()
void onStartCommand(Intent intent, int flags, int startId)
IBinder onBind(Intent intent)
boolean onUnbind(Intent intent)
```

The `onCreate()` is the lifecycle callback that is called once when the service is created that might be used to allocate Service resources.

The `onDestroy()` is the lifecycle callback called when the service is going to be destroyed and might be used to free Service resources.

The `onStartCommand()` is the lifecycle callback invoked when a started Service is explicitly started with the `startService()` command.

`onBind()` is the lifecycle callback called when the service is bound to a Service client – `bindService()`.

The onUnbind() is the callback called when the service is unbound from a client - unbindService():

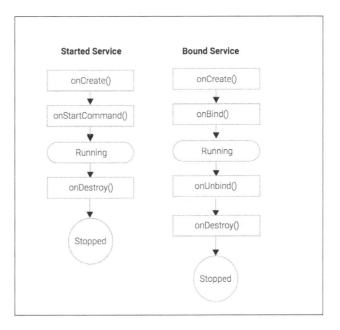

Also, just like Activity, Service does not automatically entail a separate background thread or process, and as a result, performing intensive or blocking operations in a Service callback method can lead to the annoying ANR dialog.

However, there are several ways in which services are different to activities, those ways are listed as follows:

- A Service does not provide a user interface.
- There can be many services active at the same time within an application.
- A Service can remain active even if the application hosting it is not the current foreground application, which means that there can be many services of many apps are active at the same time.
- Because the system is aware of services running within a process, it can avoid killing those processes unless absolutely necessary, allowing the background work to continue. Services have a higher priority than inactive or invisible activities.

Services in Android can be classified based on how the clients interact with it, taking the next forms:

- **Started Service**: This is a kind of service that is explicitly started when any object on the system invokes `startService()` and it will continue to run until it stops itself by calling `stopSelf()` or it is explicitly destroyed with `stopService()`.

- **Bound Service**: This is a kind of service that is started when the first client binds to it and runs until it has clients are connected. Service clients attach to a Service by calling `bindService()`, and the service will be destroyed when all the clients unbind, calling `unbindService()`.

- **Hybrid Service**: This Service is started when an object on the system calls `startService()` and might have clients connected to it during its lifecycle, by calling `bindService()`. Like the started Service, it runs indefinitely until the service is stopped, stops itself, or is killed by the system.

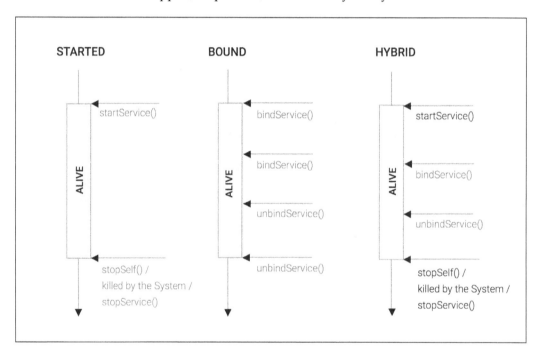

The Service can be also classified by its boundaries, taking the following forms:

- **Local Service (LS)**: The Service runs on the same process as the other Android components and therefore the shared memory could be used to send Java Objects between client and Server.

- **Internal Remote Service (IRS)**: The Service runs on a separate process but it can only be used by the components that belong to the application that defines it. To access it, an IPC technique (Messenger or AIDL) is required to interact with the remote process.

- **Global Service (GS)**: The Service runs on a separate process and could be accessed by other applications. For instance, with IRS, an IPC communication technique must be used by the client to access it.

Started service

As described previously, a started Service is a service that is initiated when the `Context` method `startService()` is invoked by any entity on the system that has access to a Context object or is a Context itself, such as an Activity:

```
ComponentName startService(Intent service)
```

 An Intent is a messaging object that can carry data (action, category, extras, and so on) and that you can use to request an action from another Android component.

The `startService()` function basically starts a service with an intent, and returns to the user a component name that can be used to verify that the correct service was resolved and invoked.

To simplify the Service resolution, we pass an Intent created from the current context with the Service class that needs to be started:

```
startService(new Intent(this,MyStartedService.class));
```

When the system receives the first `startService(intent)` request, it builds up the Service by calling `onCreate()` and forwards the intent from the first `startService` and the subsequent Intents to the `onStartCommand` function to be processed according to the order of `startService` calls:

```
int onStartCommand(Intent intent, int flags, int startId)
```

The onStartCommand should return an int that defines the Service restart behavior applied by the system in cases where the system kills it to release resources. Like explained before, the system maintains a list of Android running entities on the system ordered by rank, and once the available system resources are low it destroys the entities with lower rank first to free up resources.

The most common restart int values are defined by the following Service static fields:

- START_STICKY: If the Service process is terminated by the system, the Service is going to be restarted and no processed Intents will be delivered to the onStartCommand function. When no start Intents are pending for delivery, a null Intent is passed to the onStartCommand function. If a start request didn't return before the system kills the Service, the start request is submitted again on the restarted Service passing START_FLAG_RETRY on the onStartCommand second argument.

- START_NOT_STICKY: If the Service is terminated by the system, the Service is only restarted when there is at least one pending start request to be delivered.

- START_REDELIVER_INTENT: If the Service is terminated by the system, the Service will be restarted redelivering the last delivered start Intent and any pending requests. This kind of service is similar to START_STICKY, but instead of delivering a null Intent in the start command, the last successfully delivered Intent is dispatched. When the start request is redelivered, the flag START_FLAG_REDELIVERY is passed in on the onStartCommand second argument.

The onStartCommand, which executes on the main Thread, is the entry point for your service, so in cases where you execute long running operations on your Service, the offload of your operation into a background thread is imperative for keeping your application responsiveness at bearable levels.

In the next code snippet, we are going to create a basic Service that offloads the Intent processing to a background thread. The SaveMyLocationService Service subclass is going to receive an address location in a String and consume it in an operation that could occupy the CPU for a long period. First, we are going to create the background thread, that will retrieve the locations from a queue and consume them until it receives a signal to stop:

```
public class SaveMyLocationService extends Service {
  boolean shouldStop = false;
  Queue<String> jobs = new LinkedList<String>();

  Thread thread = new Thread() {
    @Override
```

```
    public void run() {
      while (!shouldStop) {
        String location = takeLocation();
        if (location != null) {
          consumeLocation(location);
        }
      }
    }
  };


  @Override
  public void onCreate() {
    super.onCreate();
    thread.start();
  }

String takeLocation() {
  String location = null;
  synchronized (jobs) {
    if (jobs.isEmpty()) {
      try {
        jobs.wait();
      } catch (InterruptedException e) {
        Thread.currentThread().interrupt();
        return null;
      }
    }
    location = jobs.poll();
  }
  return location;
}
void consumeLocation(String location) {...}
}
```

In the previous code, we basically constructed the foundations for our asynchronous processing. The single thread that is started when the Service's onCreate() callback is invoked on the main Thread, is going to monitor the jobs queue for new location requests. The Thread will wait in the background efficiently, using a Java monitor, until it gets notified with notify() when a new location is submitted.

When our background thread finds new locations in the queue, the `takeLocation()` that is waiting on the Java monitor returns and forwards the new request to the `consumeLocation()` to execute the business logic requested. The jobs are going to be processed sequentially following the order of insertion.

Once the `shouldStop` is set to true, the `run()` function will return and the thread will be terminated.

We'll need to register the Service in our AndroidManifest file, using a `<service>` element as follows:

```
<service android:name=".chapter5.SaveMyLocationService"/>
```

In the next step we are going to implement the `onStartCommand`, the function that will receive the request from the system in the first place and forward it to our thread to be processed in background:

```
@Override
public int onStartCommand(Intent intent, int flags, int startId) {
    super.onStartCommand(intent, flags, startId);
    String location = intent.getStringExtra(LOCATION_KEY);
    synchronized (jobs) {
        jobs.add(location);
        jobs.notify();
    }
    return START_STICKY;
    }
```

On the `onStartCommand`, we received the intent object from the system and the location passed as a String on the Intent extras. Next, we push it to our queue of jobs used to store the jobs in sequence. Later, we return the START_STICKY flag, which means that we want the Service restarted after the system shuts down our application and the pending intents delivered in case the system shuts down the system to free up resources.

Finally, we have to implement the callback function to stop our background processing infrastructure. This function is going to be called when the system forces the service to terminate or any component sends a `stop` command:

```
@Override
public void onDestroy() {
    super.onDestroy();
    synchronized (jobs) {
        shouldStop = true;
        jobs.notify();
    }
}
```

In the `onDestroy()` function, we mainly ask our thread to terminate, setting the `shouldStop` as true and by notifying the thread to finish the `run()` function. In case you allocated objects in your `onCreate()` function, this callback should be used to liberate any resources that you created during the Service lifecycle.

Now we are going to create a simple Activity that is able to start the service and stop the service:

```
public class SaveMyLocationActivity extends Activity {

    ...

    void onStartServiceClick() {
        Intent intent = new Intent(this, SaveMyLocationService.class);
        intent.putExtra(SaveMyLocationService.LOCATION_KEY,
                        getCurrentLocation());
        startService(intent);
    }

    void onStopServiceClick() {
        Intent intent = new Intent(this,SaveMyLocationService.class);
        stopService(intent);
    }
}
```

In our Activity, we created a start button that calls `onStartServiceClick()`, and a stop button that calls `onStopServiceClick()`, but for brevity we omitted the code.

Once the **start** button is clicked, our Activity will submit a new save location request, with the current location retrieved from the `getCurrentLocation()` function, to our service calling `startService()`.

Clicking on the **stop** button will result in a `stopService()`, which sends a stop request to our Service that leads to a `onDestroy()` invocation on our Service.

It is essential to mention that if the service is stopped and started repeatedly, a new thread is created to replace the older one. As mentioned before, the thread creation is an expensive operation, so in order to reduce the burden of the thread creation, the developer should keep the Service running as long it may be needed.

Our custom service is able to handle the `onStartCommand()` asynchronously very well but in the next section, we will focus our attention on the `IntentService` class, a special-purpose subclass of `Service` that comes in the Android SDK that makes it very easy to implement a task queue to process work on a single background thread.

Building responsive apps with IntentService

The IntentService class is a specialized subclass of Service that implements a background work queue using a single HandlerThread. When work is submitted to an IntentService, it is queued for processing by a single HandlerThread, and processed in order of submission on the onHandleIntent function:

```
abstract void onHandleIntent(Intent intent);
```

If the user exits the app before the queued work is completely processed, the IntentService will continue working in the background. When the IntentService has no more work in its queue, it will stop itself to avoid consuming unnecessary resources.

 The system may still kill a background app with an active IntentService, if it really needs to (to reclaim enough memory to run the current foreground process), but it will kill lower priority processes first, for example, other non-foreground apps that do not have active services.

The IntentService class gets its name from the way in which we submit work to it by invoking startService with an Intent:

```
startService(new Intent(context, MyIntentService.class));
```

As we do with our previous example, we can call startService as often as we like, which will start the IntentService if it isn't already running, or simply enqueue work to an already running instance if there is one.

If we want to pass some data to a Service, we can do so by supplying a data URI or extra data fields via an Intent:

```
Intent intent = new Intent(context, MyIntentService.class);
intent.setData(uri); intent.putExtra("param", "some value");
startService(intent);
```

We can create an IntentService subclass by extending android.app. IntentService and implementing the abstract onHandleIntent method.

We must invoke the single-argument constructor with a name for its background thread (naming the thread makes debugging and profiling much easier).

```
public class MyIntentService extends IntentService {

    public MyIntentService() {
```

```
    super("myIntentService");
  }
  protected void onHandleIntent(Intent intent) {
    // executes on the background HandlerThread.
  }
}
```

We'll need to register the IntentService in our AndroidManifest file, using a <service> element as follows:

```
<service android:name=".chapter5.MyIntentService"/>
```

If we want our IntentService to only be used by the components of our own application, we can specify that it is not public with an extra attribute:

```
<service android:name=".chapter5.MyIntentService"
        android:exported="false"/>
```

Let's get started by implementing an IntentService to retrieve the number of SMSs in the inbox from a particular mobile number:

```
public class CountMsgsIntentService extends IntentService {

public static final String NUMBER_KEY = "number";

public CountMsgsIntentService() {
    super("CountThread");
}

@Override
protected void onHandleIntent(Intent intent) {
  String phoneNumber = intent.getStringExtra(NUMBER_KEY);
  Cursor cursor = getMsgsFrom(phoneNumber);
  int numberOfMsgs = cursor.getCount();
    // Return will be adressed later
    ...
}
// Retrieve the number of messages in the inbox for a
// specific number
private Cursor getMsgsFrom(String phoneNumber) {
  String[] select = {
    Telephony.Sms._ID,
    Telephony.Sms.ADDRESS,
    Telephony.Sms.BODY,
  };
```

```
        String whereClause =
          Telephony.Sms.ADDRESS + " = '" + phoneNumber + "'";
        Uri quri = Uri.parse("content://sms/inbox");
        return getContentResolver().query(
            quri,
            select, // Columns to select
            whereClause, // Clause to filter results
            null, // Arguments for the whereClause
            null);
    }
}
```

Once the request is received on the `IntentService`, the request is pushed to the internal `Looper` queue and as soon as it get chance to process it, the `IntenService` invokes the `onHandleIntent` method with the Intent we passed in on the `startService()` method.

Next, we query the SMS Inbox Content Provider using the `phoneNumber` received, and after that we count the records retrieved.

Notice that we're declaring a public static constant name for the argument parameter, just to make it easy to use the correct name from any client `Activity` that wants to invoke the Service.

We can now invoke this `IntentService` as follows:

```
void triggerIntentService(String phone) {
    Intent intent = new Intent(this,
                                    CountMsgsIntentService.class);
    intent.putExtra(CountMsgsIntentService.NUMBER_KEY, phone);
    startService(intent);
}
```

The code above receives the `phoneNumber` as an argument and submits a new start request to `IntentService` to be processed sequentially following the submission order.

So far so good, but you've probably noticed that we haven't done anything with the result we retrieved. In the next section, we'll look at some of the ways in which we can send results from services to activities or fragments.

Handling results

Any `Service` — including subclasses of `IntentService` — can be used to start background work from which the originating `Fragment` or `Activity` doesn't expect a response.

However, it is very common to need to return a result or display the result of the background work to the user. We have several options for doing this:

- Send a `PendingIntent` to the `Service` from the originating `Activity`, allowing the `Service` to callback to the `Activity` via its `onActivityResult` method

- Post a system notification allowing the user to be informed that the background work was completed, even if the application is no longer in the foreground

- Send a message to a `Handler` in the originating `Activity` using `Messenger`

- Broadcast the result as an `Intent`, allowing any `Fragment` or `Activity` — including the originator — to receive the result of background processing

We'll learn about `BroadcastReceiver`, long-running tasks with `Service`, later, but now we'll return results with `PendingIntent` and alert the user with system notifications.

Posting results with PendingIntent

When we invoke an `IntentService`, it does not automatically have any way to respond to the calling Activity; so if the `Activity` wants to receive a result, it must provide some means for the `IntentService` to reply.

Arguably the easiest way to do that is with `PendingIntent`, which will be familiar to any Android developer who has worked with multiple activities using the `startActivityForResult` and `onActivityResult` methods, as the pattern is essentially the same.

 A PendingIntent is a token that you give to a foreign application component (Service, BroacastReceiver, or other applications) that allows the foreign entity to use your application's permissions to execute a predefined piece of code.

First, we'll add a few static members to `CountMsgsIntentService` to ensure that we use consistent values between it and the calling `Activity`:

```
public static final String PENDING_RESULT = "pending_result";
public static final String RESULT = "result";
public static final int RESULT_CODE = "countMsgs".hashCode();
```

We'll also need to define a static member in our Activity for the `REQUEST_CODE` constant, which we can use to correctly identify the results returned to our `onActivityResult` method:

```
private static final int REQUEST_CODE = 0;
```

Now, when we want to invoke `CountMsgsIntentService` from our `Activity`, we'll create a `PendingIntent` for the current `Activity`, which will act as a callback to invoke the Activity `onActivityResult` method.

We can create a `PendingIntent` with the `createPendingResult` method of the Activity, which accepts three parameters: an `int` result code, an Intent to use as the default result, and an `int` that encodes some flags for how the `PendingIntent` can be used (for example, whether it may be used more than once):

```
PendingIntent pending = createPendingResult(REQUEST_CODE,
                                            new Intent(), 0);
```

We pass the `PendingIntent` to the `IntentService` by adding it as an extra to the Intent we launch the `IntentService` with:

```
private void triggerIntentService(String phone) {
    PendingIntent pending = createPendingResult(
                          REQUEST_CODE, new Intent(), 0);
    Intent intent = new Intent(this,CountMsgsIntentService.class);
    intent.putExtra(CountMsgsIntentService.NUMBER_KEY, phone);
    intent.putExtra(CountMsgsIntentService.PENDING_RESULT,
                pending);
    startService(intent);
}
```

To handle the result that will be returned when this `PendingIntent` is invoked, we need to implement `onActivityResult` in the `Activity`, and check for the result code:

```
protected void onActivityResult(int req, int res, Intent data) {

    if (req == REQUEST_CODE &&
```

```
      res == CountMsgsIntentService.RESULT_CODE) {

    // Retrieve the count from result Intent
     int result = data.getIntExtra(
               CountMsgsIntentService.RESULT, -1);

    // Update UI View with the result
      TextView msgCountBut = (TextView) findViewById(
                          R.id.msgCountTv);
   msgCountBut.setText(Integer.toString(result));
     }
     super.onActivityResult(req, res, data);
  }
```

The `IntentService` can now reply to the calling `Activity` by invoking one of the `PendingIntent` send methods with the appropriate request code. Our updated `onHandleIntent` method looks as follows:

```
@Override
protected void onHandleIntent(Intent intent) {

  String phoneNumber = intent.getStringExtra(NUMBER_KEY);
  Cursor cursor = countMsgsFrom(phoneNumber);
  int numberOfMsgs = cursor.getCount();

  try {
  Intent result = new Intent();
  result.putExtra(RESULT, numberOfMsgs);
  PendingIntent reply = intent.getParcelableExtra(
                   PENDING_RESULT);
    reply.send(this, RESULT_CODE, result);
  } catch (PendingIntent.CanceledException exc) {
  Log.e("CountMsgsIntentService", "reply cancelled", exc);
  }
}
```

The additional code creates a new Intent object and populates it with our counter result retrieved from the cursor, and sends the result back to the calling Activity using the received `PendingIntent`. Additionally, we handle the `CanceledException`, in case the calling `Activity` decided that it wasn't interested in the result anymore and canceled the `PendingIntent`.

That's all there is to it—our `Activity` will now be invoked via its `onActivityResult` method when the `IntentService` completes its work. As a bonus, we will even receive the result if the `Activity` has restarted, for example, due to configuration changes such as a device rotation.

What if the user left the `Activity` (or even left the application) while the background work was in progress? In the next section, we'll use notifications to provide feedback without interrupting the user's new context.

Posting results as system notifications

System notifications appear initially as an icon in the notification area, normally at the very top of the device screen. Once notified, the user can open the notification drawer to see more details.

Notifications are an ideal way to inform the user of results or status updates from services, particularly when the operation may take a long time to complete and the user is likely to be doing something else in the meantime.

Let's post the result of our message counter as a notification, with a message containing the result that the user can read when they open the notification drawer. We'll use the support library to ensure broad API level compatibility, and add one method to `CountMsgsIntentService`, as follows:

```
private void notifyUser(String phoneNumber, int msgsCount) {

    String msg = String.format(
        "Found %d from the phone number %s", msgsCount, phoneNumber);

    NotificationCompat.Builder builder =
        new NotificationCompat.Builder(this)
            .setSmallIcon(R.drawable.ic_sms_counter_not)
            .setContentTitle("Inbox Counter")
            .setContentText(msg);

    // Gets an instance of the NotificationManager service
    NotificationManager nm = (NotificationManager) getSystemService(
                        Context.NOTIFICATION_SERVICE);
    // Sets an unique ID for this notification
    nm.notify(phoneNumber.hashCode(), builder.build());
}
```

Each notification has an identifier that we can use to control whether a new notification is posted or an existing one is reused. The identifier is an int, and is the first parameter to the notify method. Since our countMsgsFrom value is an int, and we would like to be able to post multiple notifications, it makes sense to use phoneNumber as the ID for our notifications so that each different request can produce its own separate notification.

To post a notification containing the result of our service request, we just need to update onHandleIntent to invoke the notifyUser method:

```
@Override
protected void onHandleIntent(Intent intent) {

    String phoneNumber = intent.getStringExtra(NUMBER_KEY);
    Cursor cursor = countMsgsFrom(phoneNumber);
    int numberOfMsgs = cursor.getCount();
    notifyUser(phoneNumber,numberOfMsgs);
    ...
}
```

Now that we've learned the basics of using IntentService, let's consider some real-world applications.

Applications of IntentService

Ideal applications for IntentService include just about any long-running task where the work is not especially tied to the behavior of a Fragment or Activity, and particularly when the task must complete its processing regardless of whether the user exits the application.

However, IntentService is only suitable for situations where a single worker thread is sufficient to handle the workload, since its work is processed by a single HandlerThread sequentially following the order of submission, and we cannot start more than one instance of the same IntentService subclass.

A use case that Intent Service is ideally suited for is one-shot, long–running tasks that could be processed in the background without user intervention:

- Uploading data to remote servers
- Database or data backups
- Time consuming file data processing
- Communication with web service resources (WSDL or REST)
- Periodic time operations such as alarm processing, calendar event processing, and so on

A use case that `IntentService` is ideally suited for is uploading data to remote servers because:

- The upload usually must complete, even if the user leaves the application
- A single upload at a time usually makes best use of the available connection, since bandwidth is often asymmetric (there is much smaller bandwidth for upload than download)
- A single upload at a time gives us a better chance of completing each individual upload before losing our data connection

Let's see how we might implement a very simple `IntentService` that uploads images to a simple web service via HTTP POST.

HTTP uploads with IntentService

For this example, we'll create a new `Activity`, `UploadArtworkActivity`, to allow the user to pick an album artwork to upload. We'll start with the code for `AlbumListActivity` that we created in *Chapter 4, Exploring the Loader*.

Our new `UploadArtworkActivity` only needs a small modification to add an `OnItemClickListener` interface to the `GridView` of images, so that tapping an image triggers its upload. We can add the listener as an anonymous inner class in `onCreate` as follows:

```
grid.setOnItemClickListener(new AdapterView.OnItemClickListener() {
  @Override
  public void onItemClick(AdapterView<?> parent, View view,
                          int position, long id) {
    Cursor cursor = (Cursor) mAdapter.getItem(position);
    int albumId = cursor.getInt(
      cursor.getColumnIndex(MediaStore.Audio.Albums._ID));
    Uri sArtworkUri = Uri.parse(
      "content://media/external/audio/albumart");
    Uri albumArtUri = ContentUris.
                        withAppendedId(sArtworkUri, albumId);
    Intent intent = new Intent(UploadArtworkActivity.this,
                        UploadArtworkIntentService.class);
    intent.setData(albumArtUri);
    startService(intent);
  }
});
```

This looks like quite a dense chunk of code, but all it really does is use the position of the tapped thumbnail to move the `Cursor` to the correct row in its result set, extract the ID of the album that was tapped, create a `Uri` for its artwork file, and then start `UploadArtworkIntentService` with an Intent containing that Uri.

We'll extract the details of the upload into a separate class, so `UploadArtworkIntentService` itself is just a fairly sparse `IntentService` implementation. In `onCreate`, we'll set up an instance of our `ImageUploader` class, which will be used to process all uploads added to the queue during this lifetime of the Service:

```
public void onCreate() {
  super.onCreate();
  mImageUploader = new ImageUploader(getContentResolver());
}
```

The implementation of `ImageUploader` itself is not all that interesting — we just use Java's `HTTPURLConnection` class to post the image data to the server. The complete source code is available on the Packt Publishing website, so we'll just list two critical methods — upload and pump — and leave out the housekeeping:

```
public boolean upload(Uri data, ProgressCallack callback) {
  HttpURLConnection conn = null;
  try {
    int len = getContentLength(data);
    URL destination = new URL(UPLOAD_URL);
    conn = (HttpURLConnection) destination.openConnection();
    conn.setRequestMethod("POST");
    ...
    OutputStream out = null;
    try {
      pump(in = mContentResolver.openInputStream(data),
           out = conn.getOutputStream(),
           callback, len);
    } finally {
      if (in != null )
        in.close();
      if (out != null )
        out.close();
      int responseCode = conn.getResponseCode();
      return (( responseCode >= 200) &&
              (responseCode < 400));
    }
  } catch (IOException e) {
```

```
            Log.e("Upload Service", "upload failed", e);
            return false;
        } finally {
        conn.disconnect();
        }
    }
}
```

The `pump` method just copies 1 KB chunks of data from the `InputStream` to the `OutputStream`, pumping the data to the server, and invokes the progress callback function, as follows:

```
    private void pump(InputStream in, OutputStream out,
                    ProgressCallack callback, int len)
    throws IOException {

        int length, i = 0, size = 1024;
        byte[] buffer = new byte[size]; // 1kb buffer
        while ((length = in.read(buffer)) > -1) {
            out.write(buffer, 0, length);
            out.flush();
            if (callback != null)
                callback.onProgress(len, ++i * size);
        }
    }
```

Each time a 1 KB chunk of data is pushed to the `OutputStream`, we invoke the `ProgressCallback` method, which we'll use in the next section to report the progress to the user.

Reporting progress

For long-running processes, it can be very useful to report progress so that the user can take comfort in knowing that something is actually happening.

To report progress from an `IntentService`, we can use the same mechanisms that we use to send results—for example, sending `PendingIntents` containing progress information, or posting system notifications with progress updates.

We can also use other techniques that we'll cover later in the chapter, broadcasting intents to registered receivers.

Whichever approach we take to report progress, we should be careful not to report progress too frequently, otherwise we'll waste resources updating the progress bar at the expense of completing the work itself!

Let's look at an example that displays a progress bar on notifications in the drawer—a use case that the Android development team anticipated and therefore made easy for us with the setProgress method of NotificationCompat.Builder:

```
Builder setProgress(int max, int progress, boolean indeterminate);
```

Here, max sets the target value at which our work will be completed, progress is where we have got to so far, and indeterminate controls which type of progress bar is shown. When indeterminate is true, the notification shows a progress bar that indicates something is in progress without specifying how far through the operation we are, while false shows the kind of progress bar that we need—one that shows how much work we have done, and how much is left to do.

We'll need to calculate progress and dispatch notifications at appropriate intervals, which we've facilitated through our ProgressCallback class. Now we need to implement the ProgressCallback and hook it up in UploadArtworkIntentService:

```java
private class ProgressNotificationCallback
    implements ImageUploader.ProgressCallack {
    private NotificationCompat.Builder builder;
    private NotificationManager nm;
    private int id, prev;

    public ProgressNotificationCallback(
        Context ctx, int id, String msg) {
        this.id = id;
        prev = 0;
        builder = new NotificationCompat.Builder(ctx)
            .setSmallIcon(android.R.drawable.stat_sys_upload_done)
            .setContentTitle("Uploading Artwork")
            .setContentText(msg)
            .setProgress(100, 0, false);
        nm = (NotificationManager)
            getSystemService(Context.NOTIFICATION_SERVICE);
        nm.notify(id, builder.build());
    }

    public void onProgress(int max, int progress) {
```

```
      int percent = (int) ((100f * progress) / max);
      if (percent > (prev + 5)) {
        builder.setProgress(100, percent, false);
        nm.notify(id, builder.build());
        prev = percent;
      }
    }

    public void onComplete(String msg) {
      builder.setProgress(0, 0, false);
      builder.setContentText(msg);
      nm.notify(id, builder.build());
    }
  }
```

The constructor of `ProgressNotificationCallback` consists of familiar code to post a notification with a progress bar.

The `onProgress` method throttles the rate at which notifications are dispatched, so that we only post an update as each additional 5 percent of the total data is uploaded, in order not to swamp the system with notification updates.

The `onComplete` method posts a notification that sets both the integer progress parameters to zero, which removes the progress bar.

To complete the code, we implement `onHandleIntent` to display the notification drawer and deliver the upload result:

```
@Override
protected void onHandleIntent(Intent intent) {
  Uri data = intent.getData();

  // Unique id per upload, so each has its own notification
  int id = Integer.parseInt(data.getLastPathSegment());
  String msg = String.format("Uploading %s.jpg", id);

  ProgressNotificationCallback progress =
    new ProgressNotificationCallback(this, id, msg);

  // On Upload sucess
  if (mImageUploader.upload(data, progress)) {
    progress.onComplete(
      String.format("Upload finished for %s.jpg", id));
  // On Upload Failure
  } else {
```

```
        progress.onComplete(
          String.format("Upload failed %s.jpg", id));
    }
  }
}
```

Tap an artwork image to start uploading and you'll see a notification appear. Slide open the notification drawer and watch the progress bar ticking up as your image uploads.

We are finished with started services, so now it is time to move to a different type of Service, the Bound Service.

Bound Service

A Bound Service is an Android Service that defines a client interface and allows several entities to bind it by invoking `bindService()` and creating a relation between each order that facilitates the interaction with a request-response model.

The `Service` instance will be created when the first client attempts to connect to it and will be alive until the last client disconnects from it using the `unbindService()` function.

In order to create the connection between the client and the server, the service must implement the `onBind()` function and return an `IBinder` object that implements a lightweight remote procedure mechanism to perform in-process or cross-process calls:

```
    IBinder onBind(Intent intent)
```

When all the clients disconnect from the Service, calling `unbindService()`, the service `onUnbind()` member method is called:

```
    boolean onUnbind (Intent intent)
```

A Bound Service might reside in the same process (LS), in a different process that belongs to the application (LIS), or in an another application process (GS), so the technique to communicate with the service and the `IBinder` type returned depends entirely on the service process location, as mentioned before.

In the next section, we are going to explain how to interact and bind to a local Service to initiate an asynchronous action on the Service.

The remote binding with AIDL or with Messenger are other techniques used in advanced use cases where inter-process communication is required, though in this book we are not going to cover it.

For a smooth start, first we are going to cover a local `Service` binding.

Communicating with a Local Service

A local bound service is the most common type of bound `service`, and given that the server and the client run on the same process, there is no need to use an **inter-process communication (IPC)** technique to send requests and receive responses between them. Moreover, both entities, the service client and server, share the same address memory space within the process, making the exchange of requests and responses quite easy using Java Objects.

Since we are within the same process, the `Binder` object returned by the `onBind()` `Service` method might define a method to return the `Service` class instance object. In this manner, we can use the public `Service` class functions to submit new requests to the `Service` in the same way as we invoke a regular object method.

Let's demonstrate this with an example, creating a bound service that creates an SHA1 cryptographic digest from a string that we type in a UI `EditText`.

Primarily, we will start by implementing our own `Binder`:

```
public class Sha1HashService extends Service {

  // Instance Binder given to clients
  private final IBinder mBinder = new LocalBinder();

  public class LocalBinder extends Binder {
    Sha1HashService getService() {
      // Return this instance of LocalService
      // so clients can call public methods
      return Sha1HashService.this;
    }
  }
  @Override
  public IBinder onBind(Intent intent) {
    return mBinder;
  }
}
```

Our binder, `LocalBinder`, extends from the `Binder` class, and provides a `getService()` method to retrieve the instance of our `Service`. Then, when any client connects to our `Service`, the `onBind()` function will return our `LocalBinder` instance object.

An `Activity` or `Fragment` that wants to directly interact with this `Service` first needs to bind to it using the `bindService` method and secondly supply a `ServiceConnection` to handle the `onServiceConnected()`/`onServiceDisconnected()` callbacks.

The `ServiceConnection` implementation simply casts the `IBinder` received to the concrete class defined by the `Service`, obtains a reference to the `Service`, and records it in a member variable of the `Activity`:

```
public class Sha1Activity extends Activity {

  Sha1HashService mService;
  boolean mBound = false;

  // Defines callbacks for service binding,
  // passed to bindService()
  private ServiceConnection mConnection = new ServiceConnection()
  {
    @Override
    public void onServiceConnected(ComponentName name,
                                   IBinder service) {

      // We've bound to LocalService,
      // cast the IBinder and get LocalService instance
      Sha1HashService.LocalBinder binder =
        (Sha1HashService.LocalBinder) service;
      mService = binder.getService();
      mBound = true;

      // After this the Activity can invoke the Service methods
    }

    @Override
    public void onServiceDisconnected(ComponentName arg0) {
      mBound = false;
      mService = null;
    }
  };
}
```

When we lose the connection with Service unexpectedly, due to a service crash or an unexpected error in the Android system, `onServiceDisconnected` gets called to notify the client that the connection to the service is considered lost.

We can make the `Activity` bind and unbind during its `onStart()` and `onStop()` lifecycle method, because we only need to interact with the service when the `Activity` is visible on the screen. We should try to avoid the bind and unbind `onResume()` and `onPause()` `Activity` callbacks to reduce the number of connect and disconnect transitions in your application's lifecycle:

```
@Override
protected void onStart() {
    super.onStart();
    // Bind to LocalService
    Intent intent = new Intent(this, Sha1HashService.class);
    bindService(intent, mConnection, Context.BIND_AUTO_CREATE);
}

@Override
protected void onStop() {
    super.onStop();
    // Unbind from the service
    if (mBound) {
        unbindService(mConnection);
        mBound = false;
    }
}
```

Once the `Activity` starts, we call the `Context.bindService()`, passing an Intent that explicitly defines the `Service` class that we want to bind, our `ServiceConnection` instance, and the optional flag `Context.BIND_AUTO_CREATE` that means that the System will keep the Service running as long as this bind exists.

In Hybrid Services (Bound/Started), after we bind to a Service, we can access the Service by calling `startService(Intent)` and process Service calls over `onStartCommand(Intent, int, int)`.

This is great—once the binding is made, we have a direct reference to the `Service` instance and can call its methods! However, we didn't implement any methods in our `Service` yet, so it's currently useless.

Let's create a method on `Sha1HashService` to calculate the digest in the background and return the result to the `Activity`.

First, to execute this task in background we need to setup the execution engine, so to achieve that we are going to set up our own `Executor` based on the `ThreadPool` class supplied in `java.util.concurrent`. The Executor will support concurrency, from two to four concurrent threads, and request queueing up to 32 queued jobs:

```java
public class Sha1HashService extends Service {

    private static final int CORE_POOL_SIZE = 2;
    private static final int MAXIMUM_POOL_SIZE = 4;
    private static final int MAX_QUEUE_SIZE = 32;
    private static final BlockingQueue<Runnable> sPoolWorkQueue =
        new LinkedBlockingQueue<Runnable>(MAX_QUEUE_SIZE);

    private ThreadPoolExecutor mExecutor;

    // Factory to set the Thread Names
    private static final ThreadFactory sThreadFactory =
    new ThreadFactory() {
      private final AtomicInteger mCount = new AtomicInteger(1);
      public Thread newThread(Runnable r) {
        Thread t = new Thread(r, "SHA1HashService #" +
                                    mCount.getAndIncrement());
        t.setPriority(Thread.MIN_PRIORITY);
        return t;
      }
    };

    @Override
    public void onCreate() {
      super.onCreate();
      mExecutor = new ThreadPoolExecutor(CORE_POOL_SIZE,
                                    MAXIMUM_POOL_SIZE, 1,
                                    TimeUnit.SECONDS,
                                    sPoolWorkQueue,
                                    sThreadFactory);
      mExecutor.prestartAllCoreThreads();
    }
```

When the Service is created, immediately after the first binding, the `ThreadPool` is started and the core threads (2) are started with `prestartAllCoreThreads`, ready to process the incoming requests as soon as they arrive in the Service. If the clients submit requests at such a pace that the core threads are not able handle them, the thread pool will increase the number of worker threads in the pool until it reaches four threads.

Now that we have the executor in place, we will create the public method that receives the request to digest a `String`:

```
void getSha1Digest(final String text) {

  Runnable runnable = new Runnable() {
    @Override
    public void run() {
      try {
          // Execute the Long Running Computation
          final String digest = SHA1(text);
        } catch (Exception e) {
          Log.e("Sha1HashService", "Hash failed for "+ text, e);
        }
      }
    };
    // Submit the Runnable on the ThreadPool
    mExecutor.execute(runnable);
}

private String SHA1(String text) throws Exception {
  MessageDigest md = MessageDigest.getInstance("SHA-1");
  md.update(text.getBytes("iso-8859-1"), 0, text.length());
  byte[] sha1hash = md.digest();
  return convertToHex(sha1hash);
}
private String convertToHex(byte[] data) {
  ...
}
```

Since `Sha1Activity` has a direct object reference to `Sha1HashService`, we can now go ahead and invoke its `getSha1Digest` method directly — taking care to check that the `Service` is actually bound first, of course:

```
// Invoke the Sha1Hash Service to calculate the digest
//   when the hash button is pressed
queryButton.setOnClickListener(new View.OnClickListener() {
  @Override
  public void onClick(View v) {
    EditText et = (EditText)findViewById(R.id.text);
    if (mService != null) {
      mService.getSha1Digest(et.getText().toString());
    }
  }
});
```

Taking the text retrieved from our `EditText` view, we call our Service `getSha1Digest` to calculate the typed text digest. This is a very convenient and efficient way of submitting work to a `Service` — there's no need to package up a request in an Intent, so there's no excess object creation or communication overhead.

Since `getSha1Digest` is asynchronous, we can't return a result directly from the method invocation, and `Sha1HashService` itself has no user interface, so how can we present results to our user?

One possibility is to pass a callback to `Sha1HashService` so that we can invoke methods of our `Activity` when the background work completes. Let's define a generic callback interface for the activity to implement:

```
public interface ResultCallback<T> {
    void onResult(T data);
}
```

There is a serious risk that by passing an `Activity` into the `Service`, we'll expose ourselves to memory leaks. The lifecycles of `Service` and `Activity` do not coincide, so strong references to an `Activity` from a `Service` can prevent it from being garbage collected in a timely fashion.

The simplest way to prevent such memory leaks is to make sure that `Sha1HashService` only keeps a weak reference to the calling `Activity` so that when its lifecycle is complete, the `Activity` can be garbage collected, even if there is an ongoing calculation in the Service.

It is really important to remember that whenever we update the UI during the `ResultCallback.onResult`, we must do it in the UI Thread; therefore, it is essential to create a `Runnable` object with the result and post it on the main `Looper`.

The modified `Sha1HashService` is shown in the following code:

```
private void postResultOnUI(final String result,
    final WeakReference<ResultCallback<String>> refCallback) {

    // Retrieve the main Thread Looper
    Looper mainLooper = Looper.getMainLooper();
    final Handler handler = new Handler(mainLooper);
    handler.post(new Runnable() {
      @Override
      public void run() {
        if ( refCallback.get() != null ) {
          refCallback.get().onResult(result);
        }
      }
    }
```

```
    });
  }

  public void getSha1Digest(final String text,
                            ResultCallback<String> callback) {

    final WeakReference<ResultCallback<String>> ref =
      new WeakReference<ResultCallback<String>>(callback);

    Runnable runnable = new Runnable() {
      @Override
      public void run() {
        try {
          // Execute the Long Running Computation
          final String digest = SHA1(text);
          // Execute the Runnable on UI Thread
          postResultOnUI(digest, ref);
        } catch (Exception e) {
          Log.e("Sha1HashService", "Hash failed", e);
        }
      }
    };
    // Submit the Runnable on the ThreadPool
    mExecutor.execute(runnable);
  }
```

We invoke the callback on the main thread using `postResultOnUI`, so that `Sha1Activity` can interact with the user interface directly in the callback method. We can implement the callback as a method of `Sha1Activity`:

```
public class Sha1Activity extends Activity
  implements ResultCallback<String> {

  @Override
    public void onResult(String data) {
        // Updates the result view with the digest string
        TextView et = (TextView)findViewById(R.id.hashResult);
        et.setText(data);
    }
  }
```

Now we can directly invoke methods in `Sha1HashService` and return results via a callback method of `Sha1Activity` by passing the `Activity` itself as the callback:

```
if ( mService != null ) {
  mService.getSha1Digest(et.getText().toString(),
                         Sha1Activity.this);
}
```

Our service uses their local `ThreadPool` executor to handle the requests in an asynchronous way, although we might have used the `AsyncTask` public static executors: `SERIAL_EXECUTOR` to execute our digest calculation in a serialized way, or the `THREAD_POOL_EXECUTOR` to calculate the digest concurrently and independently:

```
void getSha1Digest(final String text,
                   ResultCallback<String> callback) {

  AsyncTask.SERIAL_EXECUTOR.execute(runnable);
  // or
  AsyncTask.THREAD_POOL_EXECUTOR.execute(runnable);
}
```

Notice that the `AsyncTask` executors are a system-shared resource, a shared group of threads, used by all the `AsyncTasks` in the system; therefore, our processing might suffer a delay when all the executor threads are occupied doing work. In most use cases there is no need to create our own custom group of working threads and the `AsyncTask` executors should be used.

This direct communication between `Sha1Activity` and `Sha1HashService` is very efficient and easy to work with. However, there is a downside: if the `Activity` restarts because of a configuration change, such as a device rotation, the `WeakReference` to the callback will be garbage collected and `Sha1HashService` cannot send the result.

In the next section we are going to explore a mechanism that sends the results back to an Activity, or an other part of the application, even after a configuration change – Broadcast Intents.

Broadcasting results with intents

Broadcasting an `Intent` is a way of sending results to anyone who registers to receive them. This can even include other applications in separate processes if we choose, but if the `Activity` and `Service` are a part of the same process, broadcasting is best done using a local broadcast, as this is more efficient and secure:

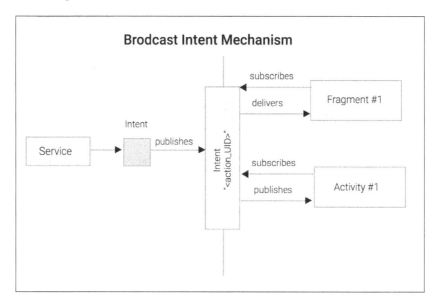

We can update `Sha1HashService` to broadcast its results with just a few extra lines of code. First, let's define two constants to make it easy to register a receiver for the broadcast and extract the result from the broadcast Intent object:

```
public static final String DIGEST_BROADCAST =
        "asynchronousandroid.chapter5.DIGEST_BROADCAST";
public static final String RESULT = "digest";
```

Now we can implement the method that does most of the work using the `LocalBroadcastManager` to send an Intent object containing the calculated result. We're using the support library class `LocalBroadcastManager` here for efficiency and security – broadcasts sent locally don't incur the overhead of interprocess communication and cannot be leaked outside of our application:

```
private void broadcastResult(String digest) {
    Intent intent = new Intent(DIGEST_BROADCAST);
    intent.putExtra(RESULT, digest);
    LocalBroadcastManager.getInstance(this).
      sendBroadcast(intent);
}
```

The `sendBroadcast` method is asynchronous and will return immediately without waiting for the message to be broadcast and handled by receivers. Finally, we invoke our new `broadcastResult` method from `getSha1Digest`:

```
void getSha1Digest(final String text) {
  Runnable runnable = new Runnable() {
    @Override
    public void run() {
      try {
        // Execute the Long Running Computation
        final String digest = SHA1(text);
        // Broadcast Result to Subscribers
        broadcastResult(digest);
      ...
  }
}
```

Great! We're broadcasting the result of our background calculation. Now we need to register a receiver in `Sha1Activity` to handle the result. Here's how we might define our `BroadcastReceiver` subclass:

```
private static class DigestReceiver extends BroadcastReceiver {

  private TextView view;

  @Override
  public void onReceive(Context context, Intent intent) {
    if (view != null) {
      String result = intent.getStringExtra(
                          Sha1HashService.RESULT);
      view.setText(result);
    } else {
      Log.i("Sha1HashService", " ignoring - we're detached");
    }
  }

  public void attach(TextView view) {
    this.view = view;
  }
  public void detach() {
    this.view = null;
  }
};
```

This `DigestReceiver` implementation is quite simple—all it does is extract and display the result from the Intent it receives—basically fulfilling the role of the Handler we used in the previous section.

We only want this `BroadcastReceiver` to listen for results while our `Activity` is at the top of the stack and visible in the application, so we'll register and unregister it in the `onStart()` and `onStop()` lifecycle methods. As with the `Handler` that we used previously, we'll also apply the attach/detach pattern to make sure we don't leak View objects:

```
@Override
protected void onStart() {
  super.onStart();
    . . .
  mReceiver.attach((TextView) findViewById(R.id.hashResult));
  IntentFilter filter =
    new IntentFilter(Sha1HashService.DIGEST_BROADCAST);
  LocalBroadcastManager.getInstance(this).
  registerReceiver(mReceiver, filter);
}

@Override
protected void onStop() {
  . . .
  LocalBroadcastManager.getInstance(this).
  unregisterReceiver(mReceiver);
  mReceiver.detach();
}
```

Of course, if the user moves to another part of the application that doesn't register a `BroadcastReceiver`, or if we exit the application altogether, they won't see the result of the calculation.

If our Service could detect unhandled broadcasts, we could modify it to alert the user with a system notification instead. We'll see how to do that in the next section.

Detecting unhandled broadcasts

In the previous sections, we used system notifications to post results to the notification drawer—a nice solution for when the user has navigated away from our app before the background work has completed. However, we don't want to annoy the user by posting notifications when our app is still in the foreground and can display the results directly.

Ideally, we'll display the results in the app if it is still in the foreground and send a notification otherwise. If we're broadcasting results, the Service will need to know if anyone handled the broadcast and if not, send a notification.

One way to do this is to use the sendBroadcastSync synchronous broadcast method and take advantage of the fact that the Intent object we're broadcasting is mutable (any receiver can modify it). To begin with, we'll add one more constant to Sha1HashService:

```
public static final String HANDLED = "intent_handled";
```

Next, modify broadcastResult to use the synchronous broadcast method and return the value of a Boolean extra property; HANDLED from the Intent:

```
void broadcastResult(final String text) {
  Intent intent = new Intent(DIGEST_BROADCAST);
  intent.putExtra(RESULT, digest);
  // Synchronous Broadcast
  LocalBroadcastManager.getInstance(Sha1HashService.this).
    sendBroadcastSync(intent);
  boolean handled = intent.getBooleanExtra(HANDLED, false);
}
```

Because sendBroadcastSync is synchronous, all registered BroadcastReceivers will have handled the broadcast by the time sendBroadcastSync returns. This means that if any receiver sets the Boolean extra property HANDLED to true, broadcastResult will return true.

In our BroadcastReceiver, we'll update the Intent object by adding a Boolean property to indicate that we've handled it:

```
@Override
public void onReceive(Context context, Intent intent) {
  if (view != null) {
    String result = intent.getStringExtra(
                    Sha1HashBroadCastUnhService.RESULT);
    intent.putExtra(Sha1HashBroadCastUnhService.HANDLED, true);
    view.setText(result);
  } else {
    Log.i("Sha1HashService", " ignoring - we're detached");
  }
}
```

Now if Sha1Activity is still running, its BroadcastReceiver is registered and receives the Intent object and will set the extra Boolean property HANDLED with the value true.

However, if Sha1Activity has finished, the BroadcastReceiver will no longer be registered and Sha1HashService will return false from its broadcastResult method.

> There's one final complication: unlike sendBroadcast, which always invokes BroadcastReceivers on the main thread, sendBroadcastSync uses the thread that it is called with.

Our BroadcastReceiver interacts directly with the user interface, so we must call it on the main thread. To broadcast the intent on the main thread synchronously, we create an anonymous Runnable to execute the broadcast:

```
private void broadcastResult(final String text,
                             final String digest) {

    Looper mainLooper = Looper.getMainLooper();
    Handler handler = new Handler(mainLooper);
    handler.post(new Runnable() {
      @Override
      public void run() {
        Intent intent = new Intent(DIGEST_BROADCAST);
        intent.putExtra(RESULT, digest);
        LocalBroadcastManager.getInstance(Sha1HashService.this).
        sendBroadcastSync(intent);
        boolean handled = intent.getBooleanExtra(HANDLED,
                                                 false);

        if (!handled) {
          notifyUser(text, digest);
        }
      }
    });
}
```

Now that we have the broadcast function in place, we can call it from the getSha1Digest to generate an Android notification when the intent is not handled by a Receiver:

```
void getSha1Digest(final String text) {
    ...
    final String digest = SHA1(text);
    // Execute the Runnable on UI Thread
    broadcastResult(text, digest);
    ...
}
```

This does just what we want—if our `BroadcastReceiver` handles the message, we don't post a notification; otherwise, we will do so to make sure the user gets their result.

So far we have been binding to a Service that runs within the same process, where the client shares the memory address space with the Service. In the next section we are going to detail how to interact with Services that run in remote processes using the Android IPC-specific techniques.

Applications of Services

With a little bit of work, `Services` give us the means to perform long-running background tasks, and free us from the tyranny of the `Activity` lifecycle. As opposed to `IntentService`, directly sub-classing a `Service` also gives us the ability to control the level of concurrency.

With the ability to run as many tasks as we need and to take as long as is necessary to complete those tasks, a world of new possibilities opens up.

The only real constraint on how and when we use `Services` comes from the need to communicate results to a user-interface component, such as a `Fragment` or `Activity`, and the complexity this entails.

Ideal use cases for `Services` tend to have the following characteristics:

- Long-running (a few hundred milliseconds and upward):
- Not specific to a single Activity or Fragment class
- Must complete, even if the user leaves the application
- Does not require user intervention to complete
- Operations that require state between different calls
- Requires more concurrency than `IntentService` provides, or needs control over the level of concurrency

There are many applications that exhibit these characteristics, but the stand-out example is, of course, handling concurrent downloads from a web service.

To make good use of the available download bandwidth and to limit the impact of network latency, we want to be able to run more than one download at a time (but not too many). We also don't want to use more bandwidth than necessary by failing to completely download a file and having to restart the download later. So ideally, once a download starts, it should run to completion even if the user leaves the application.

Summary

In this chapter, we explored the very powerful `Service` component, putting it to use to execute long-running background tasks with or without a configurable level of concurrency.

We explored the incredibly useful `IntentService` — an ideal construct for performing long-running background tasks off the main thread, surviving well beyond the lifecycle of the initiating `Activity`, and even continuing to do useful work when the application is no longer in the foreground.

We learned how to send work to an `IntentService` with parameterized Intents, how to process that work in the background by implementing `onHandleIntent`, and how to send results back to the originating `Activity` using a `PendingIntent`.

For cases where the application is no longer in the foreground or an operation is particularly long-running, we saw how to post notifications to the notification drawer, complete with progress updates.

We also saw the wide range of communication mechanisms available for delivering results back to the user: direct invocation of local `Service` methods; broadcasting results to registered parties with `BroadcastReceiver`; and, if the user has already left the application, raising system notifications.

In the next chapter, we'll add one other weapon to our arsenal: the ability to run background tasks at specific times — even when the device is asleep — by scheduling alarms with `AlarmManager`.

6

Scheduling Work with AlarmManager

Maintaining the responsiveness of foreground apps has been our primary focus throughout this book, and we've explored numerous ways to shift work away from the main thread and run work in the background.

In all of our discussions so far, we wanted to get the work done as soon as possible, so although we moved it to a background thread, we still performed the work concurrently with ongoing main thread operations, such as updating the user interface and responding to user interaction.

In this chapter we will learn how to defer work with `AlarmManager` to run at some distant time in the future, initiating work without user intervention, and even waking up the device from an idle state if it is really necessary. Meanwhile, we will introduce you to some power saving features introduced with Android Marshmallow 6 and explain how to adapt your application to this new paradigm.

In this chapter we will cover the following topics:

- Scheduling alarms with AlarmManager
- Canceling alarms
- Scheduling repeating alarms
- Scheduling alarms in Doze Mode
- Setting up an alarm clock
- Debugging AlarmManager alarms
- Handling alarms with Activities
- Handling alarms with BroadcastReceivers

- Staying awake with WakeLocks
- Restoring alarms on system boot
- Applications of AlarmManager

Introducing AlarmManager

In *Chapter 2, Performing Work with Looper, Handler, and HandlerThread,* we learned how to schedule work on a `HandlerThread` using `postDelayed`, `postAtTime`, `sendMessageDelayed`, and `sendMessageAtTime`. These mechanisms are fine for short-term scheduling of work while our application is running in the foreground.

However, if we want to schedule an operation to run at some point in the distant future, we'll run into problems. First, our application may be terminated before that time arrives, removing any chance of the Handler running those scheduled operations. Second, the device may be asleep, and with its CPU powered down it cannot run our scheduled tasks.

 The solution to this is to use an alternative scheduling approach, one that is designed to overcome these problems: `AlarmManager`.

`android.app.AlarmManager` is a class that has been available in the Android SDK since the first version, delivering an advanced API to fire off Intents in the future at one specific time or time window defined by the user. The schedules are managed by the Android system, taking into account the device power cycles and states to keep energy consumption at a low level.

Moreover, `AlarmManager` is a system service that provides scheduling capabilities far beyond those of Handler. Being a system service, AlarmManager cannot be terminated and has the capacity, under certain conditions, to wake the device from sleep to deliver scheduled alarms.

The leading features of `android.app.AlarmManager` are as follows:

- **Ability to wake up the device from idle states**: The user is able to control how the system should handle your alarm when it is in energy saving mode
- **Cancel Alarms**: a mechanism to cancel a previously created alarm based on Intent comparison
- **Update Alarms**: a mechanism to update an existing scheduled alarm

- **Exact and Inexact Alarms**: an API that is able to control the exactness of our scheduling
- **Scheduling managed by the Android system**: The alarms will fire even when your application is not running, and without consuming any application resources to manage the timers

Scheduling alarms with AlarmManager

As we said before, all the alarm operations are managed through the singleton object `AlarmManager`, an Android global system service that can be retrieved by any class with access to a `Context` instance. As an example, in an `Activity` we can get the `AlarmManager` from any member method by using the following code:

```
AlarmManager am = (AlarmManager)getSystemService(ALARM_SERVICE);
```

Once we have a reference to the `AlarmManager`, we can schedule an alarm to deliver a `PendingIntent` object to a `Service`, an `Activity` or `BroadcastReceiver`, at a time of our choosing. The simplest way to do that is using the `set` method:

```
void set(int type, long triggerAtMillis, PendingIntent operation)
```

When we set an alarm, we must also specify a `type` flag—the first parameter to the `set` method. The `type` flag sets the conditions under which the alarm should fire and which clock to use for our schedule.

There are two conditions and two clocks, resulting in four possible `type` settings.

The first condition specifies whether or not the device will be woken up if it is in a sleeping state at the time of the scheduled alarm—whether the alarm is a `wakeup` alarm or not.

The clocks provide a reference time against which we set our schedules, defining exactly what we mean when we set a value to `triggerAtMillis`. We could base our schedules on the following time references:

- The elapsed-time system clock—`android.os.SystemClock`—measures time as the number of milliseconds that have passed since the device booted, including any time spent in deep sleep. The current time according to the system clock can be found using this code term:

  `SystemClock.elapsedRealtime()`

- The real-time clock (Unix Time) - measures time in milliseconds since the Unix epoch. The current time according to the real-time clock can be found as follows:

```
System.currentTimeMillis()
```

In Java, `System.currentTimeMillis()` returns the number of milliseconds since midnight on January 1, 1970, Coordinated Universal Time (UTC) — a point in time known as the Unix epoch.

UTC is the internationally recognized successor to **Greenwich Mean Time** (**GMT**) and forms the basis for expressing international time zones, which are typically defined as positive or negative offsets from UTC.

Given these two conditions and two clocks, these are the four possible `type` values we can use when setting alarms:

- `android.app.AlarmManager.ELAPSED_REALTIME`: This schedules the alarm relative to the system clock. If the device is asleep at the scheduled time it will not be delivered immediately; instead, the alarm will be delivered the next time the device wakes.

- `android.app.AlarmManager.ELAPSED_REALTIME_WAKEUP`: This schedules the alarm relative to the system clock. If the device is asleep, it will be woken to deliver the alarm at the scheduled time.

- `android.app.AlarmManager.RTC`: This schedules the alarm in UTC relative to the Unix epoch. If the device is asleep at the scheduled time, the alarm will be delivered when the device is next woken.

- `android.app.AlarmManager.RTC_WAKEUP`: This schedules the alarm relative to the Unix epoch. If the device is asleep it will be awoken, and the alarm is delivered at the scheduled time.

We will start setting an alarm at a particular time, to go off 24 hours after the initial boot. We'll use the `TimeUnit` class from the `java.lang.concurrent` package to calculate times in milliseconds. To set the previous alarm, we need to calculate the number of milliseconds in 24 hours, as shown in the following code:

```
long delay = TimeUnit.HOURS.toMillis(24L);
am.set(AlarmManager.ELAPSED_REALTIME, delay, pending);
```

We can set an alarm to go off five minutes from now, using the system time, by adding five minutes to the current time. Using the system clock, it looks like this:

```
long delay = TimeUnit.MINUTES.toMillis(5L);
long time = System.currentTimeMillis() + delay;
am.set(AlarmManager.RTC, time, pending);
```

To set an alarm for 9:00 pm today (or tomorrow, if it's already past 9:00 pm today), we can use the `Calendar` class to do some time calculations:

```
Calendar calendar = Calendar.getInstance();
// Tomorrow at 9 if already passed 9pm today
if (calendar.get(Calendar.HOUR_OF_DAY) >= 21) {
    calendar.add(Calendar.DATE, 1);
}
calendar.set(Calendar.HOUR_OF_DAY, 21);
calendar.set(Calendar.MINUTE, 0);
calendar.set(Calendar.SECOND, 0);
am.set(AlarmManager.RTC, calendar.getTimeInMillis(), pending);
```

None of the examples so far will wake the device if it is sleeping at the time of the alarm. To do that, we need to use one of the `WAKEUP` alarm conditions, for example:

```
am.set(AlarmManager.ELAPSED_REALTIME_WAKEUP, delay, pending);
am.set(AlarmManager.RTC_WAKEUP, time, pending);
```

It is also important to understand that when the alarm clock time is in the past, the alarm will sound immediately after we invoke the `AlarmManager` set alarm functions.

Setting alarms in recent Android versions

If our application targets an API level below 19 (KitKat), scheduled alarms will run exactly at the alarm time. For applications targeting KitKat or later, the schedule is considered inexact and the system may re-order or group alarms to minimize wake-ups and save battery.

After API Level 23, the Android Development team went a little further and Doze mode was introduced on the Android System to reduce battery consumption when the device is unplugged from the power adapter, motionless, and not used by the user for a long period of time.

The Doze system will try to decrease the device's wake-up frequency deferring background jobs, network updates, syncs, and our precious alarm until the device exits Doze mode or a recurring maintenance window runs to execute pending jobs, certain alarms, or synchronization with the network. After the maintenance window finishes, the device would enter Doze mode again if it was not used in the meantime:

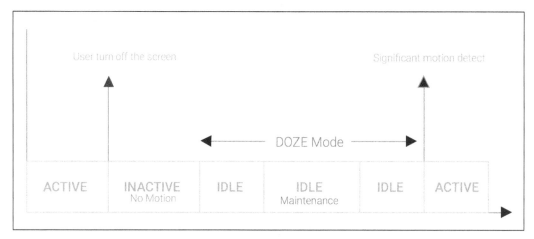

Figure 6.1: Doze Mode Timeline

Doze mode is likely to impact your application and will defer your alarms until a maintenance window comes in, unless you use the methods `setAndAllowWhileIdle()` and `setExactAndAllowWhileIdle()` to allow the execution of your alarms in a deep idle state.

Moreover, the number of times that the Doze Mode maintenance window runs will be less frequent in cases of long-term inactivity, so the impact of this new mechanism on our scheduling will increase, hence causing more unpredictable jitters at the alarm time.

During the doze mode the applications are also not allowed to access the network, the WakeLocks are ignored and Wi-Fi scans are not executed.

If we need precision scheduling and you are targeting Marshmallow or later, we shall use the new `setExactAndAllowWhileIdle()` method introduced at API level 23:

```
am.setExactAndAllowWhileIdle(AlarmManager.RTC_WAKEUP,
                             time, pending);
```

The Android system has protection that prevents abuse for exact alarms that fire off too frequently. AlarmManager only wakes up the device and dispatches one alarm per minute, and in low power mode it can be as low as one every 15 mins.

If your application targets a version between KitKat (API Level 19) and Marshmallow (API Level 23), the setExact method is enough for timing precision:

```
am.setExact(AlarmManager.RTC_WAKEUP, time, pending);
```

But we'll need to check that the methods exist before we try to call it; otherwise, our app will crash when run under earlier API levels. Lets sketch out our new exact alarm code:

```
if (Build.VERSION.SDK_INT >= 23) {
    // Wakes up the device in Doze Mode
    am.setExactAndAllowWhileIdle(AlarmManager.RTC_WAKEUP, time,
                                 pending);
} else if (Build.VERSION.SDK_INT >= 19) {
    // Wakes up the device in Idle Mode
    am.setExact(AlarmManager.RTC_WAKEUP, time, pending);
} else {
    // Old APIs
    am.set(AlarmManager.RTC_WAKEUP, time, pending);
}
```

This will deliver our alarm at exactly the specified time on all platforms.

Don't forget that you should only use exact scheduling when you really need it, for example, to deliver alerts to the user at a specific time. For most other cases, allowing the system to adjust our schedule a little to preserve battery life is usually acceptable.

Android Marshmallow API Level 23 also comes with the setAndAllowWhileIdle function, which allows us to create an alarm to sound in Doze mode, but with less exactness compared to setExactAndAllowWhileIdle().

The system will try to batch these kinds of alarm across the entire system, minimizing the number of times the device wakes up, and hence reducing the energy consumption of the system. Here is the code to create an alarm that triggers, even in Doze mode, 10 hours from now:

```
long delay = TimeUnit.HOURS.toMillis(10L);
long time = System.currentTimeMillis() + delay;

if (Build.VERSION.SDK_INT >= 23) {
    am.setAndAllowWhileIdle(AlarmManager.RTC_WAKEUP, time, pending);
}
```

Testing your alarms in Doze Mode

In order to test your application's behavior in doze mode, the Android SDK team added some new commands to the dumpsys tool to manually change the device's power state from the command line.

It is also important to remember that Doze mode requires that your device is unplugged from the charger. To force the device to a state where it is disconnected from the charger, we should run the following command on a command line with access to SDK Tools:

```
# Emulate a charger unplug
adb shell dumpsys battery unplug
# Emulate a charger plug in
adb shell dumpsys battery set ac 1
```

Then, to enter idle mode, we should turn off the screen and run the following commands:

```
// Enable the doze mode, step required on Android Emulator
adb shell dumpsys deviceidle enable
// To goes directly go IDLE mode
adb shell dumpsys deviceidle force-idle
```

After the device is put in idle mode, we can enable the maintenance window by running the following command:

```
// Goes from IDLE -> IDLE_MAINTENANCE state
adb shell dumpsys deviceidle step
```

If we run the same step again the device goes back to an idle state; however, if we want to go back to an active state, we should run the next command:

```
// Goes from IDLE,IDLE_MAINTENANCE -> ACTIVE state
adb shell dumpsys deviceidle disable
```

With these handy commands we are able to verify that the alarm sounds even in deep idle states.

Setting a Window alarm

One more addition in KitKat is setWindow(), which introduces a compromise between exact and inexact alarms by allowing us to specify the time window within which the alarm must be delivered. This still allows the system some freedom to play with the schedules for efficiency, but lets us choose just how much freedom to allow.

Here's how we would use sentindo() to schedule an alarm to be delivered within a 3 minute window — at the earliest 5 minutes from now and at the latest 8 minutes from now — using the real-time clock:

```
if (Build.VERSION.SDK_INT >= 19) {
  long delay = TimeUnit.MINUTES.toMillis(5L);
  long window = TimeUnit.MINUTES.toMillis(3L);
  long time = System.currentTimeMillis() + delay;
  am.setWindow(AlarmManager.RTC_WAKEUP, time, window, pending);
}
```

Debugging AlarmManager alarms

The Android System comes with a handy diagnostic tool that outputs to the developer a list of registered alarms on the device. To get a list, we run the following command from the command line:

adb shell dumpsys alarm

After we have created the exact 5 minute alarm on Android API Level 23, the system will output our registered alarm on the command output:

```
. . .
Batch{bfce57 num=1 start=6199180 end=6199180 flgs=0x5}:
RTC_WAKEUP #0: Alarm{
 d38d44 type 0 when 1449181419460
    com.packpublishing.asynchronousandroid}
 tag=*walarm*:my_alarm
 type=0 whenElapsed=+58s670ms when=2015-12-03 22:23:39
```

```
window=0 repeatInterval=0 count=0 flags=0x5
operation=PendingIntent{a58bbe0: PendingIntentRecord{
  466e99 android broadcastIntent}}
```

The Alarm system tries to organize the alarm execution in batches for battery saving purposes, so in the first line we have information about the alarm batch that our alarm belongs to.

The details of the batch output format are shown in the following list:

- `bfce57`: Batch internal identifier number
- `num=1`: Number of alarms in this batch
- `start=6199180`: It refers to the time, in terms of elapsed milliseconds since system boot, at which the batch should be started
- `end=6199180`: It refers to the time, in terms of elapsed milliseconds since system boot, at which the batch will end

Inside the batch, our alarm gets detailed over the following fields:

- `d38d44`: An internal identifier number used by the system
- `type 0 (RTC_WAKEUP)`: Alarm type
- `when`: Alarm time based on the clock time (milliseconds since epoch)
- `tag=*walarm*:my_alarm`: Action specified on Intent
- `com.packpublishing.asynchronousandroid`: Application package that created the alarm
- `whenElapsed=+58s670ms`: Refers to the time since the system started at which this alarm will be triggered
- `when= 2015-12-03 22:23:39`: The date/time at which this alarm will be triggered
- `window= 180000`: Refers to the value specified in the window field when the `setWindow()` method is used
- `repeatInterval=0`: Used in repeating alarms to specify the interval between repeats
- `count=0`: Number of times the alarm sounded
- `operation= PendingIntent...`: Pending intent that will be triggered

Canceling alarms

Once the alarm is set, it can be canceled very easily by invoking the `AlarmManger.cancel` method with an intent that matches the alarm that we want to cancel.

The process of matching uses the `filterEquals` method of Intent, which compares the action, data, type, class, component, package, and categories of both `Intent` to test for equivalence. Any extras we may have set in the Intent are not taken into account.

In the following code, we will show you how to create an alarm that fires off in 1 hour and the cancel code to dismiss it using different intent instances:

```
// Function to set the Alarm
void set1HourAlarm(long time) {
  AlarmManager am= (AlarmManager) getSystemService(ALARM_SERVICE);
  long time = in1HourTime();
  am.set(AlarmManager.RTC, time, createPendingIntent(time));
}

// Cancel the alarm
void cancel1HourAlarm(long time) {
  AlarmManager am= (AlarmManager) getSystemService(ALARM_SERVICE);
  // Remove the alarms matching the Intent
  am.cancel(createPendingIntent(time));
}

// Creates the Pending Intent to set and cancel the alarm
PendingIntent createPendingIntent(long time) {
  Intent intent = new Intent("my_alarm");
  PendingIntent pending = PendingIntent.
    getBroadcast(this, ALARM_CODE, intent,
              PendingIntent.FLAG_UPDATE_CURRENT);
  // extras don't affect matching
  intent.putExtra("exactTime", time);
  return pending;
}
// Calculate the Time
long in1HourTime() {
  long delay = TimeUnit.MINUTES.toMillis(5L);
  long time = System.currentTimeMillis() + delay;
  return time;
}
```

Since in our example we use the same method to construct the set and cancel `PendingIntent`, both will have the same action and match, so if the `AlarmManager.cancel` runs and it finds a match, the Android system will remove the alarm previously set from the list of enabled alarms.

 To debug the cancellation of your alarm you could verify again with an `adb shell dumpsys` alarm that the alarm disappeared from the system alarm batches.

It is important to realize that whenever we create alarm using a pending intent with the `FLAG_UPDATE_CURRENT`, we implicitly update any existing alarm with the new Intent and its extras.

Scheduling repeating alarms

As well as setting a one-off alarm, we have the option to schedule repeating alarms using `setRepeating()` and `setInexactRepeating()`. Both methods take an additional parameter that defines the interval in milliseconds at which to repeat the alarm. Generally, it is advisable to avoid `setRepeating()` and always use `setInexactRepeating()`, allowing the system to optimize device wake-ups and giving more consistent behavior on devices running different Android versions:

```
void setRepeating(
    int type, long triggerAtMillis,
    long intervalMillis, PendingIntent operation);

void setInexactRepeating(
    int type, long triggerAtMillis,
    long intervalMillis, PendingIntent operation)
```

`AlarmManager` provides some handy constants for typical repeat intervals:

```
AlarmManager.INTERVAL_FIFTEEN_MINUTES
AlarmManager.INTERVAL_HALF_HOUR
AlarmManager.INTERVAL_HOUR
AlarmManager.INTERVAL_HALF_DAY
AlarmManager.INTERVAL_DAY
```

Let's now build up an example that creates a repeating alarm to be delivered approximately 2 hours from now, then repeating every 15 minutes or so thereafter like this:

```
Intent intent = new Intent("my_alarm");
PendingIntent broadcast = PendingIntent.getBroadcast(
   this, 0, intent,PendingIntent.FLAG_UPDATE_CURRENT);
long start = System.currentTimeMillis() +
            TimeUnit.HOURS.toMillis(2L);
AlarmManager am = (AlarmManager)
                 getSystemService(ALARM_SERVICE);
am.setRepeating(
  AlarmManager.RTC_WAKEUP, start,
  AlarmManager.INTERVAL_FIFTEEN_MINUTES, broadcast);
```

From API level 19, all repeating alarms are inexact—that is, if our application targets KitKat or above, our repeat alarms will be inexact even if we use setRepeating(). To have similar inexact behavior across all the Android versions you should use the setInexactRepeating() (API Level 3) rather than setRepeating():

```
am.setInexactRepeating(
  AlarmManager.RTC_WAKEUP, start,
  AlarmManager.INTERVAL_FIFTEEN_MINUTES, broadcast);
```

The inexact repeating tells the system that your alarm time could be adjusted to reduce the device waking up frequently and increase the system's overall power efficiency.

If we really need exact repeat alarms, we can use setExact()/ setExactAndAllowWhileIdle(), instead, and schedule the next alarm while handling the current one.

Later, we might increase the repeating alarm interval and even change the Intent Extras by calling the setRepeating() with an Intent that matches the previous Intent and the flag FLAG_UPDATE_CURRENT, as shown in the following code:

```
Intent intent = new Intent("my_alarm");
PendingIntent broadcast = PendingIntent.getBroadcast(
   this, 0, intent, PendingIntent.FLAG_UPDATE_CURRENT);
// Updates the delivery intent extras
intent.putExtra("my_int",3);
am.setRepeating(
  AlarmManager.RTC_WAKEUP, System.currentTimeMillis(),
  AlarmManager.INTERVAL_HALF_HOUR, broadcast);
```

Scheduling an alarm clock

From API Level 21, `setAlarmClock`, which sets a new alarm and displays a status bar alarm icon, was introduced in the `AlarmManager` class:

```
void setAlarmClock(AlarmClockInfo info, PendingIntent operation)
```

In the next example we are going to create an alarm clock that goes off tomorrow at 10:00 pm:

```
Intent intent = new Intent("my_clock_alarm");
Calendar calendar = Calendar.getInstance();
calendar.add(Calendar.DATE, 1);
calendar.set(Calendar.HOUR_OF_DAY, 22);
calendar.set(Calendar.MINUTE, 0);
calendar.set(Calendar.SECOND, 0);


PendingIntent broadcast = PendingIntent.getBroadcast(
                            AlarmClockActivity.this, 0, intent,
                            PendingIntent.FLAG_UPDATE_CURRENT);


// Only applies to newer versions
If ( Build.VERSION.SDK_INT >= 21 ) {

  AlarmClockInfo alarmInfo = new AlarmClockInfo(
     calendar.getTimeInMillis(),
     // Create a Pending intent to show Alarm Details
     createShowDetailsPI());
  am.setAlarmClock(alarmInfo, broadcast);

} else {

  am.set(AlarmManager.RTC_WAKEUP,
       calendar.getTimeInMillis(), broadcast);
}
...
PendingIntent createShowDetailsPI() {
   ntent showIntent = new Intent(AlarmClockActivity.this,
                            ShowAlarmActivity.class);
   return PendingIntent.getActivity(AlarmClockActivity.this, 0,
                          showIntent,
                          PendingIntent.
                            FLAG_UPDATE_CURRENT);
}
```

If you are using a recent device, once we set the previous alarm we see the clock icon on the system status bar:

To cancel the alarm clock, we have to invoke the `cancel` method with a matching intent:

```
Intent intent = new Intent("my_clock_alarm");
PendingIntent broadcast = PendingIntent.getBroadcast(
  this, 0, intent, PendingIntent.FLAG_UPDATE_CURRENT);
am.cancel(broadcast);
```

Handling alarms

So far we have learned how to schedule exact and inexact alarms over the `AlarmManager Service` singleton, so at this point we are ready to take a look at how to handle the alarm in any Android application component.

Essentially, we can schedule anything that can be started with a `PendingIntent`, which means we can use alarms to start Activities, Services, and `BroadcastReceivers`. To specify the target of our alarm, we need to use the static factory methods of `PendingIntent`:

```
PendingIntent.getActivities(Context, int,Intent[],int)
PendingIntent.getActivity(Context,int, Intent, int)
PendingIntent.getService(Context,int, Intent, int)
PendingIntent.getBroadcast(Context,int, Intent, int)
```

All static methods offered to create a pending intent, receiving as arguments a Context object, an integer request code to identify the pending intent, an Intent or an array of Intents that will be delivered to the component, and finally an integer to specify the `PendingIntent` flags.

The `PendingIntent` flags used on the factory method play an important role in Intent handling, so it is crucial to understand the flags that we can use to indicate how the system should process an intent that already exists, to make an Intent immutable or to set an intent that is only delivered once:

- `FLAG_CANCEL_CURRENT`: Indicates that the system should invalidate and generates a new Intent.

- `FLAG_NO_CREATE`: If the `PendingIntent` does not already exist, a new intent is not created and factory method returns `null`.

- `FLAG_ONE_SHOT`: Indicates that the pending intent created can only be used once.

- `FLAG_UPDATE_CURRENT`: Indicates that if the pending intent already exists, the Pending Intent is replaced with this one, including all the extras.

- `FLAG_IMMUTABLE`: Indicates that the pending intent created cannot be modified afterwards. This flag is only available since API Level 23.

In most cases we want to completely replace an existing Intent with a new one, so using `FLAG_UPDATE_CURRENT` is the right flag value to use.

In the following sections, we'll see build up examples for each type of `PendingIntent` that can be used with `AlarmManager`.

Handling alarms with Activities

Starting an `Activity` from an alarm is as simple as registering the alarm with a `PendingIntent` created by invoking the static `getActivity` method of `PendingIntent`.

When the alarm is delivered, the `Activity` will be started and brought to the foreground, displacing any app that was currently in use. Keep in mind that this is likely to surprise and perhaps annoy users!

When starting Activities with alarms, we will probably want to set `Intent.FLAG_ ACTIVITY_CLEAR_TOP`; so that if the application is already running, and our target `Activity` is already on the back stack, the new intent will be delivered to the old `Activity` and all the other activities on top of it will be closed:

```
Intent intent = new Intent(context, HomeActivity.class);
intent.setFlags(Intent.FLAG_ACTIVITY_CLEAR_TOP);
PendingIntent pending = PendingIntent.getActivity(
    Context, 0, intent, PendingIntent.FLAG_UPDATE_CURRENT);
```

Not all Activities are suited to being started with `getActivity`. We might need to start an `Activity` that normally appears deep within the app, where pressing back does not exit to the home screen, but returns to the next `Activity` on the back-stack.

Let's imagine a situation where we want to start an `Activity` that is going to display the details about the model, and we want have an `Activity` that lists the models on the backstack.

This is where `getActivities` comes in. With `getActivities`, we can push more than one `Activity` onto the back-stack of the application, allowing us to populate the back-stack to create the desired navigation flow when the user presses "back". To do this, we create our `PendingIntent` by sending an array of Intents to `getActivities`:

```
Intent first = new Intent(context, ListActivity.class);
Intent second = new Intent(context, DetailActivity.class);
first.setFlags(Intent.FLAG_ACTIVITY_CLEAR_TOP);

PendingIntent pending = PendingIntent.getActivities(
    context, 0,
    new Intent[]{first, second},
    PendingIntent.FLAG_UPDATE_CURRENT);
```

The array of Intents specifies the `Activity` to launch, in order. The logical sequence of events when this alarm is delivered is as follows:

1. If the application is already running, any Activities on the back-stack above `ListActivity` are finished and removed, because we set the `Intent.FLAG_ACTIVITY_CLEAR_TOP` flag.

2. `ListActivity` is (re)started.

3. `DetailActivity` is started and placed on the back-stack above `ListActivity`. The `DetailActivity` becomes the foreground `Activity`.

Handling alarms with `Activity` is good to know about, but is not a technique we will use often, since it is so intrusive. We are much more likely to want to handle alarms in the background, which we'll look at next.

Handling alarms with BroadcastReceiver

We met `BroadcastReceiver` already in *Chapter 5, Interacting with Services*, where we used it in an `Activity` to receive broadcasts from a `Service`. In this section, we'll use `BroadcastReceiver` to handle alarms set on the `AlarmManager`.

`BroadcastReceivers` can be registered and unregistered dynamically at runtime like we did in *Chapter 5, Interacting with Services*, with `Service`, or statically in the Android manifest file with a `<receiver>` element, and can receive alarms regardless of how they are registered.

It is more common to use a statically registered receiver for alarms, because these are known to the system and can be invoked by alarms to start an application if it is not currently running.

Let's implement a static defined `BroadcastReceiver` that is able to dispatch an SMS to a phone number when an alarm sounds. First we will define our `BroadcastReceiver` in the manifest file:

```
<receiver android:name=".chapter6.SMSDispacther">
  <intent-filter>
    <action android:name="sms_dispacther"/>
  </intent-filter>
</receiver>
```

The `<intent-filter>` element gives us the opportunity to say which Intents we want to receive by specifying the action, data, and categories that should match.

Now its time to write the code to set up the schedule. To do that, we will create an Activity that is going to provide a form to set the destination number, the number of hours to defer the message dispatch, and the message text to send.

On the `SMSDispatchActivity` activity we will build a `PendingIntent` for the `sms_dispatcher` action, passing the arguments required over the Intent extras:

```java
public class SMSDispatchActivity extends Activity {
  // UI Code omitted for brevity
  ...
  private OnClickListener mSubmit = new OnClickListener() {
    ...
    // Calculate the scheduled time
    // time = now + N*hours
    long delay = TimeUnit.HOURS.toMillis(hours);
    long time = System.currentTimeMillis() + delay;

    // Store the UI Form on the Intent
    intent.putExtra(SMSDispatcher.TO_KEY, phoneMumber);
    intent.putExtra(SMSDispatcher.TEXT_KEY, text);

    // Create the Broadcast Pending Intent
    PendingIntent broadcast = PendingIntent.getBroadcast(
      getBaseContext(), 0, intent,
      PendingIntent.FLAG_UPDATE_CURRENT);

    // Set an exact Alarm
    if (Build.VERSION.SDK_INT >= 23) {
      am.setExactAndAllowWhileIdle(AlarmManager.RTC_WAKEUP, time,
                                   broadcast);
    } else if (Build.VERSION.SDK_INT >= 19) {
      am.setExact(AlarmManager.RTC_WAKEUP, time, broadcast);
```

```
        } else {
          am.set(AlarmManager.RTC_WAKEUP, time, broadcast);
        }
      }
    }
  }
```

When this alarm is due, `AlarmManager` will wake the device even in deep idle states —if it isn't already awake—and deliver the Intent to the `BroadcastReceiver` is `onReceive` method. The Alarm Manager will hold a wake lock as long as the alarm receiver's `onReceive()` runs. Therefore, it guarantees that the device will remain awake at least until `onReceive` completes, which means we can be sure of getting some work done before the device will be allowed to return to sleep.

Working with BroadcastReceiver

When the system delivers an alarm to our `BroadcastReceiver` it does so on the main thread, so the usual main thread limitations apply; we cannot perform networking and we should not perform heavy processing or use blocking operations.

In addition, a statically registered `BroadcastReceiver` has a very limited lifecycle. It cannot create user interface elements other than toasts or notifications posted via `NotificationManager`, the `onReceive` method must complete within 10 seconds or its process may be killed, and once `onReceive` completes, the receiver's life is over.

Since the work that we need in response is not intensive, we can simply complete it during `onReceive`:

```java
public class SMSDispatcher extends BroadcastReceiver {

  public static final String TO_KEY = "to";
  public static final String TEXT_KEY = "text";

  @Override
  public void onReceive(Context context, Intent intent) {
     // Retrieve the Destination number and the
    // message from the intent extras
    String to = intent.getStringExtra(TO_KEY);
    String text = intent.getStringExtra(TEXT_KEY);

    Log.i("SMS Dispatcher", "Delivering message to " + to);
    SmsManager sms = SmsManager.getDefault();
    sms.sendTextMessage(to, null, text, null, 0), null);
  }
}
```

That's it; once the alarm fires off, the `BroadcastReceiver.onReceive` gets called dispatching an SMS to the destination number with the text specified on the UI Form.

We can make this more useful by delivering a notification to the user when we receive the message delivery report from the mobile network.

First, we will add a new action on the `AndroidManifest.xml` to be processed by our `BroadcastReceiver`:

```
<receiver android:name=".chapter6.SMSDispatcher">
  <intent-filter>
      <action android:name="sms_dispatch"/>
  </intent-filter>
  <intent-filter>
      <action android:name="sms_delivered"/>
  </intent-filter>
</receiver>
```

Next, we will change the `onReceive` method to process both kinds of `Intent`:

```
@Override
public void onReceive(Context context, Intent intent) {

    if ( intent.getAction().equals(DELIVERED_ACTION) ) {
      processDispatch(context, intent);
    } else if (intent.getAction().equals(DISPATCH_ACTION)) {
      processDelivered(context, intent);
    }
}
```

Next, update the code to dispatch the message to set up a new `PendingIntent` for the message delivery report:

```
void processDispatch(Context context, Intent intent) {
  ...
  Intent deliveredIntent = new Intent("sms_delivered");
  deliveredIntent.putExtra(SMSDispatcher.TO_KEY, to);
  deliveredIntent.putExtra(SMSDispatcher.TEXT_KEY, text);
  sms.sendTextMessage(to, null, text, null,
    PendingIntent.getBroadcast(context,
      DISPATCH_ACTION.hashCode(), deliveredIntent, 0));
}
```

Finally, we add the code to process the message delivery report intent and inform the user, in the notification drawer, if the message was delivered with success:

```
void processDelivered(Context context, Intent intent) {
  String to = intent.getStringExtra(TO_KEY);
  String text = intent.getStringExtra(TEXT_KEY);
  String title = null;
  switch (getResultCode()) {
  case Activity.RESULT_OK:
    title = "Message Delivered to " + to;
    break;
  default:
    title = "Message Delivery failed to " + to;
    break;
  }
  NotificationCompat.Builder builder = new
    NotificationCompat.Builder(context)
      .setContentTitle(title)
      .setContentText(text)
      .setSmallIcon(android.R.drawable.stat_notify_chat)
      .setStyle(new NotificationCompat.BigTextStyle()
        .bigText(text));
  NotificationManager nm = (NotificationManager)
                    context.getSystemService(
                      Context.NOTIFICATION_SERVICE);
  nm.notify(intent.hashCode(), builder.build());
}
```

Although we can spend up to 10 seconds doing work in our `BroadcastReceiver`, we really shouldn't—if the app is in the foreground when the alarm is triggered the user will suffer noticeable lag if `onReceive` takes more than a hundred milliseconds to complete on the main Thread. Exceeding the 10 second budget will cause the system to kill the application and report a background ANR.

Moreover, if we try to execute the `onReceive` work in a background thread and the `onReceive` returns, the Android system is allowed to recycle the component. Whenever no other Android component is running, the system could consider the process to be empty and aggressively kill it, stopping our background work immediately.

To avoid the UI glitching, and the `BroadcastReceiver` recycling, on Android API Level 11, the `BroacastReceiver.goAsync` method was announced to delegate work to a background thread for up to 10 seconds – we'll discuss this in the next section.

Asynchronous work with goAsync

If our application targets a minimum API level of 11, we can use a feature of `BroadcastReceiver.goAsync` to handle the `onReceive` execution in a parallel line of execution:

```
public final PendingResult goAsync()
```

With `goAsync` we can extend the lifetime of a `BroadcastReceiver` instance beyond the completion of its `onReceive` method, provided the whole operation still completes within the 10 second budget.

If we invoke `goAsync`, the system will not consider the `BroadcastReceiver` to have finished when `onReceive` completes. Instead, the `BroadcastReceiver` lives on until we call finish on the `PendingResult` returned to us by `goAsync`. We must ensure that finish is called within the 10 second budget, otherwise the system will kill the process with a background ANR.

Using `goAsync`, we can offload work to background threads using any appropriate concurrency construct—for example, an `AsyncTask`—and the device is guaranteed to remain awake until we call finish on the `PendingResult`.

Let's update our SMS dispatcher to send the message asynchronously:

```
public void onReceive(final Context context, final Intent intent) {
    ...
    final PendingResult result = goAsync();
    AsyncTaskCompat.executeParallel(
      new AsyncTask<Void, Void, Void>() {
        @Override
        protected Void doInBackground(Void... params) {
          try {
            // ... do some work here, for up to 10 seconds
            processDispatch(context, intent);
          } finally {
            result.setResultCode(Activity.RESULT_OK);
            result.finish();
          }
          return null;
        }
    });
    ...
}
```

AsyncTaskCompat has been available in the Android Support Library since version 21.0.0 and allows the developer to execute multiple AsyncTask in parallel on a pool of threads in a backward compatible fashion.

This is nice, though its utility is limited by the 10 second budget and the effects of fragmentation (it is only available to API level 11 or above). In the next section, we'll look at scheduling long-running operations with services.

Handling alarms with Services

Just like starting Activities, starting a Service from an alarm involves scheduling an appropriate PendingIntent instance, this time using the static getService method:

```
Intent intent = new Intent(this,SMSDispatcherIntentService.class);
intent.putExtra(SMSDispatcherIntentService.TO_KEY, phoneNumber);
intent.putExtra(SMSDispatcherIntentService.TEXT_KEY, text);
PendingIntent service = PendingIntent.getService(
    context, 0, intent, PendingIntent.FLAG_UPDATE_CURRENT);
am.set(AlarmManager.RTC_WAKEUP, time, service);
```

As you already know, the Service should be globally defined on the Android Manifest with a service element. Given that we are calling it explicitly using the class name, we only need to define the service class:

```
<service android:name=".chapter6.SMSDispatcherIntentService" >
</service>
```

We almost certainly want our Service to do its work off the main thread, so sending work to an IntentService this way seems ideal, and an IntentService will also stop itself when the work is finished. This works reliably if the device is awake.

However, if the device is asleep we have a potential problem. AlarmManager documentation tells us that the only guarantee we have about the wakefulness of the device is that it will remain awake until a BroadcastReceiver is onReceive method completes.

Since directly starting a Service does not involve a BroadcastReceiver, and in any case is an asynchronous operation, there is no guarantee that the Service will have started up before the device returns to sleep, so the work may not get done until the device is next awakened.

This is almost certainly not the behavior we want. We want to ensure that the Service starts up and completes its work, regardless of whether the device was awake when the alarm was delivered. To do that, we'll need a `BroadcastReceiver` and a little explicit power management, as we'll see next.

Staying awake with WakeLocks

Earlier in this chapter we learned that we can use a `BroadcastReceiver` to handle alarms, and even do work in the background for up to 10 seconds, though only on devices running API level 11 or greater.

In the previous section, we saw that handling alarms directly with services is not a reliable solution for scheduling long-running work, since there is no guarantee that our `Service` will start up before the device returns to sleep.

We have a problem! If we want to perform long-running work in response to alarms, we need a solution that overcomes these limitations.

What we really want is to start a `Service` to handle the work in the background, and to keep the device awake until the `Service` has finished its work. Fortunately, we can do that by combining the waking guarantees of `BroadcastReceiver` to get the `Service` started, then keep the device awake with explicit power management using `PowerManager` and `WakeLock`.

As you might guess, `WakeLock` is a way to force the device to stay awake. `WakeLocks` come in various flavors, allowing apps to keep the screen on at varying brightness levels or just to keep the CPU powered up in order to do background work. To use `WakeLocks`, our application must request an additional permission in the manifest:

```
<uses-permission android:name="android.permission.WAKE_LOCK" />
```

There are four different kinds of wakelock that may affect the system power management differently:

- `PowerManager.PARTIAL_WAKE_LOCK`: Ensures that the CPU is on, leaving the screen and the keyboard in the current state (idle or awake).

- `PowerManager.SCREEN_DIM_WAKE_LOCK`: Ensures that the CPU is on, the screen is on and may be in a dimmed state, and the keyboard could remain off.

- `PowerManager.SCREEN_BRIGHT_WAKE_LOCK`: Ensures that the CPU is on, the screen is on full brightness, and the keyboard could remain off.

- `PowerManager.FULL_WAKE_LOCK`: Ensures that the CPU is on and the screen and keyboard backlight are at full brightness.

To keep the CPU powered up while we do background work in a `Service`, we only need `PARTIAL_WAKE_LOCK`, which won't keep the screen on, and which we can request from the `PowerManager` like this:

```
PowerManager pm = (PowerManager)ctx.getSystemService(
                   Context.POWER_SERVICE);
WakeLock lock = pm.newWakeLock(
  PowerManager.PARTIAL_WAKE_LOCK, "my_app");

// Acquire the Power Lock
lock.acquire();

// Do your work here while CPU will stay on …

// Release the Power lock
lock.release();
```

We'll need to acquire a `WakeLock` during our `BroadcastReceiver` is `onReceive` method, and find some way to hand it to our `Service` so that the `Service` can release the lock once its work is done.

Unfortunately, `WakeLock` instances are not parcelable, so we can't just send them to the `Service` in an Intent. The simplest solution is to manage the `WakeLock` instance as a static property that both the `BroadcastReceiver` and the target Service can reach.

This is not difficult to implement, but we don't actually need to implement it ourselves—we can use the handy v4 support library class, `WakefulBroadcastReceiver`.

`WakefulBroadcastReceiver` exposes two static methods that take care of acquiring and releasing a partial `WakeLock`. We can acquire the `WakeLock` and start the `Service` with a single call to `startWakefulService`:

```
ComponentName startWakefulService(Context context, Intent intent);
```

And when our Service has finished its work, it can release the `WakeLock` with the corresponding call to `completeWakefulIntent`:

```
boolean completeWakefulIntent(Intent intent);
```

Now, we will update our SMS schedule `BroadcastReceiver` to acquire the wakelock and dispatch the intent over the `startWakefulService`:

```
public class WakefulSMSDispatcher extends BroadcastReceiver {

    @Override
    public void onReceive(Context context, Intent intent) {
```

```
        // Forward intent to SMSDispatcherIntentService class,
        // the wakeful receiver is needed in case the
        // schedule is triggered while the device
        // is asleep otherwise the service may not have time to
        // receive the intent.
        intent.setClass(context, SMSDispatcherIntentService.class);
        WakefulBroadcastReceiver.startWakefulService(context, intent);
    }
}
```

We must make sure to release the WakeLock once the Service has finished its work, otherwise we'll drain the battery by keeping the CPU powered up unnecessarily. Let's implement the IntentService that receives the intent from the wakeful BroadcastReceiver and sends the message in the service background thread:

```
public class SMSDispatcherIntentService extends IntentService {

    @Override
    protected void onHandleIntent(Intent intent) {
        try {
            ...
            sms.sendTextMessage(to, null, text, null, null);
        } finally {
            WakefulBroadcastReceiver.completeWakefulIntent(intent);
        }
    }
}
```

This is great—by using a statically registered BroadcastReceiver we've ensured that we receive the alarm, even if our application is not running when the alarm is due. When we receive the alarm, we acquire a WakeLock, keeping the device awake while our Service starts up and does its potentially long-running work.

Once our work is done, we release the WakeLock to allow the device to sleep again and conserve power.

Resetting alarms after a system reboot

The AlarmManager service is a convenient class to schedule working on your Android application; however, when the device shuts down or reboots, all your alarms will be lost since the system does not retain them between system restarts.

To reset the alarm, we should persist your alarms and create a `BroadcastReceiver` that sets our alarms whenever a system boot happens:

```
public class BootBroadcastReceiver extends BroadcastReceiver {

  @Override
  public void onReceive(Context context, Intent intent) {
    // Retrieve the persisted alarms
    List<SMSSchedule> persistedAlarms = getStoredSchedules();
    // Set again the alarms
    ...
  }
  List<SMSSchedule> getStoredSchedules() {...}
}
```

In order to store our alarms, we created a `POJO` class `SMSSchedule` as the model for our schedules.

Second, in the Android Manifest we have to register our `BroadcastReceiver` to receive the boot event:

```
<receiver
    android:name=".chapter6.BootBroadcastReceiver"
    android:enabled="true" >
    <intent-filter>
        <action android:name="android.intent.action.BOOT_COMPLETED" />
    </intent-filter>
</receiver>
```

Finally, we will add the permission to receive the boot complete event:

```
<uses-permission android:name="android.permission.RECEIVE_BOOT_
COMPLETED" />
```

Now after a system reboot, we re-create our alarms and they fire off even after a system reboot. We also advise that the alarms using `ELAPSED_REALTIME` should be adjusted after a system reboot since the the clock where those alarms are based is going to be restarted.

Applications of AlarmManager

`AlarmManager` allows us to schedule work to run without user intervention.

This means that we can arrange to do work pre-emptively, for example, to prepare data that our application will need to present to the user when they next open the application, or to alert the user to new or updated information with notifications.

Ideal use cases include things like periodically checking for new e-mails, SMS scheduling, time notifications, periodic data processing, downloading new editions of periodical publications (for example, daily newspapers and magazines), or uploading data from the device to a cloud backup service.

The `AlarmManager` is able to start future work effectively but the API should be used carefully to keep your application battery power consumption at low levels. To achieve that, the developer should try to keep the alarm frequency under certain levels and use the exact set functions that force the device to wake up only in cases where it is really necessary.

Summary

In this chapter, we learned to schedule work for our applications to perform at some time in the distant future, either as a one-shot operation or at regular intervals.

We learned to set alarms relative to the system clock or real time, how to wake the device up from a deep sleep and doze mode, how to cancel alarms when we no longer need them, and how to set exact alarms on the most recent Android versions.

In the meantime, we introduced the reader to Doze Mode, a new power management feature that saves battery cycles by deferring jobs and tasks to a maintenance window. We learned how to test our alarms taking into account the new power management states introduced by the doze mode.

We learned how to debug alarms created with `AlarmManager` and how to analyze the information printed from the `dumpsys` commands.

Our exploration covered various options for responding to alarms, including bringing an `Activity` to the foreground or doing work directly in a `BroadcastReceiver`, synchronously or asynchronously.

Finally, we arranged for an `IntentService` to be launched with a `WakeLock` to keep the CPU from powering down while our long-running background work is completed, and to finish we learned how to re-create the alarms after a system boot using a boot `BroadcastReceiver`.

The `AlarmManager` is a very useful class to schedule work in the background but it has some major disadvantages. First, it does not take into account the device current context, like if the device is connected to the charger, or whether the device is connected to a Wi-Fi network. Second, we can only schedule our background work based on the time condition.

To solve these issues, the Android team introduced in Android Lollipop API Level 5.0 the `JobScheduler` API; an API that allows the execution of background work based on a number of time and context criteria.

In the next chapter we are going to explain how to exercise the `JobScheduler` API to schedule tasks that will only run when the appropriate energy and environment device conditions are met.

7
Exploring the
JobScheduler API

So far, we have been scheduling background work using a time condition in the Handler facilities for the short-term future, and the Android Alarm Manager for the long-term future.

Those APIs that are able to execute future tasks at an exact and inexact time in the future are used to trigger events, refresh data in the background, or execute tasks without user intervention. AlarmManager, which we covered in detail in the previous chapter, is able to wake up the device from deep idle states and execute work even without considering the device's battery state.

In this chapter, we will learn how to work with JobScheduler to execute jobs in the background when several prerequisites are fulfilled and taking into account the energy consumption context of the device.

In this chapter, we will cover the following:

- Introduction to JobScheduler
- Setting the JobScheduler running criteria
- Controlling the execution of your job with criteria
- How to schedule work with JobService
- Executing repeating tasks with JobScheduler
- Retrieving the list of pending JobScheduler schedules
- How to cancel a task in JobScheduler

Introduction to JobScheduler

The Android development team, under the project Volta umbrella, introduced in the API Level 21 Lollipop release some enhancements and features in order to improve the power usage on the Android platform. Apart from the tools introduced to monitor and follow the battery usage in the Android platform, a new API for scheduling background was officially released to help the developer. It saves extra power cycles when the jobs used to support the developer's application do not need a time of execution, and can be deferred until the device has better battery and network context.

The API was not created to completely replace `AlarmManager`; however, the `JobScheduler` API is able to perform a better battery management and supply extra behaviors.

The main features introduced with Scheduler API are as follows:

- **Less power consumption**: The job task could be delayed until the device is powered to the charger or they are grouped to run in batches on a regular basis

- **Persistent jobs across reboots**: We are able to install job schedules that persistent task across device reboots

- **Better network bandwidth management**: The job could be delayed until a higher bandwidth network is available, such as when a Wi-Fi network connection is available

- **Less intrusive execution**: The job could be delayed until the user is not interacting with the device

`JobScheduler` is a singleton system service that we can retrieve via a `Context` object instance, using a code similar to the following:

```
JobScheduler js = (JobScheduler)
        getSystemService(Context.JOB_SCHEDULER_SERVICE);
```

The `JobScheduler` singleton service instance object helps us to manage our running jobs and provides us with member functions to schedule, cancel, and retrieve a list of deferred jobs.

Once we have a reference to the `JobScheduler` service, we can schedule a job by passing `JobInfo` to the `JobScheduler.schedule` function:

```
int schedule(JobInfo job);
```

JobInfo is the object used in this framework where we specify all the information about the job itself, all the conditions that should be fulfilled to initiate the job execution, and the unit of work called JobService that will be started to execute the work required.

To build a JobInfo object, a common factory pattern, known Software Engineering as Builder and materialized in the static inner-class JobInfo.Builder, is available to construct the JobInfo object passed to JobScheduler. The pattern provides us with a way to construct a multi-parameter JobInfo on a clean, step-by-step basis and by using the Builder setter functions to define the JobInfo parameters.

First, we will have to build a JobInfo.Builder object using the following constructor:

```
Builder(int jobId, ComponentName jobService)
```

jobId is an internal number used to identify your job in the JobScheduler service and the second argument is used to set the JobService derived class that will be invoked when the system verifies that all the pre-requisites are met to execute the job.

Let's write some code to show this:

```
ComponentName jobSrvc= new ComponentName(ctx, MyJobService.class);
JobInfo.Builder jobIBuilder = new JobInfo.Builder(MY_JOB_ID,
                                                  jobSrvc);
```

Setting running criteria

With the Builder object reference, we can start setting up the job parameters and the pre-requisites using the member function available in the Builder object.

Let's consider a couple of examples. In our first example, the job should only start when there is a Wi-Fi network available, so to achieve that, we have to use the following code to set the network availability pre-requisite:

```
jobIBuilder.setRequiredNetworkType(JobInfo.NETWORK_TYPE_UNMETERED);
```

An unmetered network connection means that you have a connection where you don't have a limited amount of data usage per month and you are not charged when you go over the usage limit. When a network type is not specified, as a condition, the default value is NETWORK_TYPE_NONE, meaning that the job will run in any network context and even without any network connection. Apart from the previous network type criteria, there is NETWORK_TYPE_ANY, which determines that the job could run when there is network connectivity available.

To specify a job to run only when the device is plugged in and charging:

```
jobIBuilder.setRequiresCharging(true);
```

When a job should only run when the device is in idle mode:

```
jobIBuilder.setRequiresDeviceIdle(true);
```

Idle mode means that the job should only run when the device is not in use and has not been used for some time. This could be the best time to execute heavier computations because the user will not notice that the device resources have been allocated to your job, thereby the computation does not interfere with the user interactions. By default, any job will not require idle mode to run.

Persist your job execution across device reboots as follows:

```
jobIBuilder.setPersisted(true);
```

Such as an `AlarmManager` job, the job schedule will only survive a reboot if your application holds the permissions to receive the completed boot. To achieve that, add the following line to the `Android Manifest` file:

```
<uses-permission
android:name="android.permission.RECEIVE_BOOT_COMPLETED" />
```

In those cases where you want to schedule a periodic task, you can set the interval in milliseconds between subsequent executions:

```
long interval = TimeUnit.HOURS.toMillis(5L);
jobIBuilder.setPeriodic(interval);
```

This is an inexact interval since the Android system will try to group the jobs in batches in order to save some battery cycles.

When you want to define a maximum defer time to run your job, we can specify a time deadline where the job has to run, then it will run regardless of whether or not the other criteria are met:

```
long maxExecutionTime = TimeUnit.MINUTES.toMillis(5L);
jobIBuilder.setOverrideDeadline(maxExecutionTime);
```

In the following code, we set one hour as the maximum time to defer this job, so, if the other pre-requisites are not fulfilled, after one hour the job is going to run by the system independently of the other criteria:

```
jobIBuilder.setOverrideDeadline(TimeUnit.HOURS.toMillis(1L));
```

On the other hand, we can also specify a minimum defer time to this job as a criterion:

```
jobIBuilder.setMinimumLatency(TimeUnit.SECONDS.toMillis(120));
```

With the values used above, our job will never run on the next `120` seconds since we set a maximum latency time as a prerequisite to our job.

 setMinimumLatency and setOverrideDeadline are not applicable for periodic jobs criteria shall be avoided that it is in your recurrent jobs schedules. If any one of these criteria are used on recurrent jobs, an IllegalArgumentException exception will be thrown when the build is called.

When the job fails, in order to specify a retry policy, we have to specify the `backoff` initial value that determines the interval between retries and the retry increase policy. The `JobScheduler` API provides two policies that define the way in which the retry time increases between subsequent tries:

- `BACKOFF_POLICY_LINEAR`: The interval time between retries increases linearly — `initial_backoff_millis * num_retries`

- `BACKOFF_POLICY_EXPONENTIAL`: The interval time between retries increases exponentially — `initial_backoff_millis * 2 ^ (num_retries)`

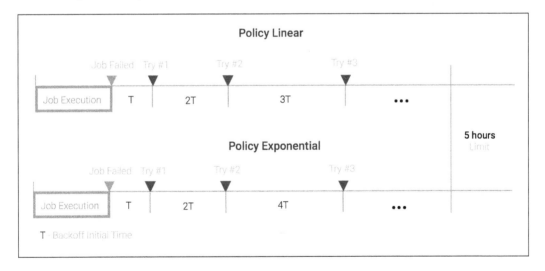

The `backoff` interval will increase until we reach a backoff of five hours (`JobInfo.MAX_BACKOFF_DELAY_MILLIS`) and the initial default value is `30` seconds (`JobInfo.DEFAULT_INITIAL_BACKOFF_MILLIS`).

Now, in the following examples we are going to show you how to create a linear and an exponential backoff policy for our `jobInfo` object:

```
// Initial Backoff of 10 minutes that grows linearly
jobIBuilder.setBackoffCriteria(TimeUnit.MINUTES.toMillis(10L),
JobInfo.BACKOFF_POLICY_LINEAR);

// Initial Backoff of 3 minutes that grows exponentially
jobIBuilder.setBackoffCriteria(TimeUnit.MINUTES.toMillis(3),
JobInfo.BACKOFF_POLICY_EXPONENTIAL);
```

The `builder` class also provides us a method to set some parameters to forward the job over a `PersistableBundle` object:

```
PersistableBundle bundle = new PersistableBundle();
bundle.putInt(MY_JOB_ARG1,2);
jobIBuilder.setExtras(bundle);
```

 A `PersistableBundle` is a special kind of bundle that can be saved and restored later. Its main purpose is to pass arguments to the deferred job execution.

As soon as we have all the criteria to schedule our defined job, we are able to construct our `JobInfo` and use it to incorporate the job execution in our application:

```
JobInfo.Builder jobIBuilder = ...
// Set Criterias
JobInfo jobInfo = jobIBuilder.setRequiresCharging(true)

setRequiresDeviceIdle(true).

                                    ...
                                    build();
```

Scheduling a job

With the criteria already defined and the `JobInfo` object, we have all the entities required to set up the job for our application. So now let's show you how to create a job with a real example.

Our example will synchronize the user account information stored in a device file with an HTTP web service over a job scheduled using the Scheduler API. The user interface will provide us a UI where we can update the user information, a button to save the information on an internal file, and a button to set up the synchronization job that will upload the account information to the web service.

First, let's start by defining our job pre-requisites and parameters:

- Our job should only run when the device is charging to save the battery
- Our job should only run when an unmetered network is available to save mobile network bandwidth
- Our job should only run when the device is idle because we don't want to slow down the UI responsiveness
- Our job must run at least once within eight hours of being scheduled
- Our job should run even after device reboot

The `JobInfo` object requires an `ID` to identify the job in all the `JobSchedule` methods, so it is a good idea, in order to ensure consistency, to use a `public static int` to identify it:

```
static final int ACC_BACKUP_JOB_ID ="AccountBackJobService"
hashCode();
```

Subsequent calls to cancel or list jobs created must use the same `jobId` defined here.

Since we use a file to store the account information internally on the device, the filename used to retrieve account information needs to be passed to the job as an argument. The same principle applies to the remote web service endpoint.

To forward the required parameters, we have to build `PersistableBundle`, passing the filename and endpoint path as bundle parameters:

```
private static final String SYNC_FILE = "account.json";
private static final String SYNC_PATH = "account_sync";
private static final String SYNC_PATH_KEY = "path";
...
PersistableBundle bundle = new PersistableBundle();
// Forward filename where the account information is stored
bundle.putString(SyncTask.SYNC_FILE_KEY,SYNC_FILE);
// Forward the HTTP Path used to upload the account information
bundle.putString(SyncTask.SYNC_PATH_KEY,SYNC_PATH);
```

Once the criteria are stated and we have the identifier and the class name of our service, we are able to create our `JobInfo` using the `Builder` inner class, as shown in the following code:

```
ComponentName serviceName = new ComponentName(this,
  AccountBackupJobService.class);

// Setup the Job Information and criterias over a builder
JobInfo jobInfo = new JobInfo.
```

```
Builder(ACC_BACKUP_JOB_ID, serviceName)
  .setRequiresCharging(true)
  .setRequiredNetworkType(JobInfo.NETWORK_TYPE_UNMETERED)
  .setRequiresDeviceIdle(true)
  .setPersisted(true)
  .setOverrideDeadline(TimeUnit.HOURS.toMillis(8L))
  .setExtras(bundle)
  .build();
```

Now we are ready to schedule the job with the `JobScheduler` service:

```
// Get a Reference to the Service
JobScheduler jobScheduler = (JobScheduler)
  getSystemService(JOB_SCHEDULER_SERVICE);

int result = jobScheduler.schedule(jobInfo);

if ( result == JobScheduler.RESULT_FAILURE ) {
  // Failed to setup the job
  Toast.makeText(AccountInfoActivity.this,
              "Failed to setup a sharedpref backup job",
              Toast.LENGTH_SHORT).show();
} else {
  // Schedule Success
  Toast.makeText(SharedPrefActivity.this,
              "SharedPrefBack job successfully scheduled",
              Toast.LENGTH_SHORT).show();
}
```

The JobScheduler's `schedule` method will return RESULT_FAILURE in the case of failure and in the case of success will return the job identifier that we defined in the `JobInfo.Builder` constructor.

Now, since we have just scheduled our job, it's time to write the backup behavior in the `JobService` subclass. In the next section, we will detail how to implement a `JobService` that plays well with the `JobScheduler` framework.

Implementing the JobService

Our `JobService` subclass is the entity that is going to do the hard work and receive the callbacks as soon as all the criteria specified in the `JobInfo` are met. To implement our own service, we have to extend from `JobService` and override the start and stop callbacks, as shown in the following code:

```
public class AccountBackupJobService extends JobService {
    @Override
    public boolean onStartJob(JobParameters params) {
      // Start your job here
        return false;
    }
    @Override
    public boolean onStopJob(JobParameters params) {
        // Stop your job here
        return false;
    }
}
```

The `onStartJob` callback function runs on the main thread, and if the job needs to do asynchronous processing then it should return `true` to indicate it's still doing work on a background thread. The `callback` function also receives the extra parameters specified in the `JobInfo` bundle.

`onStopJob` is automatically invoked by the system when it requires to cancel the job execution because the criteria specified in the `jobInfo` are no longer fulfilled.

For example, our job requires to run the work while the device is in an idle state, so, if the device leaves the idle mode because the user started to interact with the device, `onStopJob` will get called to abandon the execution for the meantime.

In this function, we should release any resources allocated to our job and stop any background processing in place. This function returning `boolean` would indicate whether you'd like to retry this job following the same criteria specified in the job creation or abandon the job execution. You should use `true` to reschedule this job based on the retry criteria specified during the job creation.

Before we add our Service business logic, we must add our `Service` class to `AndroidManifest.xml` and we must protect our service with the `android.permission.BIND_JOB_SERVICE` permission:

```
<service
    android:name=".chapter7.AccountBackupJobService"
    android:exported="true"
    android:permission="android.permission.BIND_JOB_SERVICE" />
```

There are two important things to recall about your `JobService` implementation:

1. One, the `onStartJob` and `onStopJob` callbacks will run on the main thread, and it is your responsibility to hand over your service's long running executions to separate threads to prevent the appearance of any ANR dialog in your application due to a blocking operation in the main thread.

2. Second, the Android system will acquire and hold a `WakeLock` for you while your `JobService` callbacks are running or until you explicitly call the `jobFinished` method in the case that you return `true` in the `onStartJob` function. If you don't, tell the system that your job execution is finished. The `WakeLock` will keep your device awake and burn your device's battery in vain. This could make your user angry and create a reason to uninstall your application, because your application will waste resources and battery and affect the user experience.

Now that we have learned the theory about the `JobService`, let's write the code to execute the account synchronization with the remote server away from the main thread on a background processing line.

Considering the Android constructs learned until now, we will use the `AsyncTask` construct learned in *Chapter 3, Exploring the AsyncTask*, for its simplicity, and create an `AsyncTask` subclass to upload the account information using the created for this purpose:

```
public class Result<T> {
    public T result;
    public Exception exc;
}

public class SyncTask extends
    AsyncTask<JobParameters, Void, Result<JobParameters>> {

    // Parameter Keys for parameter arguments
    public static final String SYNC_FILE_KEY = "file";
    public static final String SYNC_ENDPOINT_KEY = "http_endpoint";

    // Variable used to store a reference to the service
    private final JobService jobService;

    // Constructor
    public SyncTask(JobService jobService) {
        this.jobService = jobService;
    }
    ...
}
```

As a starting point, we specified the generic `AsyncTask` class parameter types, setting `JobParameters` as the parameter for `doInBackground` and `Result` as the type returned from `doInBackground` and passed to the `onPostExecute` function.

Later, we create the final constant keys used to pass information in the bundle.

The `Result` type is also recovered from previous sessions to return an error when something wrong happens during the background execution.

Without going into too much detail, we will implement the `doInBackground` code responsible for uploading the data to the remote web service:

```
@Override
protected Result<JobParameters> doInBackground(
   JobParameters... params) {

  Result<JobParameters> result = new Result<JobParameters>();
  HttpURLConnection urlConn = null;
  try {
    URL url;
    ...
         // Retrieve the file to upload from the parameters
         // passed in
    String file = params[0].getExtras().
                                 getString(SYNC_FILE_KEY);
         // Remote WebService Path
    String endpoint = params[0].getExtras().
                                 getString(SYNC_ENDPOINT_KEY);
    url = new URL ("http://<webs_host>:<webs_port>/"
                        + endpoint);
    ...
    // Load the account information stored internally
    String body = Util.loadJSONFromFile(jobService, file);
    // Write the information to the remote service
            uploadJsonToServer(urlConn, body);
    // Process Server Response
          ...
  } catch (Exception e) {
    result.exc = e;
  } finally {
     if ( urlConn != null) {
      urlConn.disconnect();
     }
  }
  return result;
}
```

Some implementation details are elided here for brevity, but we have implemented the doInBackground function to read the JSON data stored internally on a device file and we uploaded it over an HttpURLConnection. The Android Activity that displays the form saves and syncs the button to the final user. The **save** button, once pressed, stores the account information in the account.json local file when the **save** button is clicked.

The **sync** button, once clicked, will schedule the job for synchronizing the data with our remote HTTP server. When the job criteria defined by us are fulfilled, doInBackground is called to execute the sync procedure in the background.

Now that we have the code to upload the data to our server, let's finish it by processing the response and server errors:

```
try {
  ...
  int resultCode = urlConn.getResponseCode();
  if ( resultCode != HttpURLConnection.HTTP_OK ) {
    throw new Exception("Failed to sync with server :" +
        resultCode);
  }
  result.result = params[0];
  ...
```

When an exception occurs, such as the server being down or a server internal error happening, the exception is propagated over our Result object to onPostExecute for further processing.

Note that we are being careful to handle the error situations, so, to notify the result of the background work to the user, we will write an onPostExecute function that runs on the main thread that is going to publish a system notification that informs the user whether the task was completed successfully or failed miserably:

```
@Override
protected void onPostExecute(Result<JobParameters> result) {

  NotificationCompat.Builder builder =
    new NotificationCompat.Builder(jobService);
  ...
  if ( result.exc != null ) {
    // Error handling
    jobService.jobFinished(result.result, true);
    builder.setContentTitle("Failed to sync account")
    .setContentText("Failed to sync account " + result.exc);
  } else {
```

```
        // Success handling
        builder.setContentTitle("Account Updated")
          .setContentText("Updated Account Sucessfully at " +
                new Date().toString());
        jobService.jobFinished(result.result, false);
      }
    nm.notify(NOTIFICACTION_ID, builder.build());
  }
```

When the task is done, we invoke `jobFinished(JobParameters params, boolean needsRescheduled)` to let the system know that we are finished with that task; however, when an exception happens, we inform the system that we were unable to finish the task with success passing `true` on the second `jobFinished` argument.

When a finished job failed and needs to be rescheduled, we pass `false` as the second `jobService.jobFinished` argument, and the Scheduler API will reschedule our job using the back-off time specified in the `JobInfo` object. However, since our job only executes on idle mode, the failed job will be added to the scheduler queue and re-executed within a future idle maintenance window without using the back-off times specified in the `JobInfo`.

It is important to always call `jobFinished` to release the `WakeLock` assigned to the job and to inform the system that it can process additional jobs.

If everything goes well, a notification should appear in the notification drawer presenting the success message and the time when the last synchronization happened successfully.

Finally, we can update the `SyncJobService` code to start and stop the `SyncTask` execution:

```
    public class SyncJobService extends JobService {

        private static final String TAG = "SyncJobService";
        SyncTask mJob = null;
        @Override
        public boolean onStartJob(JobParameters params) {
            Log.i(TAG, "on start job: " + params.getJobId());
            if ( mJob != null ){
                mJob = new SyncTask(this);
                mJob.execute(params);
                return true;
            }
```

```
            return false;
    }

    @Override
    public boolean onStopJob(JobParameters params) {
        Log.i(TAG, "on stop job: " + params.getJobId());
        if ( mJob != null ){
            mJob.cancel(true);
            mJob = null;
        }
        return true;
    }
}
```

Listing pending jobs

Unlike the `AlarmManager` API, the Scheduler API provides the ability to list all the pending schedules for your application. This handy feature could help us to recognize the jobs that are going to be executed in the future and react accordingly with that list. The list retrieved could help us to pinpoint a pending job that we would like to cancel.

The `JobScheduler` service class has an `instance` method with the following signature:

```
public List<JobInfo> getAllPendingJobs();
```

The method will return a list of `JobInfo` objects that we can use to observe job parameter sets during the job build:

- Job criteria for each job:
    - `getNetworkType()`
    - `isRequireDeviceIdle()`
    - `isRequireCharging()`
    - `getMinLatencyMillis()`
    - `isPeriodic()`
    - `getIntervalMillis()`
    - `isPersisted()`
    - `getMaxExecutionDelayMillis()`

- The `JobService` subclass that will be called back by the `JobScheduler` to execute the job—`getService()`
- Job arguments: `getExtras()`
- Retry policy: `getInitialBackoffMillis()` and `getBackoffPolicy()`

Okay, now we are ready to create an Activity that prints a list of pending jobs for our application:

```
public class JobListActivity extends Activity {

  @Override
  protected void onCreate(Bundle savedInstanceState) {
  ...
JobScheduler jobScheduler = (JobScheduler)
    getSystemService(JOB_SCHEDULER_SERVICE);

  // Get the list of scheduled jobs
  List<JobInfo> jobList = jobScheduler.getAllPendingJobs();
  // Initialize the adapter job list
  JobListRecyclerAdapter adapter =
    new JobListRecyclerAdapter(this, jobList);

  rv.setAdapter(adapter);
  // Set the Job Counter
  TextView jobCountTv = (TextView)findViewById(R.id.jobCount);
  jobCountTv.setText(Integer.toString(jobList.size()));
  }
}
```

To list the pending jobs in the UI, we have used the support library `RecyclerView` class, a more advanced version of `ListView`, which simplifies the creation of a large set of `Views`.

First, we will build up our `ViewHolder` to hold the references to the row views that will display the `jobId` and the `Service` endpoint:

```
public class JobListRecyclerAdapter extends
  RecyclerView.Adapter<JobListRecyclerAdapter.JobViewHolder> {

    ...
  public static class JobViewHolder extends
    RecyclerView.ViewHolder {
    // References to the Views
    CardView cv;
    TextView jobId;
```

```
        TextView serviceName;

    JobViewHolder(View itemView) {
      super(itemView);
      cv = (CardView)itemView.findViewById(R.id.cv);
      jobId = (TextView)itemView.findViewById(R.id.jobIdTv);
      serviceName = (TextView)
        itemView.findViewById(R.id.className);
    }
  }
}
```

To bind the `jobInfo` parameters to the current `ViewHolder`, we will write the `RecyclerView.onBindViewHolder` to set the information based on the current `JobInfo`:

```
@Override
public void onBindViewHolder(
  JobListRecyclerAdapter.JobViewHolder holder, int position) {
  // Retrieve the job for the current list row
  final JobInfo ji = mJobList.get(position);
  // Update the UI Views with the Job Info
  holder.jobId.setText(Integer.toString(ji.getId()));
  holder.serviceName.setText(ji.getService().getClassName());
}
```

Yes, thanks to `getAllPendingJobs`, we have a list of our jobs, and moreover, we can analyze that programmatically to create behavior around the current application situation.

Some code is omitted on purpose; however, the full source code is available on Packt Publishing website. Take a look at the complete source code to appreciate how the recycler view and the card view was used to build up the job list UI.

To fully manipulate the jobs at will, there is only one CRUD (create, read, update, delete) operation that we need to cover in this chapter - the delete operation. The delete job operation is delivered by the `cancel` functions and is going to be covered in detail in the next section.

Canceling a job

There are some situations where we want to provide for the users an ability to cancel the job because the environment situation has changed or it does not make sense to execute the job anymore—for example, the user changed a piece of information that the job depends on and the job is no longer applicable. The JobScheduler service offers us the support for job cancellation with the following cancel and cancelAll methods:

```
void cancel(int jobId);

void cancelAll();
```

The first method, cancel(jobId), allows us to cancel a specific job using the job identifier returned from the schedule(JobInfo job) function or the jobId available on JobInfo objects returned by the getAllPendingJobs function.

The cancelAll() method allows us to cancel the scheduled jobs that have been registered with the JobScheduler by the current application.

With JobInfo from the previous example we are able to cancel a specific job passing the job identifier:

```
final JobInfo ji = ...;
JobScheduler jobScheduler = (JobScheduler)
        mContext.getSystemService(mContext.JOB_SCHEDULER_SERVICE);
// Cancel a Specific Job based on the JobInfo->jobId
jobScheduler.cancel(ji.getId());
```

Whenever we cancel a schedule, the job will be removed from the JobScheduler future execution queue and will no longer be executed by the SyncJobService or any other JobService.

Scheduling a periodic job

So far, we have scheduled one-shot jobs, but do you know there is an option to schedule the execution of a job at periodic internals. These kinds of jobs might be the perfect construct to performing repeating backups or repeating network operations such as application user data backup.

Let's update our AccountInfoActivity to schedule the periodic execution of the account synchronization job.

We'll start by defining a new job identifier for our periodic job:

```
static final int SYNC_PER_JOB_ID = "SyncJobPerService".hashCode();
```

We can schedule a periodic job to be executed approximately every 12 hours like this:

```
JobInfo.Builder builder = new JobInfo.Builder(SYNC_PER_JOB_ID,
    serviceName);
builder.setRequiresDeviceIdle(true)
  // Persist the schedule across the device reboots
  .setPersisted(true)
  .setPeriodic(TimeUnit.HOURS.toMillis(12L))
  .setRequiredNetworkType(JobInfo.NETWORK_TYPE_UNMETERED)
  .setRequiresDeviceIdle(true)
  .setExtras(bundle);

// Schedule the repeating job
JobScheduler jobScheduler = (JobScheduler)
getSystemService(JOB_SCHEDULER_SERVICE);
jobScheduler.schedule(builder.build());
```

Now we are able to schedule the synchronization job to run periodically in the background while the device is idle and the Wi-Fi network is available. The job schedule will be persisted by the system and re-enabled after the device boots up until we explicitly cancel the job or all the jobs are cancelled through `cancelAll()`.

Applications of the JobScheduler

The `JobScheduler` API allows us to schedule work that runs asynchronously without user intervention in the future under certain conditions. This API is also able to reduce the energy consumption by deferring the job execution until the device is charging or connected to an unmetered network, such as the Wi-Fi network.

Ideal cases include things such as application database backup that could be deferred and do not require exact time execution, a periodic upload of user data to the network, and download of configuration parameters. So, typically jobs that don't have to run immediately and which data doesn't have to be ready for user consumption. Reducing your application energy consumption without compromising the user experience will increase the device battery lifetime and therefore improve the user experience.

The JobScheduler could cover most of the AlarmManager use cases, notwithstanding it provides advanced features to optimize device resources acquisition. As an additional feature, this API provides a way to create schedule that survive the device shutdown and restart.

The only big drawback is that JobScheduler was only introduced with Android 5.0 (Lollipop). Therefore, you need to target your application to an API Version 21 or higher to interact with this API.

At the time of writing in July 2016, 45 percent of Android devices run a version of Android that supports JobScheduler. To get up-to-date information about the Android market share by version, please check the Android Developer Dashboard.

Summary

In this chapter, we explored the JobSheduler API, putting it to use to schedule background work that starts when a group of conditions defined by us are met.

We learned in detail how to set the different criteria supported by the API and how to schedule based on the JobInfo object that starts a job when the device is charging and not in use.

In the meantime, we learned how to implement an asynchronous JobService that is able to run in a background execution line and finish the job execution properly by releasing all the acquired resources (WakeLock, . . .).

Later, we used the getAllPendingJobs to create a sample code to list all the pending Scheduler API jobs within our application. From the example, we learned how to cancel a specific job or all the pending jobs in our applications.

To finish, we built a persistent and recurrent schedule using the JobSheduler API, which wakes up the device and executes our job every 12 hours.

In the next chapter, we will learn how to transfer data from and to the network using effective asynchronous libraries and protocols, without even draining the battery.

8
Interacting with the Network

So far, we have been using the HttpURLConnection HTTP client to transfer data from and to the network, such as when downloading images from an HTTP server and synchronizing information with a remote HTTP server. We have been using this Android HTTP client blindly without going into much detail about the internals and the features provided by this handy framework that deals transparently with the HTTP protocol for us.

In this chapter, we'll learn more about the advanced features of HttpURLConnection and fresh techniques to communicate asynchronously and securely with a remote server using the HTTP protocol.

In the meantime, we will learn how use a customized HTTP client to communicate over secure channels, tweak the HTTP client to deal with network delays, and learn how to interact with web APIs.

In this chapter, we will cover the following:

- Introducing Android HTTP clients
- Performing HTTP requests asynchronously
- Interacting with JSON web APIs
- Interacting with XML web APIs
- Optimizing HTTP timeouts
- Communicating securely over SSL sessions
- HTTP open source libraries

Introducing Android HTTP clients

In recent times, the ability to send and receive data from remote servers has become an essential feature that all applications should enforce in order to create dynamic and impressive experiences. Today almost every application uses the network to pull up data information, execute remote business logic operations, and download or upload resources.

The network interactions that happen between the application and a remote server are typically defined as a set of request/response messages that traverse the network using a network protocol.

In general, the HTTP protocol is often used to transport messages between each peer, and the Android SDK comes with two high-level HTTP clients available out of the box to send and receive data: `AndroidHttpClient` and `HttpURLConnection`.

The HTTP communication protocol is a stateless, standard text-based application protocol maintained by **Internet Engineering Task Force (IETF)** and the **World Wide Web Consortium (W3C)** and is widely used on the Internet to exchange data between a client, normally called a user agent, and a server.

The protocol has undergone some improvements over time, but most servers and clients base their implementation on HTTP 1.1, a revision of the original HTTP 1.0, which introduced the connection re-use feature and chunked transfer encoding to the original protocol.

In a typical HTTP flow, the client, the entity that initiates the operation, sends a request to the server over a connection and waits for the server's response. On the other end, the server reads the request from the communication channel, processes the request, and sends a response back to the client. In the next figure, we can visualize a request and response example exchanged between peers:

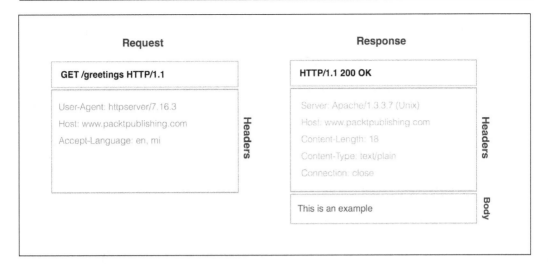

The new HTTP revision, 2.0, published in May 2015, hasn't been widely adopted and there is no official support on the Android SDK.

After a preliminary HTTP protocol introduction, we will try to compare the HTTP clients available on the Android SDK.

AndroidHttpClient

The AndroidHttpClient client library, based on the Apache HTTP client, has been deprecated since API Level 9 (Gingerbread), but it provides a large and flexible API to access HTTP servers with support for cookie management, timeout customization, basic authentication schemes, and secure communication channels.

This client is more stable than HttpURLConnection on API Level 8 (Froyo) and API Level 7 (Eclair).

On API Level 23 (Marshmallow), support for this client has been removed in favor of HttpURLConnection due to the lack of transparent response compression and response caching.

HttpURLConnection

This client framework supports secure communication sessions (HTTPS), transparent response compression, response caching, network timeout customization, network connection polling, IPV6 support, proxy servers, and streaming.

According to Google, prior to API Level 8 (Froyo), this client has some important issues that could spoil the HTTP connection re-use.

 Since Android 4.4 (KitKat), this implementation engine is based on the open source OkHttp Square library.

Given that `HttpURLConnection` is the HTTP client recommended by Google for Android versions greater than API Level 9, we will base our code examples on this HTTP client. However, this fragmentation issue can be surpassed by using different Android HTTP clients based on the API Level:

```
if (Build.VERSION.SDK_INT >= 9) {
    // After Gingerbread, use the google recommended
    // client, HttpUrlConnection
    ...
} else {
    // Prior to Gingerbread, use the Apache based
    // client, AndroidHttpClient
    ...
}
```

In the next section, we will start to write our HTTP asynchronous toolkit based on `HttpURLConnection` and explore the advanced features delivered by the client to communicate with remote peers.

Performing HTTP requests asynchronously

So far we have been using the `HttpURLConnection` client and `AsyncTask` to retrieve remote data asynchronously in our code examples.

While this solution can work in most cases, we could end up with loads of duplicate code in our applications.

In this section, we will create a neat high-level asynchronous HTTP client to perform remote requests outside of the main thread that forwards the result of the request to the application's main thread using a callback handler. This approach fits well with the application UI model because the callback handler, which executes on the main thread, is able to update the UI with the data retrieved from the server.

First of all, let's define the basic interface that our asynchronous client should honor to execute remote requests in the background:

```
public interface AsyncHTTPClient {
    void execute(HTTPRequest request, ResponseHandler handler);
}
```

The `HTTPRequest` class is a Java model used to define all the parameters required to build the HTTP request. We will omit some of the implementation details, but with the help of the `Builder` class, we will be able to define the HTTP request verb, the request URL, the HTTP headers, the HTTP query parameters, and the HTTP body:

```
public class HTTPRequest {

    final Verb mVerb;
    final String mUrl;
    final List<Header> mHeaders;
    final Map<String, String> mParameters;
    final Body mBody;

    private HTTPRequest(Builder builder) {...}
}
```

`ResponseHandler` is the class that defines the callbacks that will be invoked when a success or failure response is sent from the server, or an exception happens during the operation execution. So, we'll define an abstract `ResponseHandler` class for the subclasses to implement:

```
public abstract class ResponseHandler {

    // Method invoked when a success response is returned
    // 200 Response Code
    abstract public void onSuccess(HTTPResponse response) ;

    // Method invoked when a failure response is returned
    // 4XX, 50X
    abstract public void onFailure(HTTPResponse response) ;

    // Method Invoked when an error happens
    abstract public void onError(Throwable error);
}
```

All callback methods are forwarded automatically to the main thread when a response or an error is ready to be dispatched to the handler. All the network and input/output operations and memory allocations have to be done on the background thread to avoid any UI undesired pauses.

When the server returns an HTTP response, one of the following methods, onSuccess or OnFailure, is invoked based on the code returned by the response message. So, when any of the callbacks are called, an HTTPResponse object is delivered for further processing.

For now, the HTTPResponse class carries information about the request code, the response headers, and the response body:

```
public class HTTPResponse {

    final int mResponseCode;
    final List<Header> mHeaders;
    final Body mBody;


}
```

With the base classes and interface already defined, let's implement our asynchronous high-level client with the help of the HttpURLConnection class.

Since we already know how to construct a background-processing pipeline based on the AsyncTask class, for simplicity, we will base our implementation on this construct. In the future, you can replace AsyncTask with AsyncTaskLoader to support configuration changes:

```
public class HTTPAsyncTask extends
  AsyncTask<HTTPRequest, Void, Result<HTTPResponse>> {

  // Response Handler to be invoked In onPostExecute
  // on the UI Thread
  final ResponseHandler mHandler;

  // Handler is passed on the constructor
  public  HTTPAsyncTask(ResponseHandler handler) {
    this.mHandler = handler;
  }
  . . .
}
```

As defined in the preceding code, the input parameter type for our `AsyncTask` is `HTTPRequest` and as a result an object of type `Result<HTTPResponse>` is sent to the UI thread. The result, is a generic class, as defined in previous chapters, that is able to carry an error or an `HTTPResponse` object.

With the `HTTPAsyncTask` generic parameters already defined, now it is time to override `doInBackground` to send the HTTP request and process the response in the background:

```
@Override
protected Result<HTTPResponse> doInBackground(HTTPRequest...
params) {

  HTTPRequest request = params[0];
  Body body = null;
  HttpURLConnection conn = null;
  Result<HTTPResponse> response = new Result<HTTPResponse>();
  try {

    // Retrieve the request URL from the request object
    URL url = new URL(request.mUrl);

    // Opens up the connection to the remote peer
    conn = (HttpURLConnection) url.openConnection();

    // Set the HTTP Request verb
    conn.setRequestMethod(request.mVerb);

    // set The HTTP Request Headers
    setRequestHeaders(conn, request);

    // Allows Receiving data on the response
    conn.setDoInput(true);

    // Retrieve the response code
    int responseCode = conn.getResponseCode();

    // Build the HTTP Response Object
    HTTPResponse.Builder builder = new HTTPResponse.Builder()
    .setResponseCode(responseCode);

    // Fill the HTTP Response Headers
```

```
        fillHeaders(conn.getHeaderFields(), builder);

        // Read the Body from the Connection Input Stream
        // using a factory
        body = BodyFactory.read(conn.getContentType(),
                                conn.getInputStream());
        // Set the HTTPResponse body
        builder.setBody(body);
        // Build the HTTP Response Object
        response.result = builder.build();
      } catch (Exception e) {
        response.error = e;
      } finally {
        if ( conn != null ) {
          conn.disconnect();
        }
      }
      return response;
      }

    // Write any header to the Request Ex: Accept: text/xml
    void setRequestHeaders(HttpURLConnection con, HTTPRequest request ) {
      for (Header header : request.mHeaders) {
        con.addRequestProperty(header.getName(), header.getValue());
      }
    }
```

openConnection will establish a TCP connection with the resource specified in the URL object. Once the connection is established, and we try to retrieve the status line response code, our HTTP request headers and body are dispatched to the network.

As soon as the status line is read, we process the HTTP response headers received and we store them on our response object for further processing. As you probably already know, an HTTP response might contain data on the HTTP message body, related to the resource specified on the requested URL.

For further processing, the data will be consumed from the connection InputStream in order to build a Body object. To detect the type of data content received on the HTTP Response, the client should look into the header Content-Type content. To simplify this recognition, the HttpURLConnection class provides the member method, getContentType(), that retrieves the content directly from the header.

The body consumption and construction is done on the `BodyFactory` class shown in the following code:

```
public class BodyFactory {

  public static Body read(String mimeType,
                          InputStream is) throws IOException {
    Body result = null;
    if ( mimeType.startsWith("text") ) {
      result = new TextPlainBody(mimeType);
      result.consume(is);
    }
    return result;
  }
}
```

Since we know the content type, we are ready to consume the body and store the bytes received on a `Body` object for further processing by our `ResponseHandler`.

`Body` is an abstract class and itself is not able to read any kind of content, although we can extend the `Body` class directly to build a text body from the received data.

Our `Body` subclass, called `TextPlainBody`, will implement the abstract consume function in order to construct the body from the `InputStream`:

```
abstract void consume(InputStream is)
  throws IOException;
```

The consume code for the `TextPlainBody` is omitted for brevity, though the full source code is available to download from the Packt Publishing website. Take a look at the `TextPlainBody` source code to appreciate how we build a string using the `InputStream`.

For now, we only support the `text/*` type; however, in the next sections we are going to extend the `BodyFactory` class to support other interesting mime types, such as JSON documents.

Once the response body has been fully read, the connection with the remote server will be closed and the resources held by the connection released.

 The connection is not immediately destroyed but rather pushed to a connection pool for future use. After a finite amount of time idle (`idleTimeout`) on the pool, the connection is destroyed.

During the `doInBackground` execution, network or input/output exceptions are likely to arise, so to avoid an application crash we must catch and forward them over the `result.error` to the `postExecute` function and later to the `ResponseHandler` specified when the execution is initiated.

Unchecked exceptions that propagate out of AsyncTask's methods will crash our application, so we must test carefully and handle those if necessary.

To make our `AsyncTask` subclass useful, we have to write the `onPostExecute` function that forwards the response or an error to the `ResponseHandler` object:

```
protected void onPostExecute(Result<HTTPResponse> result) {

    if ( result.error != null ) {
      mHandler.onError(result.error);
    } else if ( result.obj.mResponseCode ==
               HttpURLConnection.HTTP_OK ) {
      mHandler.onSuccess(result.obj);
    } else {
      mHandler.onFailure(result.obj);
    }
}
```

 As stated before in *Chapter 3, Exploring AsyncTask*, the `onPostExecute` callback will be executed on the main thread, so you should avoid any time-consuming operations on the following callbacks: `onError`, `onSucess`, and `onFailure`.

All that remains is to invoke our `AsyncTask` from our `AsyncHTTPClient` subclass— `PacktAsyncHTTPClient`:

```
public class PacktAsyncHTTPClient implements AsyncHTTPClient {

    @Override
    public void execute( HTTPRequest request,
                        ResponseHandler handler) {
      // Execute the HTTP Request on the default AsyncTask Executor
      new HTTPAsyncTask(handler).execute(request);
    }
    ...
}
```

Great! Now we have a core asynchronous HTTP client implementation with support for text mime types. In the next section we will use our high-level client to retrieve a text message from a remote server.

Retrieving a text response

With our asynchronous HTTP client supporting text responses, we are able to make use of it to obtain a dynamic text so, let's create an activity that displays the text available on a remote URL resource.

First, we have to build our `HTTPRequest` using the `HTTPRequest.Builder` class:

```
protected void onCreate(Bundle savedInstanceState) {
    ...
    HTTPRequest.Builder builder = new HTTPRequest.Builder();
    // Set the HTTP Verb to GET
    builder.setVerb(HTTPRequest.Verb.GET);
    // Sets location of the remote resource
    builder.setUrl("http://<hostname>:<port>/greetings");
    // Build the request object
    HTTPRequest request =  builder.build();
    ...
}
```

We wish to draw your attention to the fact that you should replace `<hostname>` and `<port>` to make it work for your HTTP server.

As defined before, in order to execute the request over our asynchronous client, `AsyncHTTPClient`, we must provide a `ResponseHandler` object to the `execute` method. Moreover, we want to define an object that updates the UI with the text obtained.

First of all, we will extend our `ResponseHandler` abstract and create a class to process the body and forward the response to a callback that receives the text message as the input:

```
public abstract class TextResponseHandler
  extends ResponseHandler {
    // Response Callback receiving the string body
    abstract void onSuccess(String response);

    @Override
    public void onSuccess(HTTPResponse response) {
        TextPlainBody body = (TextPlainBody)response.mBody;
        // Invoke the callback that receives a string
        onSuccess(body.getContent());
    }
}
```

Next, we need to finish our `Activity` code to send the HTTP request and in the meantime we will also present a progress dialog making the user aware that something is going on in the background:

```
HTTPRequest request =  builder.build();
// Create a client Instance object
PacktAsyncHTTPClient client = new PacktAsyncHTTPClient();
// Enable a progress bar
ProgressBar pb =(ProgressBar) findViewById(R.id.loading);
pb.setVisibility(View.VISIBLE);
// Retrieve the response on the background
client.execute(request,textResponseHandler);
...
```

Now, all we need is to define our `textResponseHandler`, an anonymous inner class that implements `TextReponseHandler`, updates the `View` with the `String` received, and dismisses the indeterminate progress dialog enabled:

```
TextResponseHandler greetingsHandler = new TextResponseHandler() {

  // Invoked when request was processed with success by the server
  @Override
  void onSuccess(String response) {

    // Update the View with the String received on the
    // HTTP body
    EditText et = (EditText) findViewById(R.id.inputText);
    et.setText(response);
    dismissProgress();
  }

  // Invoked when the served returned an error
  @Override
  public void onFailure(HTTPResponse response) {
    Log.e("GreetingsActivity", "Server returned an error: " +
          response.mResponseCode + " " +
          response.mResponseMessage);
    dismissProgress();
  }

  // Invoked when an error happened
  @Override
  public void onError(Throwable error) {
```

```
        Log.e("GreetingsActivity", "Exception happened: " +
                error.getMessage(), error);
        dismissProgress();
    }
};
```

Notice that all the callback functions are going to be executed on the main thread, so in these functions you should follow the golden rule of not blocking the thread to avoid UI delays.

When the server returns an error or an exception happens during the execution, the following callback methods, `onFailure` and `OnError`, are called respectively.

Support for reading text resources from a remote server is a good starting point, although in most cases we intend to communicate with the remote server to exchange structured document formats, such as JSON, XML, or even binary data.

Interacting with JSON web APIs

Our previous `TextResponseHandler` is able to process the generic response `HTTPResponse` fulfilled with a text response and forward a String coming from JSON web APIs and forward a `String` to the `TextResponseHandler onReceive(String)` callback.

Now we want to go a little further and convert an `HTTPResponse` returned from the `doInBackground` to a **Plain Old Java Object (POJO)** that characterizes a model on our business logic. To achieve that, we must convert a JSON-structured content returned on the HTTP body to one Java defined previously.

To forward the processing to the callbacks defined above, we will create the `JSONResponseHandler`, an abstract subclass of `ResponseHandler` that implements `onSuccess(HTTPResponse)`, `onFailure(HTTPResponse)`, and convert the objects to `<ResponseType>` and `<ErrorType>` respectively:

```
public abstract class JsonResponseHandler<ResponseType, ErrorType>
extends ResponseHandler {

  abstract public void onSuccess(ResponseType response);
  abstract public void onFailure(ErrorType response);
  ...
}
```

To support the processing of different body contents, our `BodyFactory` needs an update. So, before we move on to the `JSONResponseHandler` implementation, we will update our `BodyFactory` function to support the `application/json` mimetype:

```
public class BodyFactory {

  public static Body read(String mimeType,
                          InputStream is)
    throws IOException {

    ...
    } else if ( mimeType.startsWith("application/json")){
      result = new RawBody(mimeType);
      result.consume(is);
    }
    return result;
  }
}
```

Notice that we read the content from the network and we store the data on a new `Body` class named `RawBody` that simply stores the content that comes from the HTTP Response body on an internal byte memory buffer.

 Storing the full body might work for our simple client use cases. Although, if we are willing to process bodies with megabytes of data, we must use another strategy to read and consume the body, consume the body in chunks, or save the body on a local filesystem.

With the body already with JSON web APIs stored on the device memory, we are ready to process it with the help of our `JSONResponseHandler`.

Converting Java objects to JSON

To convert the JSON document format to a plain object we will make use of one open source library that's very well known in the Android community—the Google GSON library: `https://github.com/google/gson`.

The GSON library, a library developed and maintained by Google, is able to convert Java objects to a JSON object and vice versa.

So, before you move on, make sure that you add the library to your Gradle or Eclipse project:

```
compile 'com.google.code.gson:gson:2.5'
```

To convert from a protocol encoded content body to a POJO, we will define the `BodyDecoder` interface:

```
public interface BodyDecoder <T> {
    T decode(Body body) throws Exception ;
}
```

To convert from a POJO to a `Body` object, we are going to define the `BodyEncoder` interface:

```
public interface BodyEncoder<T> {
    Body encode(T obj,String mimeType) throws Exception;
}
```

To decode a JSON document to a POJO, we will have to subclass this generic interface and write the code to deal with the JSON decoding with the help of the GSON library:

```
public class JSONConverter<POJO>
  implements BodyEncoder<POJO>, BodyDecoder<POJO> {
  // Store the Generic Type information
  private final Type pojoType;

  JSONConverter(Type pojoType) {
    this.pojoType = pojoType;
  }

  @Override
  public POJO decode(Body body) throws Exception {
    Gson gson = new Gson();
    RawBody rawBody = (RawBody) body;
    InputStream is = null;
    POJO obj = null;
    try {
      is = new ByteArrayInputStream(rawBody.getContent());
      BufferedReader bfReader =
        new BufferedReader(new InputStreamReader(is));
      obj = gson.fromJson(bfReader, pojoType);
    } finally {
      if (is != null) is.close();
    }
    return obj;
  }
}
```

Finally, we are ready to implement our generic JSONResponseHandler that forwards the converted JSON-structured documents returned on the onSuccess and onFailure methods to the generic types Response and Error.

Here is how the JsonResponseHandler code will look:

```
public abstract class JsonResponseHandler<ResponseType, ErrorType>
   extends ResponseHandler {
    // Store the Response Type class information
     private final Type responseType;
    // Store the Error Type class information
     private final Type errorType;

     JsonResponseHandler(Type responseType, Type errorType) {
         this.responseType = responseType;
         this.errorType = errorType;
     }

    // Callback invoked on the main Thread that converts
    // a body to a POJO object
    @Override
    public void onSuccess(HTTPResponse response) {
      RawBody body = (RawBody)response.mBody;

      if ( body != null ) {
        Response obj = null;
        try {
          obj = new JSONConverter<Response>(responseType).
                  decode(body);
          onSuccess(obj);
        } catch (Exception e) {
          onError(e);
        }

      } else {
        onSuccess((Response)null);
      }
    }
   @Override
   public void onFailure(HTTPResponse response) {...}
}
```

This generically typed class is able to consume the `RawBody` object forwarded from `onSuccess` or `onFailure` and expose two generic type parameters. The first `Response` is a generic type that specifies the type of POJO class for the success response (`onSuccess`) and the `Error` generic type that specifies the type of POJO class for the error function (`onFailure`).

When any of the callback functions that receive the `HTTPResponse` is invoked, with the help of the GSON library we convert the JSON document, stored on the `RawBody`, to a response/error object.

The `onFailure` function is omitted because its code is quite similar to the `onSuccess` method; however, you can take a look at the full source code on the Packt Publishing website to understand the differences.

Finally, we are ready to exercise our asynchronous client by reading a model from an HTTP JSON body:

```
Content-Type: application/json

[
  {
    "userId": 1,
    "id": 1,
    "title": "..",
    "body": "..."
  },...
]
```

To test our client we will take advantage of `JSONPlaceHolder` (http://jsonplaceholder.typicode.com/), a fake online REST API for testing and prototyping.

Before we try to access it, let's define the `User` POJO class that we will use in our example:

```
public class User {
   public int id;
   public String name;
   public String username;
   public String email;
   public String phone;
   public String website;
}
```

And we will define a POJO class for the `failure` function:

```
public class Error {
  public int resultCode;
  public String resultMessage;
}
```

To display the models returned from the fake API, we'll create a new `UserListActivity` that will implement `JSONResponseHandler` and display the name and the e-mail of all the users with the JSON document returned from `http://jsonplaceholder.typicode.com/users`.

Let's start by defining the `JsonResponseHandler<List<User>,Error>` anonymous class that receives a list of users as an argument , `List<User>`, for the success callback and an `Error` object as the argument for the failure callback.

`onSuccess(List<User>)` will update a `ListView` that displays the name followed by the e-mail:

```
JsonResponseHandler<List<User>, Error> jsonResponseHandler =
  new JsonResponseHandler<List<User>, Error>(
    new TypeToken<ArrayList<User>>() {} .getType(),
    new TypeToken<Error>() {} .getType()) {
      // On Success Callback
      @Override
      public void onSuccess(List<User> users) {
        // Update the List View with the a List Adapter that displays
        // the user name and email per user
        ListView listView = (ListView) findViewById(R.id.usersList);
        ListAdapter adapter = new UserListAdapter(
          UserListActivity.this, users);
        listView.setAdapter(adapter);
      }
      // Prints the Error object
      @Override
      public void onFailure(Error response) {
        Log.e("UserListActivity",
            "Error happened retrieving greetings " +
            response.toString());
      }
      @Override
      public void onError(Throwable error) {
      // Do Something with the exception
      }
    };
```

All that remains is to write the Activity's `onCreate` function that builds up the HTTP Request and dispatches the request, GET /users, to the `JSONPlaceHolder` API:

```
@Override
protected void onCreate(Bundle savedInstanceState) {
  super.onCreate(savedInstanceState);
  setContentView(R.layout.user_list_layout);

  HTTPRequest.Builder builder = new HTTPRequest.Builder();
  // Set the HTTP Verb to GET
  builder.setVerb(HTTPRequest.Verb.GET);
  // Sets location of the remote resource
  builder.setUrl("http://jsonplaceholder.typicode.com/users");

  // Notify the server that the client is able to receive json
  // documents
  builder.addHeader(new Header("Accept","application/json"));
  HTTPRequest request = builder.build();

  PacktAsyncHTTPClient client = new PacktAsyncHTTPClient();
  client.execute(request, jsonResponseHandler);
}
```

When the server sends back a response to our request, the `JSONResponseHandler` object will decode the JSON document with a list of 10 users and convert the document to a `List<User>` object.

The JSON data exchange format has predominantly been used on most recent APIs and web services deployed on the Internet because of its simplicity, readability, compactness, and lack of data structure rigidity.

However, XML-based remote web services, mainly based on the SOA data exchange protocol, are still around to cover advanced use cases where we want to have stricter data model schema validation and modelling, built-in namespace support, and advanced information extraction tools.

XML-based APIs have lost some traction in the industry, although the XML-based APIs are still common, so in the next section we will extend our toolkit to support the encoding and decoding of XML content on our HTTP requests.

Interacting with XML web APIs

Over the last 10 years, XML message-based APIs have been successfully used to exchange data (SOAP) and run remote procedures (XML-RPC) between applications and remote servers. Moreover, nowadays, some REST APIs are built with JSON and XML support, so it's up to the developer to decide whether they want to interact with the API using XML or JSON documents.

With this in mind, we will extend our toolkit to exchange XML messages in order to communicate with the remote server.

In the preceding sections, we implemented a ResponseHandler to decode JSON documents sent on the HTTP body, but now we want to go further and add support for sending XML documents on the HTTP Request.

If we go back into our HTTPAsyncTask details, the code required to support body transmissions on the request was lacking; therefore, this is the perfect time to rewrite the code to carry an entity body on the HTTP request:

```
@Override
protected Result<HTTPResponse> doInBackground(HTTPRequest... params) {
  ...
  if ( request.mBody != null ) {
    // Allows Sending data on the request
    conn.setDoOutput(true);
    // Specifies The Content-Type based on the Body Mime Type
    conn.setRequestProperty(
      "Content-type", request.mBody.getMimeType());
    // Retrieves the connection stream to write content
    OutputStream os = conn.getOutputStream();
    request.mBody.write(os);
  }
  // Retrieve the response code
  int responseCode = conn.getResponseCode();
  ...
}
```

In the preceding code, when a body is available on the HTTPRequest object and before we try to read the responseCode of the response status line, we retrieve the output stream from the HttpURLConnection and we write the content stored on the Body object.

Apart from the data written, the header Context-Type is set on the HTTP request header section based on the body's mimetype.

Now, we are ready to send and receive entity bodies on the HTTP request and response respectively, so now we can start to work on our XML implementation example.

In the next paragraphs, and following the JSON section, we will write the code to serialize an API Request into an XML document and the code to de-serialize XML documents, received on response, to an API Response object.

Converting Java objects to XML

To de-serialize and serialize from Java objects to XML and vice-versa, we will use the open source library SimpleXML (http://simple.sourceforge.net/); therefore, to make use of it, please add this library to your application list of external dependencies.

If you use Android Studio, here is the content to add to your `build.gradle` list of dependencies:

```
dependencies {
    ...
    compile('org.simpleframework:simple-xml:2.7.+'){
            exclude module: 'stax'
            exclude module: 'stax-api'
            exclude module: 'xpp3'
    }
}
```

With the `User` model defined previously we will build up a `APIRequest` named `GetUserInfo` that will get the user details (`GetUserInfoResponse`) for the user identifier submitted in the request.

To describe this further, let's define the API Request POJO objects:

```
@Root(name = "GetUserInfo")
@Namespace(prefix="p",
    reference="https://www.packtpub.com/asynchronous_android")
public class GetUserInfo {

    @Namespace(reference=
        "https://www.packtpub.com/asynchronous_android")
    @Element(name="UserId")
    public String userId;
            // … Setters and Getters
}
```

And let's define the API Response POJO object:

```
@Root
@Namespace(prefix = "p",
  reference = "https://www.packtpub.com/asynchronous_android")
public class GetUserInfoResponse {

  @Element(name = "User")
  @Namespace(prefix = "p",
    reference = "https://www.packtpub.com/asynchronous_android" )
  private User user = new User();
  // … Setters and Getters
}
```

The annotation for the other classes, User, Address, and Company, are quite similar to the ones above, with all the elements referring to the https://www.packtpub.com/asynchronous_android namespace, hence we will omit the POJO changes for brevity.

With the mapping between the Java objects and XML Request and response message finished, let's start to work on the code that converts the GetUserInfo object into an XML document.

To encode an XML document from a Java object, we will subclass this generic interface to encode a POJO generic type into an XML document with the help of SimpleXML:

```
public class XMLConverter<POJO>
  implements Encoder<POJO>{

  private final Class<POJO> clazz;
  XMLConverter(Class<POJO> clazz){ this.clazz = clazz; }

  @Override
  public Body encode(POJO obj, String mimeType)
    throws Exception {

    // Creates SimpleXML Serializer Instance
    Serializer serializer = new Persister();
    ByteArrayOutputStream output = new ByteArrayOutputStream();

    // Converts from obj -> xml document
    serializer.write(obj, output);

    // Build a RawBody body
```

```
        RawBody body = new RawBody(mimeType);
        output.close();

        // Stores the result on the body
        body.setContent(output.toByteArray());
        return body;
    }
}
```

Converting XML to Java objects

To decode an XML document to a Java POJO object we will add the
BodyDecoder<POJO> to the XMLConverter class definition interface and write the
code to convert the XML document to a POJO generic class with the help of the
SimpleXML library:

```
public class XMLConverter<POJO>
    implements BodyEncoder<POJO>, BodyDecoder<POJO> {

    . . .
    @Override
    public POJO decode(Body body) throws Exception {
        // Instantiate a SimpleXML Serializer
        Serializer serializer = new Persister();
        InputStream is = null;
        RawBody rawBody = (RawBody)body;
        POJO obj = null;
        try {
            is = new ByteArrayInputStream(rawBody.getContent());
            BufferedReader bfReader =
                new BufferedReader(new InputStreamReader(is));
            obj = (POJO) serializer.read(clazz, bfReader);
        } finally {
            if ( is != null ) is.close();
        }
        return obj;
    }
    . . .
}
```

With the XML serialization and deserialization already in place, let's start to write
the activity that will retrieve the user information from a remote server using the
GetUserInfo and GetUserInfoResponse defined above and display the user
information on a UI.

To test our client, we will create a fake XML WebService with the help of the mockable `https://www.mockable.io/` web application. This web application allows us to create configurable REST APIs that return a static JSON or XML document as a response to the clients, so this tool will be extremely helpful to test our client in a controlled environment.

Our fake HTTP API will return the following XML document when any HTTP request is sent to the following URI, `http://demo1472539.mockable.io/GetUserInfo`:

```
<?xml version="1.0"  ?>
<p:GetUserInfoResponse
    xmlns:p="https://www.packtpub.com/asynchronous_android">
 <p:User>
   <p:Id>12</p:Id>
   <p:Name>John</p:Name>
   <p:Username>John</p:Username>
   ...
   <p:Company>
        <p:Name>Packt</p:Name>
        ...
    </p:Company>
  </p:User>
  </p:GetUserInfoResponse>
```

In order to convert the `HTTPResponse` objects received by the `onSuccess(HTTPRequest)` and `onFailure(HTTPResponse)` callbacks to domain models, we will have to subclass the `ResponseHandler` abstract class and create the code to de-serialize a generic POJO class:

```
public abstract class XMLResponseHandler
    <Response, Error> extends ResponseHandler {

    // Class used to by Simple to convert to the ResponseTYpe
    private final Class<Response> responseClass;

    private final Class<Error> errorClass;

    XMLResponseHandler(Class<Response> responseClass,
                       Class<Error> errorClass) {
      this.responseClass = responseClass;
      this.errorClass = errorClass;
    }

    // Callback invoked with the converted Response  object instance
```

```
abstract public void onSuccess(Response response);

// Callback invoked with the converted Error object instance
abstract public void onFailure(Error response);

// Convert the body to a POJO object using the our converter
@Override
public void onSuccess(HTTPResponse response) {
  RawBody body = (RawBody)response.mBody;

  if ( body != null ) {
    Response obj = null;
    try {
      obj = new XMLConverter<Response>(responseClass)
      decode(body);
      onSuccess(obj);
    } catch (Exception e) {
      onError(e);
    }
  } else { onSuccess((Response)null); }
}
//.. Failure elided for brevity
}
```

Now we are ready to collect the GetUserInfoResponse dispatched from
our fake server, so let's implement, on our Activity, an anonymous inner
XMLResponseHandler subclass that will update the UI with user details:

```
XMLResponseHandler<GetUserInfoResponse, Error> xmlResponseHandler
  = new XMLResponseHandler<GetUserInfoResponse,Error>(
      GetUserInfoResponse.class, Error.class) {

  // Updates the UI with the user details
  @Override
  public void onSuccess(GetUserInfoResponse getUserInfoResponse) {
    TextView nameTv = (TextView)findViewById(R.id.nameValue);
    TextView emailTv = (TextView)findViewById(R.id.emailValue);

    nameTv.setText(getUserInfoResponse.getUser().name);
    emailTv.setText(getUserInfoResponse.getUser().email);

  }
  @Override
  public void onFailure(Error response) {
```

```
    // Do Something with the Error
  }
  @Override
  public void onError(Throwable error) {
    // Do Something with the Throwable
  }
};
```

To finish our `Activity`, we will have to build the request and ask our asynchronous client to execute our demand in the background with the help of the `HTTPAsyncTask` class:

```
HTTPRequest.Builder builder = new HTTPRequest.Builder();
// Set the HTTP POST Verb
builder.setVerb(HTTPRequest.Verb.POST);

// Set location of the remote resource
builder.setUrl("http://demo1472539.mockable.io/GetUserInfo");

// Tell the Server that you are able to consume
// application/xml contents on the response
builder.addHeader(new Header("Accept", "application/xml"));

// Build the Request Body object
GetUserInfo query = new GetUserInfo();
query.setUserId("123");
try {
  // Encode the POJO into a XML Document
  Body body = new XMLConverter<GetUserInfo>(GetUserInfo.class)
              .encode(query, "application/xml");
  builder.setBody(body);
} catch (Exception e) {
  // Catch and display and error to the user
  ...
}
PacktAsyncHTTPClient client = new PacktAsyncHTTPClient();
client.execute(builder.build(), xmlResponseHandler);
```

Once the response is returned from the fake server, the UI will be updated to show the user name, e-mail, and other properties, based on the XML specified on the fake endpoint.

Nothing is mentioned about the error flow; however, I will challenge you to create a fake endpoint that returns an error object to exercise the `onError` callback. The full source code with the error flow is available to download from the Packt Publishing website. Take a look at it to appreciate how error handling is implemented. The error XML document might be something similar to this:

```
<?xml version="1.0"?>
<p:Error
    xmlns:p="https://www.packtpub.com/asynchronous_android">
 <p:ResultCode>1000</p:ResultCode>
 <p:ResultMessage>The LDAP Server is down</p:ResultMessage>
</p:Error>
```

So far, we have covered most common formats (Text, XML, and JSON) used in the industry to exchange data between HTTP clients and servers. Each of these formats has its own strengths; however, for its compactness and simplicity (easy parsing, syntax, and so on), the JSON format has been widely adopted by API designers, electronics manufacturers, and **Software as a Service** (**SaaS**) vendors.

During this process, we will build up a core framework that could be easily extended to support different data exchange formats, such as YAML or binary protocols. Therefore, you might write your own `BodyEncoder`, `BodyDecoder`, and `ResponseHandler` to fit a standard data format or even your own data format.

In this section, we will introduce the reader to a set of timeouts available on the `HttpUrlConnection` used to accommodate network delays on the request execution.

Customizing HTTP timeouts

When `HttpUrlConnection` connects, reads, or writes content over a low bandwidth network (2G, 3G, and so on), the exposure to unpredictable communication delays can not be avoided. Moreover, apart from the mobile network delays, the HTTP servers might introduce significant response delays (server latency) when they are experiencing high volumes of traffic.

Although the default timeout values used by the the `HttpUrlConnection` are long enough to cope with these delays, there are some special use cases where you might want to customize the default values according to your needs. For example, when on the way to the application server, the HTTP request travels through some proxies.

`HttpUrlConnection` offers us two member methods that can be used to change the default timeouts:

```
void setConnectTimeout(int timeoutMillis)
void setReadTimeout(int timeoutMillis)
```

`setConnectTimeout(int)` is able to redefine the maximum time in milliseconds that our client is allowed to wait until the TCP connection to the remote host is established (server is down). `ConnectTimeoutException` will be thrown whenever the connection fails, for example, if the server is down or is not able to respond in time due to lack of resources, so you should be careful and handle this exception cleanly in your code.

When the hostname resolves into multiple addresses, the client will try to connect one after the other and the timeout will be applicable multiple times. If the timeout is set to 0, the connection will be blocked until the TCP timeout expires, which on Android is normally several minutes.

`setReadTimeout(int)` defines the maximum time that our client is allowed to be blocked on the read operation until any available data is allowed to be read. The default value 0 will block the read operation indefinitely until data becomes available, the connection is dropped by the remote peer, or an error occurs on the socket. When the timeout is longer than 0 and no data is available when the timeout expires, a `SocketTimeoutException` will be thrown.

Now that we understand the meaning of each timeout, let's update our `HTTPRequest.Builder` with some new setter methods:

```
public class HTTPRequest {
  ...
  public static class Builder {

    private int mReadTimeout = 0; // Default Value
    private int mConnectTimeout = 0; // Default Value

    public void setConnectTimeout(int connectTimeoutMs) {
      this.mConnectTimeout = connectTimeoutMs;
    }
    public void setReadTimeout(int readTimeoutMs) {
      this.mReadTimeout = readTimeoutMs;
    }
  }
}
```

Finally, we have to update `HTTPAsyncTask` to set the timeouts specified on
the `HTTPRequest`, on the `HttpURLConnection` object used to connect to the
remote server:

```
public class HTTPAsyncTask extends
  AsyncTask<HTTPRequest, Void, Result<HTTPResponse>> {
  @Override
  protected Result<HTTPResponse> doInBackground(
    HTTPRequest... params) {
      conn = (HttpURLConnection) url.openConnection();
      conn.setReadTimeout(request.mReadTimeout);
      conn.setConnectTimeout(request.mConnectTimeout);
      ...
  }
}
```

It's highly recommended that you test your customized timeouts under several
network latency levels and take into account the time that your server could defer
the response for a couple of seconds when it is under load.

A typical network delay could go from 80-120 ms on an LTE mobile network
to 150-550 ms on a GPRS mobile network

When you run your application on the Internet and you have to deal with
sensitive data, such as personal information, payment information, or business
documentation, it is really important to protect your communication channels with a
security layer that hides the exchanged data from an outside attacker or avoids any
spoofing attacks. In the next section, we will expand our high-level client to support
a secure SSL connection channel to the remote server.

Communicating securely over SSL sessions

So far, we have been using plain connections to communicate with a remote HTTP
server. Despite the fact that these kinds of connections might fit your application
requirements when the data exchanged is not sensitive, there are use cases where
we must use a secure channel to send or receive, preventing any third party from
reading or changing the data exchanged on the network.

In order to setup an SSL session with a remote server, our client, with the help of some cryptographic tools, will create a cryptographic communication channel where all the data is encrypted with a symmetric cipher that uses a secret key exchanged during the secure connection handshake. Apart from that, the content received and encrypted with a previously exchanged secret key is validated against other peer public keys to prove that the data is coming and signed from the right source.

During the connection establishment, as part of the SSL handshake, the server has to prove that it holds a private key for a trusted certificate. A trusted certificate is a certificate that is available from our list of trusted **Certificate Authorities** (**CAs**) or it was signed by one of the certificates available from your trusted CAs.

 The Android platform comes out-of-the-box with a list of well-known trusted CAs that help us to assure the identity of most servers on the Internet.

Therefore, when we are contacting to a server with a certificate signed by a well-known CA, the code used before to create an HTTPS connection does not require any changes:

```
URL url = new URL("https://packtpub.com");
con = (HttpsURLConnection) url.openConnection();
```

This code example will create an SSL connection using the default cryptographic cipher suite specified on the Android platform and validate the server against the platform CAs.

Although this can work in most of the cases, it might be necessary to use a specific CA, a list of trusted certificates, or only the safest ciphersuite (TLSv1)i In the cases where the developer has to build their own `SSLContext` and specify their own `TrustManagers` and `KeyManagers` in order to connect successfully to the remote server.

In the next paragraphs we are going to extend our client to use private keys and CAs stored on Java keystores in order to validate and communicate with a server of which the **Certificate authority** (**CA**) is managed by us.

First of all, we will create an `SSLOptions` class where we define the cipher suite that we want to use in our SSL session:

```
public class SSLOptions {

  enum CipherSuite {
    DEFAULT("Default"), // Supported on Android API Level > 9
    SSL("SSL"), // Supported on Android API Level > 9
```

```
      SSLv3("SSLv3"), // Supported on Android API Level > 9
      TLS("TLS"), // Supported on Android API Level > 1
      TLSv1("TLSv1"), // Supported on Android API Level > 1+
      TLSv1_1("TLSv1.1"), // Supported on Android API Level > 16+
      TLSv1_2("TLSv1.2"); // Supported on Android API Level > 16+
   ...
   }
   // Cipher Suite used on the connection
   final CipherSuite cipherSuite;
   final SSLContext sslContext;

   public SSLOptions(Context ctx, Builder builder)
     throws Exception {
     ...
     // Build up our own SSLContext
     sslContext = SSLContext.
     getInstance(cipherSuite.toString());
     // Will use the Android default KeyManager and TrustManager
     sslContext.init(null,null,new SecureRandom());
   }

   public static class Builder {
     private CipherSuite cipherSuite = CipherSuite.DEFAULT;
     ...
     SSLOptions build(Context ctx) throws Exception {
       return new SSLOptions(ctx, this);
     }
   }
 }
}
```

With the preceding code we are able the control the cipher suite used by our SSLContext; however, in order to use our own private key, certificates, and trusted CAs, we will have to initialize the SSLContext with our own TrustManager and KeyManager:

```
   void init(KeyManager[] km, TrustManager[] tm, SecureRandom sr)
```

For simplicity, we will load our KeyManagers and TrustManager from a keystore file stored on the application assets directory. The Java keystore is available on the Packt Publishing website. So, before we go any further, download the asynchronous_ client.ks file from the Packt website with a ready-to-use private key, a certificate, and the custom CA certificate that signed the certificate as the trusted Authority.

> Notice that you can build your own `TrustManager` and
> `KeyManager` custom subclass that can load the private key
> and the certificates from a different source but for simplicity
> we will load them from a file.

Let's take a look at our `asynchronous_client.ks` java keystore file with the help of the keytool application.

On the command line, please run the following command to list the content of the keystore:

```
keytool -list -v -keystore asynchronous_client.ks -storetype BKS
provider org.bouncycastle.jce.provider.BouncyCastleProvider
providerpath bcprov-jdk15on-146.jar
```

```
Alias name: asynchronous_client
Entry type: PrivateKeyEntry
Certificate[1]:
Owner: C=UK,ST=Birmingham,L=Birmingham,O=Packt Publishing,OU=Packt
Publishing,CN=asynchronous_client
Issuer: C=UK,…,CN=packt
Certificate[2]:
Owner: C=UK,…,CN=packt

Alias name: ca
Entry type: trustedCertEntry
Owner: C=UK,…,CN=packt
Issuer: C=UK,…,CN=packt
```

Our keystore file, which will act as the trusted store file and keystore file, has a public and private key named `asynchronous_client` and a trusted CA named ca. The keytool requires the Bouncy Castle Provider JAR to read the the file contents, so before, please download the file from the Packt website.

Notice that since we have C=UK, ST=Birmingham, L=Birmingham, O=Packt Publishing, and CN=packt as a trusted CA, we will allow our HTTP to connect with SSL endpoints that present a certificate signed by this authority or a certificate where all intermediate certificates are trustworthy (a trusted certificate chain).

> Every Android device comes with a pre-installed list of
> trusted certificates that can be used to authenticate a secure
> remote peer.

Now that we know the details about our keystore and truststore, let's update our
SSL options to load the `KeyManager` and `TrustManager` from the `asynchronous_
client.ks`:

```
public class SSLOptions {
   final CipherSuite cipherSuite;
   final SSLContext sslContext;
   private final  String keyStore;
   private final String keyStorePassword;
   private final String trustStore;
   private final String trustStorePassword;
   ...

   public SSLOptions(Context ctx, Builder builder)
     throws Exception {
     ...
     sslContext = initSSLContext(ctx);
   }
   // Initialize the SSLContect with loaded
   private SSLContext initSSLContext(Context ctx)
     throws Exception {

     KeyManagerFactory kmf = getKeyManagerFactory(ctx);
     TrustManagerFactory tmf = getTrustManagerFactory(ctx);
     // Use the cipher suite defined SSL, SSLv3 , TLS, TLSv1,
     SSLContext result = SSLContext.getInstance(
                         cipherSuite.toString());

     result.init( kmf != null ? kmf.getKeyManagers() : null ,
                  tmf != null ? tmf.getTrustManagers() : null,
                  new SecureRandom());
     return result;
   }
}
```

Notice that we initialize SSLContext using the Keymanager list and `TrustManager`
list returned by `KeyManagerFactory` and `TrustManagerFactory` respectively.
Hence, the next step is to write the code member method to acquire our factories.
So, let's start with the `getKeyManagerFactory`:

```
KeyManagerFactory getKeyManagerFactory(Context ctx)
   throws Exception {
   KeyManagerFactory kmf = null;
   // Initialize Key store
```

```
    if ( keyStore != null ) {
      // Load the file keystore from the assets directory
      InputStream keyStoreIs = ctx.getResources().
                                  getAssets().open(keyStore);
      String algorithm = KeyManagerFactory.getDefaultAlgorithm();
      kmf = KeyManagerFactory.getInstance(algorithm);

      // Create BouncyCastle Key Store
      KeyStore ks = KeyStore.getInstance("BKS");

      // Load the Keymanagers available on the file using
      // a password
      ks.load(keyStoreIs, keyStorePassword.toCharArray());
      kmf.init(ks, keyStorePassword.toCharArray());
    }
    return kmf;
  }
```

The previous code will load up a public and private key from a BCS keystore that we previously prepared. So, all that remains is the getTrustManagerFactory function used to load our trusted CA:

```
TrustManagerFactory getTrustManagerFactory(Context ctx)
  throws Exception {

  TrustManagerFactory tmf = null;

  if ( trustStore != null) {
    InputStream keyStoreIs = ctx.getResources().
                                getAssets().open(trustStore);
    String algorithm = TrustManagerFactory.getDefaultAlgorithm();
    tmf = TrustManagerFactory.getInstance(algorithm);
    KeyStore ts = KeyStore.getInstance("BKS");
    ts.load(keyStoreIs, trustStorePassword.toCharArray());
    tmf.init(ts);
  }
  return tmf;
}
```

Now that we have the `SSLOptions` class to initialize our `SSLContext`, let's move on to the `HTTPRequest` and update our `Builder` to store the `SSLOptions`:

```
public class HTTPRequest {

  final SSLOptions mSSLOptions;

  private HTTPRequest(Builder builder) {
    this.mSSLOptions = builder.mSSLOptions;
  }

  public static class Builder {
    ...
    private SSLOptions mSSLOptions = null;

    public Builder setSSLOptions(SSLOptions options) {
      this.mSSLOptions = options;
      return this;
    }
  }
  ...
}
```

Finally, we are ready to update our `HTTPAsyncTask` to use our `SSLOptions` object in order to customize our SSL client endpoint. Hence, we will be able to verify the identity of our server that has a certificate signed by our own CA (`C=UK`, `ST=Birmingham`, `L=Birmingham`, `O=Packt Publishing`, `CN=packt`) and vice-versa:

```
@Override
protected Result<HTTPResponse>
doInBackground(HTTPRequest... params) {
  // Retrieve the request URL from the request object
  URL url = new URL(request.mUrl);
  // Opens up the connection to the remote pper
  conn = initConnection(request, url);
  ...
}

HttpURLConnection
initConnection( HTTPRequest request, URL url) throws IOException {

  HttpURLConnection genCon = (HttpURLConnection) url.
                            openConnection();

  if ( url.getProtocol().equals("https") ) {
```

```
    HttpsURLConnection con = (HttpsURLConnection) genCon;
    // Apply our SSL Options to the connection
    if ( request.mSSLOptions != null ) {
      applySSLContext(request, con);
    }
  }
  return result;
}
void
applySSLContext(HTTPRequest request, HttpsURLConnection con) {
  // Initialize the SSL Session with your own
  // keystore and truststore
  if ( request.mSSLOptions != null ) {
    SSLContext ctx = request.mSSLOptions.sslContext;
    con.setSSLSocketFactory(ctx.getSocketFactory());
    con.setHostnameVerifier(new AcceptAllHostNameVerifier());
  }
}
```

Notice that our implementation does not perform hostname verification, because the server CN might not match the server hostname used to contact the HTTP server.

However, if you want to be stricter about this, change the `setHostnameVerifier` line to use the default behavior, implement your own `HostnameVerifier`, or use the hostname verifiers available on the Android SDK, such as the Apache `X509HostnameVerifier` that checks whether the supplied hostname matches any of the supplied certificate CNs or Subject-Alts.

Finally, let's illustrate how to use our client to connect to a server that possesses a certificate with the following certificate chain:

```
// Server Certificate
Certificate[1]:
Owner: CN=asynchronous_server, OU=Packt Publishing, O=Packt
Publishing, L=Birmingham, ST=Birmingham, C=UK
Issuer: CN=packt, ..., C=UK

// CA Certificate
Certificate[2]:
Owner: CN=packt, OU=Packt Publishing, O=Packt Publishing,
L=Birmingham, ST=Birmingham, C=UK
Issuer: CN=packt, …, C=UK
```

The following code shows how to establish an SSL session with a URL where the protocol is `https`:

```
// Set the HTTP Verb to GET
builder.setVerb(HTTPRequest.Verb.GET);
// Sets location of the remote resource
builder.setUrl("https://<server_hostname>:<port>/hello_ssl");
builder.addHeader(new Header("Accept", "text/plain"));
SSLOptions.Builder sslBuilder = new SSLOptions.Builder();

// TLS Cipher Suite using the  asynchronous_client.ks
// as the truststore file and keystore file
sslBuilder.setKeyStore("asynchronous_client.ks", "123qwe")
        .setTrustStore("asynchronous_client.ks", "123qwe")
        .setCipherSuite(SSLOptions.CipherSuite.TLS);

// The Application context is required to load
// the keystore from the assets
builder.setSSLOptions(sslBuilder.build(getApplication()));

HTTPRequest request = builder.build();

PacktAsyncHTTPClient client = new PacktAsyncHTTPClient();
client.execute(request, textResponseHandler);
```

If the SSL handshake between the peers finishes with success, the server verifies our identity and our client verifies the server's identity. As a result, a cryptographic channel is opened between both entities keeping the data hidden from third-party intruders.

Summary

In this chapter, we explored in detail the `HttpUrlConnection` Android HTTP client and we built a basic and expandable asynchronous client to interact with HTTP web APIs.

In the first section, we exposed the main differences between the `HttpUrlConnection` client and the deprecated Apache HTTP client available on pre-Marshmallow SDKs.

Next, we wrote the core classes and callback interfaces for our asynchronous client and we expanded our high-level client to interact with JSON and Web APIs. Additionally, we built the code to convert from our Java models to a JSON or an XML document.

Later, we learned how to configure the HTTP timeouts and to set up secure communications that are able to use our own signed certificates, keys, and CAs. In our example, we created and prepared an SSL context to be used to establish a secure channel based on a prepared Java secure keystore.

In the next chapter, we will introduce and explore the **JNI (Java Native Interface)** to create asynchronous tasks in native code (C/C++). This interface is able to interact with compiled code that runs directly on the device's CPU.

9
Asynchronous Work on the Native Layer

In previous chapters, we have been using Java thread APIs and concurrent primitives delivered by the Android SDK to build our asynchronous constructs. A Java thread, an independent line of execution in our application, is automatically attached to the Android virtual machine and is bound to one native thread on the system. In previous chapter examples, we executed Java compiled bytecode on the JVM and used Java synchronization and concurrent primitives to solve correctness and liveness issues.

In this chapter, we will make use of the Java Native Interface (JNI) to execute code written in C/C++ and compile it to native code. The native code, which runs directly on the hardware and makes use of the native CPU **Application Binary Interface** (**ABI**), generally runs faster than the bytecode due to optimizations made by the compilers, or optimizations introduced by developers with the use of specific ABI techniques. Hence, when we perform intensive computing operations on the device this could be the way to go to obtain a performance boost on your application and to reduce the power consumption.

With this in mind, we will learn how to use the JNI interface to execute concurrent tasks on native code (C/C++), interact with Java code from the native layer, and update the UI from native code.

Later, we will learn how to create native threads and use synchronization primitives such as `mutex` and `condition` to avoid any memory consistency problems that could come up when the device multiple line of executions in parallel and they share the same memory segments.

To finish, we will start a group of threads to run background work on the native layer that dispatches the result to the UI.

In this chapter, we will cover:

- Introduction to JNI
- Android NDK
- Calling C functions from Java code
- Calling C++ member/static functions from Java code
- Accessing Java objects from native code
- Executing native background work on Java threads
- Executing asynchronous work on a native thread
- Interacting with a Java monitor from native code
- Handling Java exceptions on the native layer

Introduction to JNI

JNI is an interface that allows the execution of native code, written on C, C++, or Assembly, from the **Java Virtual Machine (JVM)**. The interface strictly defines the way that any JNI implementation should act to manage and control the interactions between Java code and the machine code. Moreover, the machine code is able to interact with the JVM and create objects, execute member functions, modify the member variables and handle Java exceptions.

The JNI, which allows you to execute machine code along with your Java code, is typically used to:

- Accelerate some critical portions of your application. Since the code runs directly on the hardware, it could make use of specific instruction sets to improve the execution:
    - Example: The use of SIMD instructions to accelerate audio or video floating-point operations.

- Integrate existing C/C++ libraries in to your Android application. You can port any legacy code or library written to the Android platform and use it on your Android application:
    - Example: The integration of open source libraries such as `opencv`, `libgdx`, and `box2d` into your application runtime.

- To use a platform dependent feature that is not accessible from the Java API:
    - Example: Low-level OS features such as poll and semaphores or native APIS such as OpenGL, OpenSL ES, or OpenMAX AL.

Notice that adding C/C++ with JNI to your project does not come free and it typically adds complexity to your project, making it harder to debug, build, and test. Therefore, you must evaluate the cost/benefit before you make the decision to use it in your application.

Android NDK (Native Development Kit)

To help with the building and construction of Android applications that require a dynamic collaboration between the Java layer and the native layer, a development kit named Android NDK is supplied on the Android Developer website (`http://developer.android.com/ndk/index.html`).

The Android NDK, the Android toolset that allows you to compile your code written in C/C++ to the several ABIs supported by Android, is also able to compile pre-existing libraries written in C or C++ to the Android platform.

Before we move on in more detail, you should install the NDK package in your development platform, following the instructions defined on `http://developer.android.com/ndk/downloads`.

At the time of writing, the latest version of NDK is 10e, so we will base our code and examples on this version for the rest of this chapter.

The Java source code that you will write in your application, compiled by Android SDK, generates Android bytecode that will be interpreted by the Android JVM on any Android device.

With your source code written in C or C++, the NDK compiler will convert it to CPU code with different instruction sets, hardware features, calling conventions, and storing conventions. Each kind of CPU architecture has its own ABI that defines how the machine code should be arranged to interact with CPU hardware.

The NDK toolset comes with tools that abstract these hardware traits and generates machine code to the following ABIs: armeabi, armeabi-v7a, arm64-v8a, x86, x86_64, mips, and mips64.

Most of the time you want to support as many devices as possible, so by default, the NDK will generate code for all the CPU architectures and instruction sets supported.

Calling C functions from Java code

The powerful JNI interface, as referred to before, is able to manage interaction in both directions, from Java to C and from C to Java.

A regular Java class declaring a method with the keyword `native` declares that the method behavior is implemented in native code. Like a regular Java method, the JNI `native` method is able to receive Java objects or primitive types as arguments and return primitive types and objects.

Let's see how a `native` method definition will look like in a Java class:

```
public class MyNativeActivity extends Activity {

  @Override
  protected void onCreate(Bundle savedInstanceState) {
    ...
    cTv.setText(isPrime(2) ? "true" : "false");
  }
  ...
  private native boolean isPrime(int number );
}
```

The preceding activity will call the native code to check whether a number is prime or not and print the result on the UI.

Notice that our function receives a primitive as an argument and return a primitive `boolean` as a result and does not have any body, like an abstract function.

With the member function declared as native, we inform the compiler that this function is going to be implemented in C/C++, in a native library that gets loaded dynamically at runtime.

With the member function now declared as native on the Java side, let's use `javah` to declare and implement our native method in the native code.

A `javah` is able to help the developer to generate native method prototypes with name conventions used by the JNI interface, the SDK becomes a handy tool that generates a header file for all your class native methods.

To use it, please go to your project directory, create a `jni` directory, and run the next `javah` to generate the header file for your native function. In Android Studio IDE, open a terminal window and go to the `src/main` directory:

```
javah  -d jni -classpath <sdk_direcory>/android.jar:../../build/
intermediates/classes/debug/  com.packpublishing.asynchronousandroid.
chapter9.MyNativeActivity
```

If everything goes as expected, the file `com_..._chapter9_MyNativeActivity.h` will be generated with our `native` method declaration:

```
JNIEXPORT jboolean JNICALL Java_com_packpublishing_
asynchronousandroid_chapter9_MyNativeActivity_isPrime
  (JNIEnv *, jobject, jint);
```

The `native` method will receive a `JNIEnv*` pointer to the JVM environment, a `jobject` reference to the actual Java object instance that invoked the method, and an integer argument.

The previous method declared in the following JNI specification, it should be declared and implemented in your code and loaded on the runtime over a shared library.

Now that we have the method declared, let's create a `source` file under `jni` called `c_functions.c`, with the `native` method implementation for our `isPrime` function:

```
#include "com_packpublishing_asynchronousandroid_chapter9_
MyNativeActivity.h"

#ifdef __cplusplus
extern "C" {
#endif

jboolean  Java_com_packpublishing_asynchronousandroid_chapter9_
MyNativeActivity_isPrime( JNIEnv *env, jobject obj, jint number) {
    int c;
    for (c = 2; c < number ; c++) {
        if (number % c == 0)
            return JNI_FALSE;
    }
    return JNI_TRUE;
}
#ifdef __cplusplus
}
#endif
```

When `MyNativeActivity.isPrime` is called, the JNI interface transparently forwards the processing to the native code function, passing a native integer primitive (`jint`). The Android JNI implementation automatically converts the Java type int value to a native type (`jint`), executes the native function, and at the end returns `jboolean` that is automatically converted by the JNI interface to a Java primitive, `boolean`.

The following table shows how Java types are mapped to native types:

Java Type	Native Type	Description
boolean	Jboolean	Unsigned 8 bits
byte	Jbyte	Signed 8 bits
char	jchar	Unsigned 16 bits
short	jshort	Signed 16 bits
int	jint	Signed 32 bits
long long	jlong	Signed 64 bits
float	jfloat	Floating Number 32 bit
double	jdouble	Floating Number 64 bit
Object	jobject	Any Java Object
Class	class	Class Object
String	jstring	String objects
void	void	

Although we have the native function declared and implemented in our source file, the JVM will not find the method until we have loaded the shared library that contains our native function. First, we will define the ndk folder in our project's root folder local.properties file:

```
ndk.dir=<Path to downloaded NDK package>/android-ndk-r10e
```

Next, in our build.gradle module configuration we will define the shared library name under the ndk configuration section:

```
apply plugin: 'com.android.library'

android {
    defaultConfig {
        minSdkVersion 9
      ...
        ndk { moduleName "mylib" }
    }
}
```

Finally, Android Studio is able to `compile c_functions.c` and generate a shared library with the name `mylib` for all the ABIs supported in the build directory:

```
├── lib
│   ├── arm64-v8a
│   │   └── libmylib.so
│   ├── armeabi
│   │   └── libmylib.so
│   ├── armeabi-v7a
│   │   └── libmylib.so
│   ├── mips
│   │   └── libmylib.so
│   ├── mips64
│   │   └── libmylib.so
│   ├── x86
│   │   └── libmylib.so
│   └── x86_64
│       └── libmylib.so
```

These libraries are going to be packed in a universal `apk` file ready to be loaded by our Android application.

All that remains is to load the library on our runtime before we try to use it in our code. To load shared libraries on the JVM runtime, the `java.lang.System` class provides a `static` method to load a shared library and its dependencies, so before we use it on our class we will add a static section to our `Activity` class to load the library as soon as the class loader loads our class:

```
public class MyNativeActivity extends Activity {
    ...
    static {
        System.loadLibrary("mylib");
    }
}
```

When the library is required, the `System` class automatically detects the ABI where the device is running and loads the required platform dependent library. Therefore, if you are running on an x86 device, `x86/libmylib.so` is going to be loaded.

Calling C++ functions from native code

So far, we have called a C function implemented in the c_functions.c source, so, in the next section, we will show you how to call a C++ member class.

First, we will add the isPrimeCPlusPlus native method to MyNativeActivty that returns String as a result. Let's see how the native function declaration will look:

```java
public class MyNativeActivity extends Activity {

    @Override
    protected void onCreate(Bundle savedInstanceState) {
        ...
      TextView cPlusTv = (TextView)
          findViewById(R.id.helloFromCPlusPlus);
      cPlusTv.setText(isPrimeCPlusPlus(4));
    }

    public native String isPrimeCPlusPlus(int number);
}
```

Running the javah tool against the new MyNativeActivity class definition will generate a new function declaration with the following signature:

```
JNIEXPORT jstring JNICALL Java_com_packpublishing_asynchronousandroid_
chapter9_MyNativeActivity_isPrimeCPlusPlus(JNIEnv *, jobject, jint);
```

Next, we are going to implement the prime function, as a class static function, on a C++ source file with the name mylib.cpp:

```cpp
#include "com_packpublishing_asynchronousandroid_chapter9_
MyNativeActivity.h"

class Math {
  public:
  static int isPrime(int number) { ...// Elided for brevity}
};

#ifdef __cplusplus
extern "C" {
#endif

jstring  Java_com_packpublishing_asynchronousandroid_chapter9_
MyNativeActivity_isPrimeCPlusPlus
```

```
(JNIEnv * env, jobject obj, jint number) {

   return (env)->NewStringUTF(
      Math::isPrime(number) ? "Is Prime" : "Is not Prime");
}


#ifdef __cplusplus
}
#endif
```

If you build your project in Android Studio, the `mylib.cpp` source file will be detected and the new function and class will be added to the `libmylib.so` shared library file.

Once we run the application, the C++ system default library will be loaded with a minimal system C++ runtime. The default C++ runtime does not provide the C++ standard library, exception support, and **RunTime Type Information** (**RTTI**). Therefore, if you want to make use of C++ standard library string classes, containers, streams, and general algorithms, you will have to explicitly load the C++ runtime required before you load your library. For a complete and up to date comparison of the C++ runtime available on Android, please check C++ Runtimes on the Android Developer website.

If we want to use a different C++ runtime than the system runtime, we must explicitly set the runtime in your module's `build.gradle` file:

```
ndk {
  moduleName "mylib"
  stl "c++_shared"
}
```

Moreover, we must load the non-default C++ runtime library before we load our library or any library that depends on it:

```
public class MyNativeActivity extends Activity {
  static {
    System.loadLibrary("c++_shared");
    System.loadLibrary("mylib");
  }
}
```

Since `c++_shared` provides a complete STL library implementation, from now on we will use this runtime as the base C++ runtime for our code examples.

Great! So far, we have learned how to interact with native methods using the JNI interface, so our next step is to learn how to access Java objects from native code.

Accessing Java objects from native code

When we call a native function, the C or C++ function receives a JNIEnv pointer to a table of JNI methods used to interact with JVM Runtime. The JNIEnv pointer provides us with a set of primitives ready to find a Java class definition, set or get Java object field values, call static or member Java object functions, create Java objects, interact with Java monitors, or deal with exceptions.

Our next example will count the number of words on an EditText UI Widget on a native function and update a TextView text with count results from the native code. Therefore, we will learn how to use JNIEnv to access a member Java object field and how to call a Java object method (TextView.setText) using the JNIEnv interface.

Let's start by defining our native function and invoke it every time the EditField content changes:

```
public class MyNativeActivity extends Activity {

    protected EditText inputTextEt = null;
    protected TextView charCountTv = null;

    @Override
    protected void onCreate(Bundle savedInstanceState) {

        // Reference stored as member fields for native access
        inputTextEt = (EditText) findViewById(R.id.inputText);
        charCountTv = (TextView) findViewById(R.id.charCount);

        // Called every time the code changes
        inputTextEt.addTextChangedListener(new TextWatcher() {
            @Override
            public void onTextChanged(CharSequence s, int start,
                                      int before, int count) {
                updateWordCounter(s.toString());
            }
            ...
        });
    }
    // Native function that calculates the number of words
    // in a string
    private native void updateWordCounter(String s);
}
```

Notice that a new function is added to `Activity` so make sure you run `javah` to generate the new native function declaration.

Next, we will define the JNI native function that counts the number of words for a string:

```
class Util {
  public:
  static int countWords(const std::string &strString) {

    ...

  };
}


Void Java_com_packpublishing_asynchronousandroid_chapter9_
MyNativeActivity_updateWordCounter(JNIEnv *env, jobject obj, jstring
text) {

    std::string content(env->GetStringUTFChars(text, 0));

    size_t word_cnt= Util::countWords(content);

    // Update the TexView with word_cnt integer


}
```

We left the native implementation because we will implement it on a step-by-step basis. As the first step, we will get the `TextView` object instance, used to present the number of words on the UI text input, from the `charCountTv` object field.

To access a Java object field or method, a `jmethodID` or `jfieldID` is always required:

```
jmethodID   GetMethodID(JNIEnv* env, jclass clazz,
                   const char*name,
                   const char* methodSignature);


jfieldID    GetFieldID(JNIEnv*, jclass clazz,
                   const char*name,
                   const char* fieldTypeCode);
```

In order to construct the `methodSignature` or the `fieldTypeCode` (TC), we have to map the Java types to type codes using the following table:

Java Type	Type Code (TC)
`boolean`	Z
`Byte`	B
`Char`	C
`double`	D
`float`	F
`Int`	I
`Long`	J
`short`	S
`Object`	L<package>;
`Void`	V

When we convert an array, always prefix the type code with the `[` character.

To create a `jfieldID` we need a single type code. However, to construct the method signature we use the following format:

```
(<Argument 1 TC ><Argument N TC>) <Return TC>
```

Let's see how we obtain the `charCountTv` `TextView` object in the native code using the instructions explained below:

```
// 1. Obtain a reference to the MyNativeActivity class definiton
jclass activityClass = env->GetObjectClass(obj);

// 2. Get the fieldId for the charCountTv TextView
    jfieldID charCountFId = env->GetFieldID(activityClass,
"charCountTv", "Landroid/widget/TextView;");

// 3. Retrieve the object using the object and the jfieldID

jobject tvObj = env->GetObjectField(obj,charCountFId);
```

Once we have the `TextView` reference, we can invoke the `setText(CharSequence)` instance method to publish the number of words found. To invoke a Java method we will make use of the JNI function `CallVoidMethod` with a `jmethodId` created from the method signature:

```
void CallVoidMethod(JNIEnv *env, jclass clazz,
                    jmethodID methodID, ...);
```

Let's see how the native code that updates the `TextView` `charCountTv` with the number of words will look:

```
// 1. Get the TextView class definition
jclass textViewClass = env->GetObjectClass(tvObj);

// 2. Get the methodId for the TextView.setText function
jmethodID setTextMId = env->GetMethodID(
        textViewClass, "setText", "(Ljava/lang/CharSequence;)V");

// 3. Invoke the SetText instance function
    env->CallVoidMethod(
        tvObj,setTextMId,env->NewStringUTF(wordCountStr);
```

To invoke `static` methods and methods with different kind of result types, the JNI interface provides us with a set of functions with the following signatures:

```
// To invoke a Class static method that returns a Java Type
<NativeType> CallStatic<Type>Method(
    JNIEnv *env, jobject obj, jmethodID methodID, ...);

// To invoke a method that returns a Java <Type>
<NativeType> Call<Type>Method(
    JNIEnv *env, jobject obj, jmethodID methodID, ...);

// To invoke a method that returns a Java <Type[]>
<NativeArrayType> Call<Type>MethodA(
    JNIEnv *env, jobject obj, jmethodID methodID, ...);
```

Now that we have the basic knowledge about how to call native functions with the JNI interface, we are ready to start using the JNI to execute asynchronous work on native code.

Executing native background work on Java threads

In previous sections, we used the JNI interface to execute native functions on the main thread. Since they run on the main thread, the functions were able to update the UI, access the `Activity` instance fields, and or update any UI widget directly.

However, as we discussed before, for long computing or intensive tasks we have to execute them on the background thread.

In previous sections, we learned how to use the `AsyncTask, Loader, Handler,` and Remote Services to execute work on background threads that don't reduce the UI responsiveness or interfere with UI rendering.

In any of these Android specific constructs, the background thread is already attached to the JVM. Hence, the background thread already possesses access to a ready to use JNI environment.

In our next example, we will make use of the `Loader` construct and build `AsyncTaskLoader,` that loads an image on the background, converts the image to gray scale in native code, and publishes the result on the UI screen.

First, we will detail how the `Loader` Java class definition will look before we start to dig into the native function details:

```java
public class GrayImageLoader extends AsyncTaskLoader<Result<Bitmap>> {

  final String fileName;
  Bitmap grayImage;

  public ToGrayImageLoader(Context ctx, String fileName) {
    super(ctx);
    this.fileName = fileName;
  }

  @Override
  public Result<Bitmap> loadInBackground() {
    Result<Bitmap> result = new Result<Bitmap>();
    try {
      BitmapFactory.Options options = new BitmapFactory.Options();
      options.inPreferredConfig = Bitmap.Config.ARGB_8888;

      // Build a RGBA 8888 Bitmap to represent the image
      Bitmap b = BitmapFactory.decodeFile(this.fileName, options);

      // Convert the Image to Gray scale on Native code
      Bitmap originalImage = BitmapFactory.decodeStream(
        getContext().getAssets().open(fileName));

      // Fill the result with the Gray Image
      result.obj = convertImageToGray(originalImage);
    } catch (Exception e) {
      result.error = e;
    }
```

```
    return result;
}

private native Bitmap convertImageToGray(Bitmap original);
...
}
```

Notice that our `Loader` will load a `Bitmap` image wrapped in a generic `Result` class, as we did in previous sections. When any exception happens on the Java or Native code, `Result.error` is filled, making the `Loader` consumer able to detect an error and react accordingly.

Our loader will receive as an argument the image filename to load from the assets and will decode the image to a `Bitmap` object in the `ARGB_8888` format and return an image in grayscale

When the native function executes in the background thread without errors, the `Result<Bitmap>` object is delivered to the `Loader` consumer in the UI Thread to be updated to the device screen.

Executing `javah` against our new `AsynTaskLoader` class should generate the `com_packpublishing_asynchronousandroid_chapter9_ToGrayImageLoader.h` header file with the following function signature:

```
JNIEXPORT jobject JNICALL Java_com_packpublishing_asynchronousandroid_
chapter9_ToGrayImageLoader_convertImageToGray(JNIEnv * env, jobject
loader, jobject bitmap);
```

To process `Bitmap` objects on the native layer, the `jnigraphics` shared library is required. Therefore, let's update our `gradle` build configuration to link our library with the `jnigraphics` shared library:

```
ndk {
    moduleName "mylib"
    stl "stlport_shared"
    ldLibs "jnigraphics", "log"
}
```

Linking our library `mylib` against `jnigraphics` will force the dynamic loader to load the `jnigraphics` library every time our library is loaded by `System.loadLibrary`. Beyond that, the `gradle` system will pack the `jnigraphics` shared library for the several ABIs required in the **application package file (APK)**.

Now that we have the method defined in the header, it is time to implement the native function that converts the original `Bitmap` to a grayscale `Bitmap`.

First, let's create the source file image.cpp that includes the jni method definition and the required jnigraphics header file:

```
#include "com_packpublishing_asynchronousandroid_chapter9_
ToGrayImageLoader.h"
#include <android/bitmap.h>
```

Next, we will implement the function that converts the original pixels to gray pixels:

```
jobject Java_com_packpublishing_asynchronousandroid_chapter9_
ToGrayImageLoader_convertImageToGray(JNIEnv * env, jobject obj,
jobject bitmap) {

    AndroidBitmapInfo info; // Image Information
    void * pixels; // Pixel Matrix
    int ret; // Jni Graphics operation result code

     // Reads the Image width, height, format,...
    if ( (ret = AndroidBitmap_getInfo(env, bitmap, & info)) < 0) {
       jclass clazz = env->FindClass("java/lang/RuntimeException");
       env->ThrowNew(clazz, "Failed to get bitmap info");
       return 0;
    }
    // Loads the bitmap pixel matrix on pixels pointer
    if ((ret = AndroidBitmap_lockPixels(env,bitmap,(void **)& pixels)) <
 0) {
       // Exception Generation Elided for brevity
    }
    // Convert each pixel to gray
    ...
    AndroidBitmap_unlockPixels(env, bitmap);
    return bitmap;
}
```

With the help of the jnigraphics library, we can read the image information using AndroidBitmap_getInfo and if everything goes well, the image info will be stored on the local variable info for further use.

However, if `AndroidBitmap_getInfo` fails we will throw an exception in JVM and return immediately from the native function because we call `return`. Under a normal situation, if we throw an exception in the JVM with `ThrowNew`, the native function does not stop and transfers control to the exception handler. Therefore, if an exception is thrown during a native code call, when the function returns, the JNI interface will detect it and transfer the execution to the exception handler.

In our example, we generate a `RuntimeException` with the `jclass` obtained from the `Findclass` JNI function.

When we finish the bitmap processing, we unlock the pixels through `AndroidBitmap_unlockPixels` and we return the `Bitmap` `jobject` to the `loadInBackground` function that originally invoked the native method from the background thread.

As you already know, the processed Bitmap will be delivered by the `AsyncTaskLoader` in the UIThread, and it could be used to update an `ImageView` or other kind of UI Widget that presents an image on the screen. Let's see how a `LoaderCallback.onLoadFinished` callback might look:

```
@Override
public void onLoadFinished(Loader<Result<Bitmap>> loader,
Result<Bitmap> data) {
    if ( data.obj != null ) {
        ImageView iv = (ImageView)findViewById(R.id.grayImage);
        iv.setImageBitmap(data.obj);
    } else {
        Log.e("<TAG>", data.error.getMessage(), data.error);
    }
}
```

In this simple example, we were able to execute asynchronous work in machine code with `AsyncTaskLoader` help, although a similar procedure could have been done with an `AsyncTask` subclass, a normal thread, or even a `HandlerThread`. These kind of Android construct use Java background threads managed by Android JVM, therefore, it is not required to explicitly attach these threads to JVM since they are part of the JVM system and have their own `JNIEnv`.

In the next chapter, we are going to learn how to create pure native threads and use them to execute background work for our Android application in a consistent and reliable way.

Executing asynchronous work on a native thread

The Android NDK is bundled with the POSIX thread C API that provides an API to create and destroy native threads, native mutual exclusion synchronization primitives, named mutexes, and condition variables, that like Java monitors, allow threads to wait until a change in a resource happens. Apart from this global API, the developer also has access to a higher level C++11 thread API available on `clang` and `gnu_stl` C++ Runtimes.

Since both of these frameworks offer the same kind of concurrent functionalities we will use C++11 thread framework for its simplicity and similarity with the Java Thread API.

First, let's update our `ndk build.gradle` to use the clang C++ Runtime that supports the thread API that we are going to use in our following code examples:

```
ndk {
    moduleName "mylib"
    stl "c++_shared"
    cppFlags.add("-frtti")
    cppFlags.add("-exceptions)
}
```

Attaching and detaching native threads from JVM

In order to interact with our JVM and execute background work concurrently for us, the native threads should be attached to the current virtual machine and build its own `JNIEnv`.

The thread `JNIEnv` is tied to a specific native thread and cannot be shared with other threads since it manages its own references and local thread environment.

To present this to you in a more practical way, in the next few paragraphs, we will build a code example that creates JVM attached native threads that execute work in the background and interact with the UI thread, publishing a `keep-alive` message using a well known Android handler construct.

To attach any thread to the JVM, we need to access the global virtual machine structure, `JavaVM`:

```
jint AttachCurrentThread(JavaVM *vm, void **p_env, void *thr_args)
```

A good way to get the JVM structures to retrieve from `JNI_OnLoad`, a function that is automatically called on our library by the JavaVM when our library gets loaded. When the callback is called by the JNI interface, we will save the JavaVM reference for future use:

```
// Java VM Global Pointer
static JavaVM* gVm = NULL;
jint JNI_OnLoad (JavaVM* vm, void* reserved) {
    gVm = vm;
    return JNI_VERSION_1_4;
}
```

With the JVM global pointer ready to be used, we are able to attach any native thread to the application JVM and start interacting with the `JNIEnv`.

As a starting point, we will create a high level C++ class that automatically attaches to the JVM, and detaches from the JVM when the instance has been destroyed. This class will be used as the base class in our thread examples, providing a common abstract interface for native thread creation.

Let's see how the `JavaThread` class definition will look:

```
#include <thread> // including the C++11 Thread Header
#include <jni.h>  // JNI Header
class JavaThread: public std::thread {
public:
  JavaThread();
  Void join(); // Wait for the thread to finish
  void entryPoint();
  void start();
  void stop();
protected:
    // Method that subclass should implement to define
    // the unit of work
    virtual void run() = 0;
    virtual void onDetach() {};JNIEnv* threadEnv = NULL; // Thread
specific JNI Environment
    std::thread thread_; // C++11 Thread
    // is Thread attached to JVM
bool isStarted = false;
    std::condition_variable startCond;
    std::mutex startMutex;
    volatile bool shouldStop = false;
    std::condition_variable stopCond;
    std::mutex stopMutex;
};
```

In this class header, we subclass the `JavaThread` from the original C++ thread class defined and we define the abstract method `run`. Any worker thread can subclass `JavaThread`, providing its own implementation of the `run` method. Additionally, the protected thread specific to the JNI interface environment is stored in `threadEnv` for future use by the thread subclasses.

Beyond that, we will introduce you to the C++ synchronization primitives, available from the thread header. `std:mutex` is a mutual exclusive primitive that only allows one thread at a time to enter a protected critical scope. If a thread is executing the critical code, another thread that tries to enter the critical section will block the execution until the thread executing the critical section releases the lock. Here is a simple example:

```
// Thread waits for his turn
mutex.lock();
...// Only one thread enters on this section
mutex.unlock();
```

The same behavior would have been achieved in Java by using the synchronized word in a Java block or a synchronized block.

The condition concurrent primitive, like a Java monitor, can be used to block a thread or a group of threads execution until another thread modifies a shared information and sends a signal to notify the waiting threads.

Now that we know what these C++ concurrency primitives are used for, let's implement the `JavaThread` that automatically attaches and detaches itself to and from JVM.

First of all, we will start the background native thread in the native `start()` by passing the `entryPoint` functions as the runtime function for the thread:

```
void JavaThread::start() {
    thread_ = std::thread(&JavaThread::entryPoint, this);
    std::unique_lock<std::mutex> lck(startMutex);
    // wait until the Thread is attached to JVM
    while (!isStarted) startCond.wait(lck);
}
```

As soon as `std::thread` creates the thread in the system it will call the `entrypoint` function in our object to initialize the JNI environment.

In the meantime, we will block the calling thread until the new thread attaches to JVM and sends a signal to the `startCond` condition variable. Next, when `std::thread` initializes the new thread in the operating system, it changes the execution control to the member function specified in the constructor, `JavaThread::entryPoint`. In this function, we will attach the native thread to the JVM, dispatching the execution to the subclass `run()` method.

Let's see how we might implement the `entryPoint` function:

```
void JavaThread::entryPoint() {

  // Attach current thread to Java virtual machine
  // and obrain JNIEnv interface pointer
  {
    // Acquires the start Mutex to access the conditional variable
    std::unique_lock<std::mutex> lck(startMutex);
    // Ataches the current thread to the JVM
    // and caches the JNIEnv
    if ( gVm->AttachCurrentThread(&threadEnv, NULL) != 0) {
      ..// Handle the error
    }
    isStarted = true;  // Changes the shared variable
    startCond.notify_all(); // Notify the thread constructor
  }
  onAttach();
  try {
    // Run the subclass method
    run();
  } catch (...) {
    // Detach current thread when an exception happens
    onDetach();
    gVm->DetachCurrentThread();
    throw;
  }
  // Detach current thread from Java virtual machine
  onDetach();
  gVm->DetachCurrentThread();
}
```

Notice that the thread is detached from the JVM even when a runtime exception is thrown during the `run` execution. When the thread is detached from the JVM, all the thread monitors are released and all the Java threads waiting for this thread are notified.

For the stopping mechanism, we will make use of a `boolean` variable and `condition` variable to notify that the `shouldStop` condition has changed. Later on, our `JavaThread` subclass will take advantage of this mechanism to stop the `run()` execution.

Let's see how the `stop` method will look:

```
void JavaThread::stop() {
    // Acquire the stop mutex
    std::unique_lock<std::mutex> lck(stopMutex);
    // Change the should stop condition
this->shouldStop =true;
    // Notify any thread waiting for this signal that shouldstop
    // condition has changed.
    stopCond.notify_all();
}
```

With the native thread base class completely defined, we are now ready to create our derived class that implements the required behavior in the `run` method.

As defined before, we will use a `Handler` construct to submit messages from the background threads to the UI thread. Since they run on the same process and share the same memory, we can safely pass a reference to a `Handler` object to the native background threads.

First, before we start to implement our `JavaThread` sub-class, we will write the `NativeThreadsActivity` and implement a `Handler` anonymous subclass to receive messages from the native threads:

```
public class NativeThreadsActivity extends Activity {
  public static final int HEALTHCHECK = 0; // Handler Message Code
  ...
  // Process the Message sent by the native threads
  Handler myHandler = new Handler() {
    public void handleMessage(Message msg) {
      switch (msg.what) {
      case HEALTHCHECK:
        TextView tv = (TextView)findViewById(R.id.console);
        tv.setText((String) msg.obj + tv.getText());
        break;
      }
    }
  };
  // Start the Native Threads when the start button is clicked
  public native void startNativeThreads(Handler handler);
```

```
    // Stop The Native Threads when the stop button is clicked
    public native void stopNativeThreads();
}
```

Once our handler receives a message with the code HEALTHCHECK it will prepend the String received on the msg.obg to a TextView on the Activity UI screen.

This class will also be responsible for starting and stopping the native threads each time we click on the **start** and **stop** button.

The start and stop button setup is omitted in the code example. However, the **start** button will invoke the native function of startNativeThreads, passing myHandler as the Handler argument and the stop button will invoke stopNativeThreads to stop the native thread execution. Additionally, we can also call stopNativeThreads on Activiy.onStop to stop the threads when the activity gets destroyed.

Now we need to implement the JavaThread that will run in the background and submit a healthcheck message to the UI thread over the handler object. Since the handler is coming from a different jniEnv, the first thing to do is to create a JNI global reference from the original handler. Let's start by implementing the constructor that creates a global Handler object reference and store the reference in a member variable:

```
class HealthCheckThread: public JavaThread {

    jobject handlerObj; // Cache the Global Reference
public:
    HealthCheckThread(JNIEnv *env_,jobject handlerObj_):
      JavaThread(),
      // Use the main threadJNIEnv to create a global ref
      handlerObj(env_->NewGlobalRef(handlerObj_)) {}
    }
```

In the constructor, we received the object reference from the main thread, we called our JavaThread default constructor, and we created a global reference to store the original reference.

JNI references explained

It's really important to understand in detail how JNI references are managed by JVM, because if we don't use them properly, we can crash the application or introduce a memory leak in the application. A memory leak will affect the application performance, increase battery consumption, and in the long term crash the application with a `java.lang.OutOfMemoryError` exception. As you know, JVM Garbage Collector (GC) manages the application memory use, cleaning up objects when they are not in use. An object is considered eligible for garbage collection when no references to that object exist in the memory, so, when the GC finds a none referred object it will release the object from the memory.

JNI supports three types of reference:

- **Local Reference** – References attached to a thread, `JNIEnv`, which is lifetime valid for the duration of a native method. The reference is passed to the native method and destroyed as soon as the method returns. The user can also create and delete local references in the native method to prevent any object from being garbage collected. Keep in mind that a local reference is valid in the `JNIEnv` where it was created. The following JNI functions are available to manage local references:

```
Jobject NewLocalRef(jobject);
void DeleteLocalRef (jobject);
```

  - JVM provides a function to allocate space in the current JNI frame to store local references. By default, it has the capacity for 16 references:

    ```
    jint EnsureLocalCapacity(jint);
    ```

- **Global Reference** – References used to keep global objects alive for an unlimited period of time. These kinds of reference can be shared between thread `JNIEnv` objects. It is critical to explicitly delete the reference from JVM when they are no longer required. When you don't free the reference from the system you are creating a memory leak in your application. Notice that when you free the reference from the system, the reference is no longer valid, so if you try to use it an exception will be thrown in the JNI interface. The following JNI functions are used to manage local references:

```
jobject NewGlobalRef (jobject);
void DeleteGlobalRef(jobject);
```

- **Weak Global Reference** – Like the global reference, but it doesn't prevent the object from being garbage collected when it is the only alive reference to the object. Weak global references in JNI are a streamlined version of Java Weak References:

```
jweak NewWeakGlobalRef(JNIEnv *env, jobject obj);
void DeleteWeakGlobalRef(JNIEnv *env, jweak obj);
```

Interacting with UI from native threads

Since we want to cache a reference to a `Handler` object that survives the `startNativeThreads` execution, it makes sense to create a global reference before we save it in a member variable. The reference will be later used in our background thread to submit messages to the UI.

Given that we created a global reference in our `HealthCheckThread` class, to release the reference in JVM and avoid any memory loss, we will delete the global reference in the `HealthCheckThread.onDetach()` function called during thread stopping:

```
class HealthCheckThread: public JavaThread {
    ...
    virtual void onDetach(){
        jniEnv()->DeleteGlobalRef(handlerObj);
    }
}
```

Next, we will update the `HealthCheckThread` and implement the `run` method that is going to submit health check messages to the `Handler` object attached to the UI thread:

```
virtual void run(){

  while (!shouldStop) {
    std::unique_lock<std::mutex> lck(stopMutex);
    // Do Work
    // ...
    sendHealthMessage();
    // Wait until a stop signal is sent
    stopCond.wait_for(lck, std::chrono::seconds(1));
  }
    }
```

The `run` function will continuously execute until `shouldStop` is `true`. Furthermore, between each cycle, the thread will send a message and block for one second unless a stop signal is sent to notify the thread to stop. In this case, the native condition variable is used to wake up the thread from the one second sleep when the stop condition is set.

All that remains regarding the `HealthCheckThread` class is to implement the `sendHealthMessage`:

```
void sendHealthMessage() {

    // Get the Handler class from the JVM
    jclass handlerClass = jniEnv()->FindClass("android/os/Handler");

    // Get the Handler.obtainMessage methodId
    jmethodID obtainMId = jniEnv()->GetMethodID(handlerClass,
"obtainMessage","(ILjava/lang/Object;)Landroid/os/Message;");
    ...
    // Build up the alive message
    std::ostringstream oss;
    oss << "Thread[" << std::this_thread::get_id()
        << "] is alive at " << ctime( & tt) << std::endl;;

    // Obtain a message object
    jobject messagObj = jniEnv()->CallObjectMethod(handlerObj,
                        obtainMId,
                        HEALTHCHECK_MESSAGE,
                        jniEnv()->NewStringUTF(oss.str().c_str()));

    // Get the Handler.senMessage methodId
    jmethodID sendMsgMId = jniEnv()->GetMethodID(handlerClass,
                        "sendMessage","(Landroid/os/Message;)Z");

    // Enqueues a new message on the main thread looper
    jniEnv()->CallBooleanMethod(handlerObj,sendMsgMId, messagObj);
    // Deletes the local references
    jniEnv()->DeleteLocalRef(handlerClass);
    jniEnv()->DeleteLocalRef(messagObj);
}
```

Before we start to use the handler object, we retrieve a `Message` from the `Handler` global message poll using the `obtainMessage` instance method. To build the string message passed in the `Message` object, we format a message using `ostringstream`, a thread ID, and the current `datetime`.

Then, we push the built `Message` to the handler object to be delivered in our
`Activity`. To finish, we delete the created local reference from the local `JNIEnv`.

Starting the native threads

Just to finish our example, we will write the native methods `startNativeThreads`
and `stopNativeThreads`. These methods will create and destroy the native threads
each time we tap on the start or stop button. The UI code is omitted for brevity. Let's
look at the `startNativeThreads` first:

```
static const int num_threads = 10;
static JavaThread* threads[num_threads];

void  Java_com_packpublishing_asynchronousandroid_chapter9_
NativeThreadsActivity_startNativeThreads
        (JNIEnv *jEnv, jobject activity, jobject handler){

    LOGI("Starting   %d Native Threads",num_threads);
    // Launch a group of threads
    for (int i = 0; i < num_threads; ++i) {
        threads[i] = new HealthCheckThread(jEnv,handler);
        threads[i]->start();
    }
}
```

In `startNativeThreads`, we create `num_thread` threads passing the main thread
`JNIEnv` and the handler reference to the `HealthCheckThread` constructor. The
`HealthCheckThread` pointer returned from the constructor is cached in a static array
for future use.

Stopping the native threads

Given that we allocate the `HealthCheckThread` object in the dynamic memory using
the C++ operator `new`, in the `stopNativeThreads`, apart from stopping the thread
execution, it is required to release the dynamic memory to avoid any memory leaks
in the native code. So, all that remains is to implement the `stopNativeThreads`:

```
void Java_com_packpublishing_asynchronousandroid_chapter9_
NativeThreadsActivity_stopNativeThreads(JNIEnv *env, jobject activity)
{

    LOGI("Stopping %d Native Threads", num_threads);

    for (int i = 0; i < num_threads; ++i) {
```

```
        // Notify the thread to stop
    threads[i]->stop();
        // This blocks the execution of the current thread until
        // HealthCheckThread native thread finishes
        threads[i]->join();
    // De-allocates memory previously allocated
        delete threads[i];
    }
}
```

The `stopNativeThreads` function will stop the created threads using the `JavaThread::stop` member function. As detailed before, the stop member function will use a condition primitive to notify the running loop that it should finish its execution. After we notify the background thread, we wait for it to finish and we destroy the object stored in the array pointer.

Great! In this section, we were able to start native threads, attach them to JVM, and interact with the main thread using a Handler object. On the way, we learned about the C++ `condition` and `mutex` concurrent primitives to synchronize the access to shared resources in the native code. Although we have been using the C++11 concurrent primitives to create and synchronize threads, we could have written our examples using the concurrent primitives provided by the POSIX `pthread` library.

The POSIX library `libpthread` also provides methods to manage native threads, mutual exclusion concurrency primitives (mutexes), and condition variables.

Handling Java exceptions in the native layer

While in Java, when an exception is thrown during a method execution, the JVM stops the normal method execution and tries to find an exception handler in the runtime to take control of execution, the same does not apply when you execute the Java method from the JNI code.

The JNI requires developers to explicitly implement the exception handling after an exception has occurred in a Java method invocation.

Moreover, when exception handling is pending, only a few JNI functions are safe to be invoked: `DeleteGlobalRef`, `DeleteLocalRef`, `DeleteWeakGlobalRef`, `ExceptionCheck`, `ExceptionClear`, `ExceptionDescribe`, `ExceptionOccurred`, `MonitorExit`, `PopLocalFrame`, `PushLocalFrame`, `Release<PrimitiveType>ArrayElements`, `ReleasePrimitiveArrayCritical`, `ReleaseStringChars`, `ReleaseStringCritical`, and `ReleaseStringUTFChars`.

There are three ways to handle Java exceptions in a native function.

The first way is to clear the pending exception with `ExceptionClear` and continue to execute the native code. This approach is seldom safe and you need to review all error flows to verify that you are handling the exception properly.

The second way is once the pending exception is detected, release the JNI allocated resources, stop the native code execution, and return the control to the Java code. In this case, the JNI will try to find a Java exception handler in the Java frame that invoked the native method.

The third way is to release the pending exception, generate a new exception with a different class type, and return from the native method with the new exception pending to be handled in Java code.

In our next example, we will follow the third because we will use most of the functions available in the JNI to handle exceptions. First, we will show you how to use the JNI exception in handling functions to clear a pending Java exception. Beyond that, we will stop the native method execution, release all the native resources, and throw a different exception to be handled in Java by the `RuntimeException` handler.

First, we will write an `Activity` that invoking the native method will spawn a pending exception in JVM:

```java
public class ExceptionActivity extends Activity {

    . . .
    OnClickListener onClickListener = new OnClickListener() {
        @Override
        public void onClick(View v) {
            try {
                // Allocate a ByteBuffer with a size of 8 bytes
                ByteBuffer byteBuffer = ByteBuffer.allocate(8);

                // Call a native function that will try to access
                // an out of bounds buffer position
                genException(byteBuffer);
                // Catches a Runtime Exception
            } catch (RuntimeException e) {
                // Prints the Exception Stack Trace to the TextView
                TextView console = (TextView)findViewById(R.id.console);
                StringWriter sw = new StringWriter();
                e.printStackTrace(new PrintWriter(sw));
                console.setText(sw.toString());
```

```
            }
        }
    };
    ...
    // Native Function that will generate and Exception
    private native void genException(ByteBuffer buffer);
}
```

Each time the `genException` button is clicked, call a native method that fails with a runtime exception (`java.lang.IndexOutOfBoundsException`).

The `onClick (View v)` method is only able to handle `java.lang.RuntimeException`, so we must handle `IndexOutOfBoundsException` in the native function and convert it to `RuntimeException`:

```
void Java_com_packpublishing_asynchronousandroid_chapter9_
ExceptionActivity_genException(JNIEnv * jniEnv, jobject activityObj,
jobject byteBuffer){

    // Get the ByteBuffer class
    jclass byteBufC= jniEnv->GetObjectClass(byteBuffer);

    jmethodID getMid = jniEnv>GetMethodID(byteBufC,"get","(I)B");

    // Trying to access a buffer position out of the buffer capacity
    jbyte byte = jniEnv->CallByteMethod(byteBuffer,getMid,32);

    if (jniEnv->ExceptionCheck()) {
        // Prints the exception  on the standard Error
        jniEnv->ExceptionDescribe();
        // Clears the exception on the JVM
        jniEnv->ExceptionClear();
        jclass excC = jniEnv>FindClass("java/lang/RuntimeException");
        jniEnv->ThrowNew(excC,"Failed to get byte from buffer");
        // Release the Allocated Resources
        jniEnv->DeleteLocalRef(excC);
        jniEnv->DeleteLocalRef(byteBufC);
        // Return with Pending RuntimeException
        return;
    }
    ...
}
```

There are two functions used to detect an exception in a JNI native function:

The ExceptionOccurred function returns a jthrowable object reference if there is a pending exception that is not handled so far, or null when no exception is ready.

The ExceptionCheck function returns jboolean when there is an outstanding unhandled exception in JVM, the function will return JNI_TRUE as the result.

Assuming that we don't want to use jthrowable returned by ExceptionOccurred, we will use ExceptionCheck to detect the exception and enter the exception handling code branch.

Thereafter, with the ExceptionDescribe function we will print the current pending throwable stack trace in the error output, and with ExceptionClear, we will clear the pending IndexOutOfBoundsException from JVM.

Given that we are only able to handle RuntimeException in the Activity function, we will attach a RuntimeException to JVM to be handled as soon as the native code returns.

To conclude, and since we are going to stop the native function execution, we must release any resource or JNI references allocated before we return from the native function.

Yes, with the help of these JNI exceptions, you should be able to detect and handle any settled unhandled exception that results from a Java method invocation. As stated before, it is extremely important to manually handle any pending exception before you try to safely invoke other JNI methods that invoke member or static functions, get or set fields on objects, or even create new objects.

Interacting with a Java monitor from native code

So far, we have been synchronizing access to shared resources in Java threads using synchronized statements or synchronized methods:

```
synchronized (obj) { ... // synchronized block }
synchronized void incrementCount() { ... // synchronized methods }
```

When we are executing a native method and want to have access to a resource or variable shared between multiple Java code and native code, the JNI offers us `MonitorEnter` and `MonitorExit` methods to control access to the mutual exclusion zone managed by a Java `synchronized` block:

```
jint MonitorEnter(JNIEnv *env, jobject obj);
jint MonitorExit(JNIEnv *env, jobject obj);
```

`MonitorEnter`, the function responsible for acquiring access to the Java monitor scope, might block when another native thread or Java thread is the owner of the monitor. When any thread acquires access to the block, JVM will make sure that no other thread enters the critical section apart from the current thread.

`MonitorExit` is the function responsible for releasing the monitor acquired previously with `MonitorEnter`, giving the chance to another thread to enter the mutual exclusion section.

 To prevent a deadlock condition, any `MonitorEnter` call must be followed by a `MonitorExit` call.

In our next code example, we will demonstrate this technique to synchronize the access to a shared object used by the Java code and the native code.

We are going to create a native thread that is constantly polling command requests from a shared queue list managed in our `Activity`.

`StatsActivity` will have a button to push commands to the shared queue list and will display the request responses sent by the native thread in a `TextView`. Whereas the UI will push commands to the request queue list in a main thread, and the native code will try to pull commands from the native code in a background thread, both need synchronized access to the shared queue list.

Our command will ask the native layer to send information about the amount of main memory that a program uses to run. As soon as it receives the response, it will print in the UI `TextView`.

To start, let's define the code to push new commands from the UI point of view:

```
public class StatsActivity extends Activity {
    // Memory RSS(Resident Set Size) SIZE Retrieve size Request
    public static final int MEM_RSS_REQUEST = 0;

    // Shared Resource between Java and Native
    Queue<Integer> requests = new LinkedList<Integer>();
```

```
    Object queueLock = new Object();

    OnClickListener onRSSReqListener = new OnClickListener() {
      @Override
      public void onClick(View v) {
        synchronized (queueLock) {
          requests.add(MEM_RSS_REQUEST);
        }
      }
    };

    @Override
    protected void onCreate(Bundle savedInstanceState) {
      ...
      RSSButton.setOnClickListener(onRSSReqListener);
    }
  }
```

Notice that, before onRSSReqListener pushes the new request command to the queue list, it acquires access to the synchronized section controlled by the queueLock object.

Given that the queueLock object is going to act as the guard object to access the shared resource we have to forward it to the native code.

Since we have already written the command request consumer, now we will move our focus to the command request consumer, the native C++ JavaThread subclass named CPUStatThread, that will process the requests and send back the command response.

As explained before, CPUStatThread will implement the run method and send us the response using Activity's Handler, so let's first implement the run method to retrieve requests from Activity in the new source code file stats.cpp:

```
#include "thread.h" // Header where JavaThread is defined

static const int RSS_REQUEST= 0;

class CPUStatThread: public JavaThread {

  // Reference to the Activity and received on the constructor
  jobject activityObj;
  ...
  virtual void run() {
    while ( !shouldStop ) {
```

```
                std::unique_lock<std::mutex> lck(stopMutex);
                processMessage();
                // Wait until a stop signal is sent
                    stopCond.wait_for(lck,std::chrono::milliseconds(200));
            }
        }
        void processMessage(){

            jclass activityClass = jniEnv()->GetObjectClass(activityObj);

            // Retrieve the QueueLock(lockObj) and the Handler
            // Fields(handlerObj) objects from Activity and
            // getNextRequest methodId
            ...
            // Acquire the queue monitor
            jniEnv()->MonitorEnter(lockObj);

            // Retrieve the next command request to be processed
            int requestCode = jniEnv()->CallIntMethod(activityObj,
                                                      getNextRequestMid);
            switch (requestCode){
              case RSS_REQUEST:
                LOGI("Received a RSS Request");
                sendRSSMessage(handlerObj);
                break;
            }
            // Release the queue monitor
              jniEnv()->MonitorExit(lockObj);
            // Release local References to avoid leaks
            ...
        }
    };
```

Our run method will retrieve the queueLock field from StatsActivity and after acquiring access to the synchronized block controlled by the queueLock, it will pull a new request from the queue using the StatsActivity's getNextRequest method:

```
    public class StatsActivity extends Activity {

        int getNextRequest(){
          return requests.size()> 0 ? requests.remove():-1;
        }
    }
```

`getNextRequest` will return -1 when nothing is available to be processed, therefore our thread will sleep for 100 milliseconds, as defined in our run method.

When an `RSS_REQUEST` is received, our native background will process it in the `sendRSSMessage` method and send a response back with the memory consumed by the process in the system.

Wrapping native data objects

So far, to send any kind of structured data from native code to Java code, we have been building and dispatching regular Java objects. However, to reduce the overhead required to convert from native types to Java types, and vice-versa, it could make sense to send native wrapped structures or object pointers to Java Runtime instead of creating a pure Java object in the native code.

The most reliable technique is to store the native address into a long member variable of the wrapper object to be compatible with 64 bit and 32 bit pointers:

```
public class MyObject {
   // Transports a pointer to original
   // native object or structure
   long nativePtr;
}
```

As you know, JVM Garbage Collector will constantly maintain the heap memory and clean the unreferenced objects for us to free more memory for next allocations required by your application. The same does not apply to native objects allocated in the dynamic memory using a `new` operator or the `malloc` function.

When we create an object in native heap, we always have to explicitly release it using the `delete` operator or `free` function, so to enforce the memory clean up on all the objects that wrap native objects we will define an interface that defines the required function to release underlying native objects:

```
public interface Disposable {
   // Releases the native objects wrapped on the object
   void dispose();
}
```

 Although we can use the `finalize` method to release any native resources when the object gets garbage collected, there is no guarantee that the GC will call `finalize` at any specific time in the future.

To demonstrate this technique in our example, we will send back using the `Handler`, a native `CPUStat` `struct` wrapped in a Java object.

Let's first define the native `CPUStat` sent when to carry the information related to the process memory consumption:

```
struct CPUStat{
    double vm; // Virtual Memory Size
    double rss; // Process Resident Memory
    // constructor
    CPUStat( double &vm_,
            double &rss_):vm(vm_),rss(rss_){}
};
```

And its Java counterpart:

```
public class JCPUStat implements Disposable {
    // Reference to the native struct stored on a long
    long nativePtr;

    public JCPUStat(long nativePtr){
        this.nativePtr = nativePtr;
    }
    native long getRSSMemory();

    @Override
    public native void dispose();
}
```

Notice that our `JCPUStat` implements the disposable object explained before, so all that remains is to write the native methods for the JCPUStat class:

```
    // Generic function to convert a nativePtr member to a T pointer
template <typename T>
T * getNativePtr(JNIEnv * env, jobject obj) {
  jclass c = env->GetObjectClass(obj);
  jfieldID nativePtrFID =  env->GetFieldID(c, "nativePtr", "J");
  jlong nativePtr = env->GetLongField(obj, nativePtrFID);
  return reinterpret_cast<T * >(nativePtr);
}

void unsetNativePtr(JNIEnv * env, jobject obj) {
  jclass c = env->GetObjectClass(obj);
  jfieldID nativePtrFID =  env->GetFieldID(c, "nativePtr", "J");
```

```
    env->SetLongField(obj, nativePtrFID, 0);
}

void Java_com_packpublishing_asynchronousandroid_chapter9_JCPUStat_
dispose(JNIEnv *env, jobject obj){

    // Retrieves the pointer to the original structure
    CPUStat *stat = getNativePtr<CPUStat>(env,obj);
    if ( stat != 0 ) {
      delete stat;  // Releases the memory allocated to stat
      unsetNativePtr(ev,obj);
    }
}
```

To simplify the native reference handling, we created two generic functions to manipulate a `nativePtr` field in wrapper objects. The first function, `getNativePtr`, will get the pointer field from the object and with help from `reinterpret_cast` we will convert the original long value stored in a `CPUStat` pointer.

After we get access to the original pointer, we can call the `delete` operator that will free the memory in the system and set the nativePtr as 0. Setting the pointer to zero will prevent a double free from happening when you call the `dispose` method twice by mistake.

Next, with the wrapper class defined, we will process the original request and build a `JCPUStat` response object to send back to `Activity` using the activity `Handler`:

```
// Function to retrieve the Memory Usage
void CPUStatThread::processMemUsage(
   double& vm_usage, double& resident_set){...}

void CPUStatThread::sendRSSMessage(jobject & handlerObj) {

   double vm, rss;
   // Read the mempory usage
   processMemUsage(vm, rss);
   jclass jCpuStatClass = jniEnv()->FindClass(
      "com.packpublishing.asynchronousandroid.chapter9.JCPUStat");

   // Find the JCPUStat Constructor
   jmethodID  jCpuConstructorMid = jniEnv()->GetMethodID(
      jCpuStatClass, "<init>", "(J)V");
   // Create a native CPUStat object
```

```
CPUStat * cpuStat = new CPUStat(vm, rss);

// Wrap the native object on a JCPUStat object
jlong nativePtr = reinterpret_cast<jlong>(cpuStat);
jobject jCpuStat = jniEnv()->NewObject(
  jCpuStatClass, jCpuConstructorMid, nativePtr);

// Get the Handler Reference and send Message
...
// Build up the Response Message with the
jobject messagObj = jniEnv()->CallObjectMethod(
    handlerObj, obtainMId, RSS_RESPONSE, jCpuStat);

// Push the message to the main Thread Handler
jniEnv()->CallBooleanMethod(handlerObj, sendMsgMId, messagObj);
// Clean up the local references
...
}
```

Our `sendRSSMessage` function will calculate the memory consumed by the process using system facilities, and build a `JCPUStat` object that wraps a native C++ structure. Afterwards, `JCPUStat` is dispatched to the main thread using the activity handler member object passed in the `sendRSSMessage` function. To finish, we cleaned up all the local references created in the local scope.

The full source code is available from the Packt Publishing website. Take a look at the complete source code to appreciate how we determined the memory consumed by the current process.

To complete the example, we will update `StatsActivity` to handle the RSS command response on the `Handler`:

```
public class StatsActivity extends Activity {
  public static final int MEM_RSS_REQUEST = 0;
  public static final int MEM_RSS_RESPONSE = 1;
  public Handler myHandler = new Handler() {
    public void handleMessage(Message msg) {
      switch (msg.what){
        case MEM_RSS_RESPONSE:
          TextView tv = (TextView) findViewById(R.id.console);
          JCPUStat stat = (JCPUStat) msg.obj;
          tv.setText("Memory Consumed is "+stat.getRSSMemory());
          // Releases the native object and frees the memory
          stat.dispose();
          break;
```

```
        }
      }
    };
    ...
    public native void startCPUStatThread();
    public native void stopCPUStatThread()
}
```

Once we get `JCPUStat` from the `Message` object, we read the RSS memory using its native method `getRSSMemory` and then we print the result on the console UI widget.

As we explained before the `JCPUStat.dispose` method is explicitly called on the Java Runtime to destroy the native object sent to us by the background thread. The JVM GC will not clean up the native objects, therefore we must call `dispose` to release native resources attached to a `Disposable` object.

`getRSSMemory` like the `dispose` method will make use of the `nativePtr` field to retrieve the RSS value stored on the native object. Let's see how it looks:

```
jlong Java_com_packpublishing_asynchronousandroid_chapter9_JCPUStat_
getRSSMemory(JNIEnv *env, jobject obj) {
    CPUStat *stat = getNativePtr<CPUStat>(env,obj);
    return (jlong)stat->rss;
}
```

For brevity, `startCPUStatThread` and `stopCPUStatThread` is omitted, as it is very similar to code used to start the native threads on previous example — see the downloadable samples for the complete code.

Great! We learned how to wrap native objects in Java objects, we defined an interface to purge native memory from a java object when the native object is no longer required and we learned how to create from native Java Objects calling the object constructor.

Summary

In this chapter we introduce you to the JNI, a standard API available on Java to interact with native code written in Assembly, C or C++ that it is available to any Android Developer with the Android NDK kit installed.

In the first section we explain how to setup a project with JNI code on Android Studio and how to call C function and C++ member functions from any Java class on your application.

Later, we use the JNI interface to execute a `Loader` asynchronous background work on a native function. The native function was able to convert a colorful image to a gray image on a Java background thread created by the `AsyncTaskLoader`.

Next, we discover how to attach and detach a pure native thread created using the C++ standard library to the JVM. The attached thread worked as a normal Java thread and managed its own JNI Environment, resources and references.

In the meantime, we also discovered the differences between JNI global and Local references and how to access a Java object field from the native code scope.

We also learned a technique to wrap native objects on Java objects and we define a concrete interface to dispose JNI resources attached to Java objects.

At the end of the chapter, we learned how to detect and handle a pending exception thrown on the JVM by a Java function.

We all the techniques explained on this chapter you should be able to integrate any code written in C/C++ in your asynchronous background execution. Beyond that, you can also make use of the native code to optimize a crucial functionality in your application or integrate with some native handy libraries.

In the next chapter, we will learn how to use the Google GCM to push and pull efficiently realtime messages from your server and how to schedule work with Google Play Services framework.

10
Network Interactions with GCM

In previous chapters, in order to update any kind of dynamic data that our examples required, we explicitly initiated a connection to a remote server, waking up the network radio and other resources required to perform the network operation. The application might fetch either fresh data or exactly the same data if nothing has changed since the last fetch.

Although this communication-fetching model might work for most use cases, it could consume battery resources and internet bandwidth in vain when the data does not change often.

This technique, commonly known as **data polling**, may also increase the server load when a great number of clients try to fetch or verify whether any data has changed.

An alternative to the polling technique is **data pushing**. In this technique, the server tells the application when new data is available or when the data has changed. When the data consumer (application) gets notified, it will initiate a new interaction with the server to retrieve the fresh data.

Since fewer synchronizations are required, it will lead to fewer network interactions, which will lead to less battery resources consumed.

In this chapter, we will introduce you to **Google Cloud Messaging** (GCM), a service delivered by Google Play Services that will help you to build applications that require data pushing or pulling messaging services. GCM delivers a framework to deliver push messages to multiple devices or group of devices in a battery-efficient way.

In this chapter, we will cover the following topics:

- Polling versus pushing messaging
- How to setup and configure **GCM** for your application
- Receiving downstream messages from the server with GCM
- Receiving downstream messages from GCM topic streams
- Sending upstream messages to your server with GCM
- Registering one shot and periodic network tasks with `GcmNetworkManager`

Introduction to GCM

Since every network interaction with your server could wake the wireless radio interface up, on a device with limited energy resources it is crucial to minimize the number of times that your application tries to hit the network to sync data.

For applications that require regular updates and up-to-date data, like a messaging application, polling in the background by setting an alarm for every x minutes, then waking up the radio and downloading your data could drain the battery in a matter of hours.

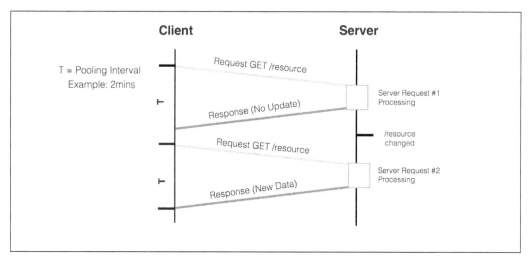

Figure 1 - Polling data from remote server

The GCM offers us a platform to efficiently deliver notifications, with less than 4096 bytes, when there is new data to be consumed or to synchronize. This interaction model reduces the network interactions, and there is no need to constantly poll the server to discover data changes.

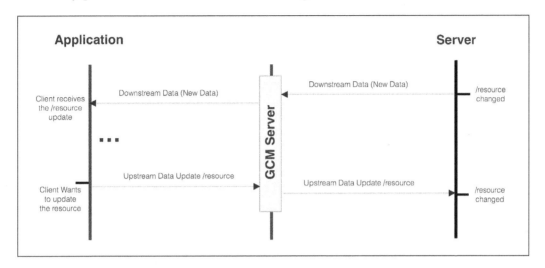

Beyond the ability to dispatch downstream messages from your server (using HTTP or XMPP protocol messages) to your Android application, the GCM framework provides a battery-efficient communication channel to dispatch upstream messages from your application to a XMPP server managed by you.

The GCM client that runs on the Android device provides a reliable and battery-efficient connection between your GCM server and the device. The connection maintained is highly optimized to minimize bandwidth and battery consumption. Therefore, the use of GCM for applications that require high-frequency network data updates, such as real-time messaging, is extremely recommended.

Beyond that, when the device is offline and is not able to contact the GCM service, the platform is able to retain the messages in queues until a maximum number of 20 queued messages, and ensure the delivery of the messages as soon as the device goes online again.

Setting up and configuring GCM for your application

To setup Google Cloud Messaging on your application you will have to register with GCM and set up a Google API Project on your Google Developers Console (`https://developers.google.com/mobile/add`):

1. First pick **Android App Platform**

2. Specify your application name

   Example: `Asynchronous Android`

3. Supply your application package name

   Example: `com.packpublishing.asynchronousandroid`

4. Select **Cloud Messaging Services** and **Enable Google Cloud Messaging**

5. Generate the configuration files and download the JSON configuration file `google-services.json` to your computer.

6. Save your credentials (Server APIKey, SenderId) to authenticate with the GCM platform

Once you have registered your application with GCM, get the `google-services.json` configuration file and copy the file into the `app/` or `mobile/` directory of your Android Studio Project.

Next, add the Google Play Services SDK to your project level and app-level `<PROJECT_DIRECTORY>/build.gradle` file and rebuild your Android Studio Project:

```
buildscript {
    repositories {
        jcenter()
    }
    dependencies {
        classpath 'com.android.tools.build:gradle:1.5.0'
        classpath 'com.google.gms:google-services:1.5.0-beta2'
    }
}
..
```

Update the application module build `< PROJECT_DIRECTORY >/app/build.gradle`:

```
apply plugin: 'com.android.application'

android {
    compileSdkVersion 23
    buildToolsVersion "21.1.1"
    defaultConfig {
        applicationId "com.packpublishing.asynchronousandroid"
        minSdkVersion 9
        targetSdkVersion 23
    }
}
dependencies {
    ...
    compile 'com.google.android.gms:play-services-gcm:8.3.0'
}
apply plugin: 'com.google.gms.google-services'
```

To use GCM on your Android application you need to have a device with Android API 8 or higher with the Google Play Store installed, or a device with API level 9 if you want to use the new GCM features delivered by the Google Play Services.

With the Google Services library dependencies declared on our build files, we can start to bootstrap the GCM infrastructure on our application.

To use GCM in your application, you have to register for the following permissions on your application `AndroidManifest.xml` file:

```
<uses-permission android:name="android.permission.INTERNET" />
<!-- Required to wakeup the device and deliver messages -->
<uses-permission android:name="android.permission.WAKE_LOCK" />

<permission android:name="<Package>.permission.C2D_MESSAGE"
        android:protectionLevel="signature"/>
<uses-permission android:name="<Package>.permission.C2D_MESSAGE"/>
    ...
</manifest>
```

 Notice that you should replace `<Package>` with your unique application package, such as `com.packpublishing.asynchronousandroid`.

Registering the GCM Receiver

In order to receive Broadcast Intents from the GCM Platform, we will add the GCM GcmReceiver, a WakefulBroadcastReceiver subclass provided by the GCM library, to our AndroidManifest.xml application element:

```
<receiver
  android:name="com.google.android.gms.gcm.GcmReceiver"
  android:exported="true"
  android:permission="com.google.android.c2dm.permission.SEND" >
  <intent-filter>
      <action
      android:name="com.google.android.c2dm.intent.RECEIVE" />
      <category android:name="<Package>" />
  </intent-filter>
</receiver>
```

This BroadcastReceiver receives an Intent when a new downstream message arrives from the GCM Server, so it is required to subscribe to Intents with action com.google.android.c2dm.intent.RECEIVE.

Setting up a registration service

In order to receive downstream messages from the GCM platform, the Android application requires a registration token. The registration token, a secret ID issued by the GCM server, must be obtained to identify the device on the service.

To obtain a registration token we will define an IntentService that will retrieve the registration token using Instance ID API. Let's start by defining it on the AndroidManisfest.xml:

```
<service android:name=".chapter10.RegistrationIntentService"
         android:exported="false">
</service>
```

Our IntentService subclass will retrieve a new registration token in the background using the SenderId returned from the GCM registration. Once the new registration token is received, it will be dispatched to our servers to be stored safely. The token is our pass key to access the GCM service, so, in order to submit notifications, the server has to present this token. On the device, the registration will be implicitly stored securely by the GCM framework.

```
public class RegistrationIntentService extends IntentService {

    @Override
```

```
protected void onHandleIntent(Intent intent) {

    SharedPreferences sharedPreferences = PreferenceManager.
      getDefaultSharedPreferences(this);

    try {
      // Get the InstanceID Singleton
      InstanceID instanceID = InstanceID.getInstance(this);

      Log.i(TAG, "\n----------------------------------------\n" +
                " GCM App instance UUID: " + instanceID.getId() +
                "\n----------------------------------------\n"
          );

      // Retrieve the Sender Id from GCM Registration
      String senderId = getString(R.string.gcm_defaultSenderId);

      // Retrieve a token with a sender ID
      String token = instanceID.getToken(senderId,
        GoogleCloudMessaging.INSTANCE_ID_SCOPE, null);

      // Save the Registration to the server
      sendRegistrationToServer(token);

    sharedPreferences.edit().
      putBoolean(MyChatActivity.SENT_TOKEN_TO_SERVER, true).
        apply();

    } catch (Exception e) {
      Log.d(TAG, "Failed to get registration token", e);
    sharedPreferences.edit().
      putBoolean(MyChatActivity.SENT_TOKEN_TO_SERVER, false).
        apply();
    }
  }
}
```

Once a registration token is received with success, we update the default application shared preferences file, setting the SENT_TOKEN_TO_SERVER to true. This property indicates whether the generated token has been sent to your server. If the property is false, we send the token to your server. Otherwise, your server should have already received the token.

If an exception happens while fetching the new token or updating our registration token on our server during the `sendRegistrationToServer` call, we will set the `SENT_TOKEN_TO_SERVER` as `false`, ensuring that a new attempt is going be executed later.

Though you would want to persist the registration to your backend server, for now, we will print the registration token to the log output. You can pick the value using `logcat` for future use in our examples.

```
private void sendRegistrationToServer(String token) {
  Log.i(TAG, " GCM Registration Token: " + token );
}
```

InstanceID listener

The first time we get `InstanceID` through `InstanceID.getInstance`, a UUID Application identifier is generated to identify the application on the GCM platform.

The instance ID may become invalid, if:

- The application explicitly deletes Instance ID (`Instance.deleteToken`)
- The device is factory reset
- The application is uninstalled
- The user clears application data

To receive a notification, each time the registration token requires a refresh, we will create a service that extends `InstanceIDListenerService`, registers to `com.google.android.gms.iid.InstanceID` intent, and includes it on the `AndroidManifest.xml`:

```
<service
  android:name=".chapter10.MyInstanceIDListenerService"
  android:exported="false">
  <intent-filter>
    <action android:name="com.google.android.gms.iid.InstanceID" />
  </intent-filter>
</service>

public class MyInstanceIDListenerService
  extends InstanceIDListenerService {
  @Override
  public void onTokenRefresh() {
    // Starts the Registration Service to obtain a new token
    Intent intent = new Intent(this,
```

```
                                        RegistrationIntentService.class);
        startService(intent);
        sharedPreferences.edit().
        putBoolean(MessagingActivity.SENT_TOKEN_TO_SERVER, false).
        apply();
    }
}
```

The `onTokenRefresh` callback will be invoked when the registration token needs to be refreshed. This may occur if the security of the previous token has been compromised, such as with a suspicious use of the token. This procedure is usually initiated by the `instanceID` provider.

Instance ID API is used to manage security tokens that authorize your application or your server to interact with the GCM Service.

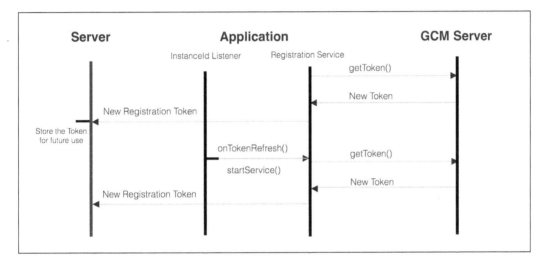

Beyond the creation of new tokens, the `InstanceID` singleton instance is able to delete tokens or even invalidate an `InstanceID`.

```
void  deleteInstanceID()
void  deleteToken(String authorizedEntity, String scope)
```

Receiving downstream messages

With the basic blocks required to set up the GCM client already in place, in our first GCM example we will send a simple downstream message through the GCM Platform and print it as a notification on the Android Notification drawer.

To handle GCM messages, we will have to implement a service that extends from `GcmListenerService` and override the `onMessageReceived(String,Bundle)` method. Since `GcmReceiver` extends `WakefulBroadcastReceiver`, it is guaranteed that the CPU is going to be awake until the service completes the delivery.

Our `GcmListenerService` subclass will receive a message from GCM and create an Android Notification as soon as it receives it.

```
public class NotificationGCMHandler extends GcmListenerService {

    public static final int NOTIFICATION_ID ="GCMNotification".
                                            hashCode();

    @Override
    public void onMessageReceived(String from, Bundle data) {

        String msgType = data.getString("type");

        // Notification Message received from GCM.
        if ( msgType.startsWith("my_notifications") ) {
            createNotification(data.getString("title"),
                            data.getString("body"));
        }
    }
    private void createNotification(String title, String body) {
        // Elided for brevity...
    }
}
```

We also need to register our `GcmListenerService` service class in the `AndroidManifest.xml` registering the service to receive the `com.google.android.c2dm.intent.RECEIVE` action:

```
<service android:name=".chapter10.NotificationGCMHandler"
        android:exported="false" >
    <intent-filter>
        <action
        android:name="com.google.android.c2dm.intent.RECEIVE"/>
    </intent-filter>
</service>
```

To instigate the initial registration with GCM, we will create an Activity that will start the `RegistrationService`'s `IntentService` to retrieve the required token. However, before we try to retrieve the token, we will have to check if the Google Play Services is available on the device, and that the version installed on this device is no older than the one required by this client.

Let's get started by implementing the `Activty.onCreate` method, triggering interaction with the GCM platform:

```
public class MyChatActivity extends Activity {
  public static final String SENT_TOKEN_TO_SERVER = "sent2Server";
  private final static int PLAY_SERVICES_RESOLUTION_REQUEST = 9000;
  @Override
  protected void onCreate(Bundle savedInstanceState) {
    super.onCreate(savedInstanceState);
    if (checkPlayServices()) {
      Log.i(LOG_TAG, "Registering to GCM");
      SharedPreferences sharedPref = PreferenceManager.
                                    getDefaultSharedPreferences(this
);
      // Registering is started when there is no available token
      boolean sentToken = sharedPref.
                          getBoolean(SENT_TOKEN_TO_SERVER, false);
      if (!sentToken) {
        //...Print an error
      }
      Intent int = new Intent(this, RegistrationIntentService.
                              class);
      startService(int);
    }
  }
}
```

Before we start the registration service, `checkPlayServices` will verify if the Google Play Services is installed on the device. If the service is not available, a dialog box is shown to the user that allows the users to download it from the Play Store or enable it on the device system settings:

```
private boolean checkPlayServices() {

  // Returns the singleton instance of GoogleApiAvailability.
  GoogleApiAvailability apiAvailability = GoogleApiAvailability.
                                          getInstance();
  // Verify if the Google Play Service installed is
  // installed and compatible with GCM Library used
```

```
    int rc = apiAvailability.isGooglePlayServicesAvailable(this);
    if ( rc != ConnectionResult.SUCCESS ) {

        // The error can be resolved with a user action
        if (apiAvailability.isUserResolvableError(rc)) {

            // Shows a user action dialog to resolve the issue
            apiAvailability.getErrorDialog(this,
               rc,PLAY_SERVICES_RESOLUTION_REQUEST).show();
        } else {
            Log.i(TAG, "This device is not supported.");
           // Finishing the Activiy
            finish();
        }
        return false;
    }
    return true;
}
```

When the `isGooglePlayServicesAvailable` returns success, we return true from the function and initiate the registration service.

When the function returns an error that can be resolved by the user, such as `SERVICE_VERSION_UPDATE_REQUIRED`, a localized dialog is shown to the user to correct the problem. The dialog could redirect the user to the Play Store if Google Play Services is out of date or missing, or to system settings if Google Play Services is disabled on the device.

If the returned cannot be solved by a user action, we simply finish the current `Activity` and print a log message because the device will not be able to register in GCM and receive the downstream message.

Yes! We finished the application GCM bootstrap, and as soon as we start the `Activity` and register with GCM, the device will be ready to receive downstream messages from GCM.

Remember that our registration service will print a registration token to the log output, so don't forget to note it when you run the `MyChatActivity` for the first time.

```
    I ...:  GCM Application Instance Identifier: <InstanceId>
    I ...:  GCM Registration Token: <Registration Token>
```

To interact with GCM you could set up an HTTP or XMPP backend server that uses the server credentials to connect to the GCM Service. For simplicity and testing we will build and submit HTTP messages directly.

To send a downstream message to our device we will have to send HTTP POST a message with a JSON object in the payload, setting the field to `to` with our noted registration token and a `data` object field with our custom notification properties: `title` and `body` and `type`.

Here is a JSON-formatted message that will generate an Android notification as soon as `NotificationGCMHandler` receives it from GCM:

```
{
  "data": {
    "title": "Hello from GCM",
    "body": "Hello from your fake server",
    "type": "my_notifications"
  },
  "to": "<DeviceRegistrationToken>"
}
```

To submit HTTP messages to the GCM platform, you can use the curl command or use the chrome web application Postman (`http://www.getpostman.com/`). Here is the curl command that will submit the previous message to GCM:

```
$ curl --request POST \
    --url https://gcm-http.googleapis.com/gcm/send \
    --header 'authorization: key=<Server API Key>' \
    --header 'Content-Type: application/json' \
    --data '{"data":{"title":"Hello from GCM","body":"Hello from
your fake server","type":"notification"},
        "to":"<DeviceRegistrationToken>"}'
```

Don't forget to replace the `<Server API Key>` with the API key generated on the Google Cloud Console registration and replace `<DeviceRegistrationToken>` with the token generated for your device. Notice that the downstream data messages have a maximum 4KB payload.

If everything goes well with your GCM setup, your data object properties are passed to your `onMessageReceived()` method in the data bundle object and the GCM service will send you back a HTTP Response (200) with a message body similar to the one below:

```
{
  "multicast_id": 6425212369847183592,
  "success": 1,
  "failure": 0,
  "canonical_ids": 0,
  "results": [{
    "message_id": "0:1456441876781708%69ee9872f9fd7ecd"
  }]
}
```

Receiving messages from topic

The downstream messages allow us to send send short (4KB) messages to alert the user of new updates, new content or even reminders.

A downstream message is a one-way communication channel where the users can receive messages, but they cannot respond to them directly or take any immediate action.

To build interactive experiences, such as a chat system, we will have to support a bidirectional communication where the user can receive downstream messages and also send upstream messages to other devices or groups of devices.

In our next example, we will build a simple group messaging system based on the GCM upstream messaging and topic messaging features. The group messaging system will allow multiple devices to publish text messages to a shared message channel.

GCM topic messaging allows your backend server to send a message to devices that have a particular topic. Once the GCM receives a message to a particular topic, it will route and deliver the message to the subscribed devices transparently using the list of subscribed devices managed on the GCM platform.

A topic is identified by the name that follows the next regular expression:

```
/topics/[a-zA-Z0-9-_.~%]+
```

To start receiving messages related to a particular topic name, a GCM-registered client application will have to subscribe in GCM with its own registration token and the desired topic stream.

First of all, we will update our `RegistrationIntentService` to subscribe our application to the `"/topics/forum"` message stream using the registration token received:

```
public class RegistrationIntentService extends IntentService {

    private static final String TOPIC_NAME = "forum";

    @Override
    protected void onHandleIntent(Intent intent) {
        ...
        // Retrieve the token
        String token = instanceID.getToken(senderId,
```

```
        GoogleCloudMessaging.INSTANCE_ID_SCOPE,null);
    ...
    // Subscribe to Topics
    subscribeTopics(token);
  }

  private void subscribeTopics(String token) {
    GcmPubSub pubSub = GcmPubSub.getInstance(this);
    try {
        pubSub.subscribe(token, "/topics/ " + TOPIC_NAME, null);
    } catch (Exception e) {
        Log.e(TAG, "Failed to subscribe to " + TOPIC_NAME, e);
    }
    ...
  }
```

To unsubscribe the device from the GCM "forum" topic, we can invoke GcmPubSub's
unsubscribe() with the registration token and topic name.

The topic messages are delivered to our GcmListenerService
(NotificationGCMHandler) in the same way the push notification GCM messages
were delivered in our previous example. The topic messages are delivered to our
application, with the from field storing the topic name /topics/forum.

I will give you an idea of what a typical topic message for our topic could look like:

```
{
  "to": "/topics/forum",
  "data": {
    "username": "heldervasc",
    "text": "I need to learn more about Android Development"
  }
}
```

The data object field is the field on the message that we might use to pass custom
properties to the application. In our example, it carries information about the
username and text written by the user.

Next, and taking into account that NotificationGCMHandler will receive the
topic messages sent from the GCM, we will update it to handle the topic messages
received, and broadcast each topic message to any local BroadcastReceiver.

Our `NotificationGCMHandler` will simply wrap the topic messages on the Intents and dispatch them to the local Activity within your process. This asynchronous communication technique, already explained in previous chapters, is faster and more secure as your messages don't leave your application:

```
public class NotificationGCMHandler extends GcmListenerService {

    public static final String FORUM_TOPIC = "/topics/forum";
    public static final String USERNAME_KEY = "username";
    public static final String TEXT_KEY = "text";
    public static final String MSG_DELIVERY = "asyncforum";

    @Override
    public void onMessageReceived(String from, Bundle data) {

        // Verify if it is a forum message
      if (from.equals(FORUM_TOPIC)) {

       // Build an intent from the forum topic message.
        Intent intent = new Intent(MSG_DELIVERY);
        intent.putExtra(USERNAME_KEY, data.getString(USERNAME_KEY));
        intent.putExtra(TEXT_KEY, data.getString(TEXT_KEY));

        // Broadcast the intent to local interested objects
        LocalBroadcastManager.
          getInstance(this).sendBroadcast(intent);
      } else ... {
        ...
      }
    }
  }
}
```

With our `GcmListenerService` forwarding the messages received from our messaging topic, it is time to build the Activity that is going to display the messages received and publish messages to the group chat using the GCM upstream messages.

Starting from the work done in the previous chapter, we will create a `MessagingActivity` that will also verify that Google Play Services is available and start the `RegistrationIntentService` when no registration token is available:

```
public class MessagingActivity extends Activity {

    @Override
    protected void onCreate(Bundle savedInstanceState) {
      super.onCreate(savedInstanceState);
```

```
        setContentView(R.layout.chat_layout);
        if (checkPlayServices()) {
          ...
        }
      }
    }
```

To receive and display the topic messages in our Activity, we will create an anonymous `BroadcastReceiver` subclass that dynamically registers and unregisters the reception of local Intents whose action is `MSG_DELIVERY`.

Since we only want to receive the topic messages when the Activity is in the foreground, we will register and unregister to the local broadcasts on `onResume` and `onPause` callbacks:

```
    public class MessagingActivity extends Activity {
        ...
      @Override
      protected void onResume() {
        super.onResume();

        // Create an intent filter to receive forum Intents
        IntentFilter filter = new IntentFilter(
          NotificationGCMHandler.MSG_DELIVERY);

        // Register the local Receive to receive the Intents
        LocalBroadcastManager.getInstance(this).
          registerReceiver(onMessageReceiver, filter);
      }

      @Override
      protected void onPause() {
        super.onPause();
        // Unregister the Local Receiver
        LocalBroadcastManager.getInstance(this).
          unregisterReceiver(onMessageReceiver);
      }
    }
```

All that remains is to display our group chat messages on the UI and implement the `BroacastReceiver` that receives the broadcast Intents and updates the UI with the message username and text.

To process the Broadcast Intent, we must override the `onReceive` method of `BroacastReceiver` in order to receive local `Intent`:

```
BroadcastReceiver onMessageReceiver = new BroadcastReceiver(){

  @Override
  public void onReceive(Context context, Intent intent) {

      TextView chatText = (TextView)findViewById(R.id.chatWindow);
      String username = intent.getStringExtra("username");
      String bodyText = intent.getStringExtra("text");
      String line = String.format("%s : %s%n", username,bodyText)
      // Prepend the message
      chatText.setText( line + chatText.getText().toString());

  }
};
```

Now, if you submit a topic message to the GCM using the following `curl` command, you will see a new message popping up on the UI `TextView`:

```
curl --request POST  \
--url "https://gcm-http.googleapis.com/gcm/send" \
--header 'authorization: <SERVER_API_KEY>'  \
--header 'Content-Type: application/json'  \
--data '{ "data": {
        "username": "heldervasc",
        "text": "Welcome to Asynchronous Android group chat"
     },
    "to": "/topics/forum"
    }'
```

Sending upstream messages

Although we are able to receive the chat group messages, we are not able to interact with the message stream from the application. Additionally, to send and process upstream messages with the GCM platform, an application server that implements the XMPP Connection Server protocol is required to connect to the GCM servers and receive upstream XMPP messages.

To deal with our group messages we built a very basic XMPP server that processes the upstream messages from the device and forwards the message to the topic message.

The basic XMPP Server source code is available from the Packt Publishing website. Grab it from the Packt website, and, before you run it, update the static fields with your `SenderID` and your `ServerKey` in the `GCMServer.java` class file.

```
private static final String SENDER_ID = "<YOUR_SENDER_ID>";
private static final String SERVER_KEY = "<SERVER_KEY>";
```

The server will connect to the GCM platform, initiate a XMPP session, and process all the messages delivered to the `<SENDER_ID>@gcm.googleapis.com`.

To generate an upstream message, we created a `EditText` on the UI and created a button that, once fired, will send an upstream message. To send an upstream message on the GCM platform, the application needs to provide the following fields:

- The address of our server on the GCM platform: `<SENDER_ID>@gcm. googleapis.com`.
- A unique message identifier (`message_id`)
- A message payload with a custom key/value pairs

Now, let's update `MessagingActivity` to send the upstream message based on the `EditText` input field. Since the upstream dispatch requires network access, and as you know we cannot perform networking on the main `Thread`, we must perform the execution off the main thread using an `AsyncTask` subclass. On the Activity class, we implemented a basic asynchronous construct named `AsyncJob` to perform the network operation in the background, catching any exception that happen during the upstream request. This special purpose class could be used in background tasks that don't produce any results:

```
public abstract class AsyncJob
  extends AsyncTask<Void, Void, Result<Void> > {

  @Override
  protected Result<Void> doInBackground(Void ...args) {
    Result<Void> result = new Result<Void>();
    try { runOnBackground() }
    catch (Throwable e)  { result.error = e; }
    return result;
  }
  @Override
  protected void onPostExecute(Result<Void> result) {
    if ( result.error != null ) { onFailure(result.error);}
    else { onSuccess();}
  }
  // Backrgound Execution Task
```

```
   abstract void runOnBackground() throws Exception;
   // Error Callback
   abstract void onFailure(Throwable e);
   // Success Function
   abstract void onSuccess();
 }
```

With `AsyncJob`, we declared three abstract methods that any `AsyncJob` subclass should provide implementations. `runOnBackground` should implement the background task, `OnFailure` should be used to handle execution exceptions, and the `onSuccess` callback is invoked to inform the developer that the job has been successfully completed.

Now we are ready to implement the `OnClicklistener` that will build up an upstream message and dispatch it to our XMPP server in the background:

```
OnClickListener sendListener = new OnClickListener() {

  @Override
  public void onClick(View v) {

    TextView msgText = (TextView) findViewById(R.id.msg);
    final String msgToSend = msgText.getText().toString();
    msgText.setText("");

    new AsyncJob() {
      @Override
      void runOnBackground() throws Exception {

        // Build the data Bundle wit our key/value pairs
        Bundle data = new Bundle();
        data.putString(USERNAME_KEY, "Helder");
        data.putString(EXT_KEY, msgToSend);
        data.putString("topic", NotificationGCMHandler.
                            FORUM_TOPIC);
        // Generate a random message Id
        String id = Integer.toString(new Random().nextInt());

        // Get the GCMMessaging instance
        GoogleCloudMessaging gcm = GoogleCloudMessaging.
          getInstance(MessagingActivity.this);

        // Sends the Message to the GCM platform
        gcm.send(getString(R.string.gcm_SenderId) +
```

```
                      "@gcm.googleapis.com", id, data);
        }
        @Override
        void onFailure(Throwable e) {
//… Handle the exception
Log.e(TAG,"Failed to send upstream message to forum",e);
        }
        @Override
        void onSuccess() {
          //.. No Exception thrown
      }
    }.execute();
  }
};
```

In our example, we created a `Bundle` object with all the payload data that we want to dispatch. Beyond that, we created a unique message ID using the `java.util.Random.nextInt` instance method.

This message receives as parameters the address following the format `<SENDER_ID>@gcm.googleapis.com`, the unique message ID string generated from the random integer, and the bundle with your payload.

Once we invoke the `GoogleCloudMessaging.send`, if an active connection is available, the new upstream message will be sent immediately, otherwise the message will be queued. Once the connectivity is re-established, the queued messages are dispatched to the GCM servers.

 If the client attempts to send more messages after the 20-message limit is reached, it returns an error.

The `GoogleCloudMessaging` API will reuse and manage the connection to the GCM platform in an efficient way, maximizing the device battery life transparently for us.

As soon as the message is received by our XMPP server, the message is dispatched to `/topics/forum` and, consequently, it will update the UI message stream with the message we typed.

GcmListenerService delivery callbacks

In some situations, when there is no connectivity with the GCM servers due to lack of network connectivity, the message could remain on the local queues for a long period of time. So, in order to discard a message that remains on the queue without being sent to the GCM Service within the time specified, the `GoogleCloudMessaging` API provides an additional send method that could receive a TTL (Time to Live) time to set the message expire time:

```
void send (String to, String msgId, long timeToLive, Bundle data)
```

This works great when you have messages that are only relevant if they arrive within a certain time frame. With a time to live of 0, we'll attempt to send and return an error immediately if we're not connected. This situation does not apply for our example, so we will keep the original code with the send method that does not discard an old unsent message.

It is important to understand that the application GCM client is only able to queue a maximum of 20 messages when there is no connection to the GCM platform for a long period of time.

Beyond the upstream expiration feature, the `GcmListenerService` also allows us to receive the upstream messages' dispatch statuses by overriding the `onMessageSent` and `onSendError` callbacks:

```
void onMessageSent(String msgId)
void onSendError(String msgId, String error)
```

The `onMessageSent` callback is invoked when the message is delivered to the GCM and the is called when there is an error dispatching the message to the GCM connection server. Notice that both callbacks are invoked with the message identifier as argument, so you should use this identifier to pinpoint the message that was sent or failed with an error.

For efficiency reasons, the GCM message delivery reports are delivered in batches, so don't expect to receive the callback execution immediately after you upload a single message.

To receive upstream messages' dispatch statuses in our chat example, we will update our `NotificationGCMHandler` and override the `onMessageSent` and `onSendError`:

```
public class NotificationGCMHandler extends GcmListenerService {
    ...
    @Override
    public void onMessageSent(String msgId) {
        super.onMessageSent(msgId);
```

```
        Log.i(TAG, "Message w/ id="+msgId+" send to GCM Server ");
    }

    @Override
    public void onSendError(String msgId, String error) {
        super.onSendError(msgId, error);
        Log.e(TAG, "Message w/ id=" + msgId +
                " send failed with error "+error);
    }
}
```

The callback methods defined in our `GcmListenerService` callbacks we print a message to the application log output with the message that was sent or failed. The dispatch of a message could fail if the message expiration time is reached or when a maximum size of upstream queued messages has been reached.

Sweet! We've finished our group chat based on the GCM platform. During our journey we learned how to send a topic message upstream and downstream using a battery-efficient API that maintains a network connection with the Google servers. The API allows us to create bidirectional communication channels between the server and a device, or between a group of devices.

Executing tasks with GCM Network Manager

Beyond the messaging framework, the GCM library comes with `GcmNetworkManager`, an API that allows us to efficiently schedule recurrent or periodic tasks on all the devices that run API level 9 (Android 2.1) and above. For devices running on API Level 21 (Lollipop) and above, GCM Network Manager uses the native `JobScheduler` API internally, covered in detail in *Chapter 7, Exploring the JobScheduler API*. In the same way as the `JobScheduler` API, it will try to batch the jobs and reduce the number of wakeups from idle state to improve the battery life of your user's device.

Moreover, with GCM Network Manager we are also able to set criteria that should meet to start the job execution, such as when the device is in a charging state or an unmetered WIFI connectivity is available. Although the GCM API offers us the same criteria offered by the `JobScheduler` API, it can be used on older and newer devices that have Google Play Services installed.

So, before you try to use it, you need to make sure that Google Play Services version is available on the device using the `GoogleApiAvailability` class, as we did for the GCM example.

Take a look at the `checkPlayServices()` function from our previous example to a more complete solution. The previous function will display dialog when any user action is required to update or install Google Play Services.

We can schedule a task execution on GCM Network Manager to run under certain conditions, such as:

- When certain network connectivity is available (any network available, unmetered network connectivity)
- When the device is plugged to the charger
- A task that runs within a predefined time window in the future
- Specify the task to run even after a reboot

While the criteria supported are the same as the Scheduler API covered previously and available on devices that run on Android Lollipop, this API requires some extra mandatory criteria that you should specify to register a service task execution on the GCM Network.

To build and construct a GCM task, two Builder classes are available: The `OneoffTask.Builder` used to create single shot tasks, and the `PeriodicTask.Builder` used register a task that runs recurrently at regular intervals.

Building a one shot task

A `OneoffTask` is a task that will execute once, within a specified time window in the future. The options available to configure a `OneoffTask` from the `OneoffTask.Builder` are:

- Execution Window Range (Mandatory)
- Tag Identifier (Mandatory)
- `GcmTaskService` subclass that runs our task(Mandatory)
- Extra Arguments (Optional)
- Job Persistence (Optional)
- Required Network (Optional)
- Charging Required (Optional)
- Update Current Task (Optional)

In our next example, we will make use of GCM Network Manager to schedule the backup of account settings. The account settings, when updated, are stored in a local file and, once the backup runs, the account details will be pushed to our XMPP server over an upstream message. For saving our account settings, we will create an Activity that displays a form to fill our personal details.

The form will have a button that, once clicked, will save our account details on a local file and register a GCM Network task execution to push our details to our network XMPP Server.

To extend the battery life and reduce our metered mobile internet usage, we will register our backup task to run only when the WIFI network is available and the device is charging, at most 4 hours after scheduling.

Before we register our task on GCM Network Manager, we will add our `GcmTaskService` to the application manifest:

```
<service
  android:name=".chapter10.MyBackupService"
  android:exported="true"
android:permission="com.google.android.gms.permission.BIND_NETWORK_
TASK_SERVICE">
  <intent-filter>
    <action
    android:name="com.google.android.gms.gcm.ACTION_TASK_READY"/>
  </intent-filter>
</service>
```

In the Android Manifest we added Intent filters required to receive GCM start broadcasts and, to protect our service from being started by programmes other than Google Play Services, we added the `com.google.android.gms.permission.BIND_NETWORK_TASK_SERVICE` permission.

Next, we are ready to register a one-off task to backup the account details stored locally on the application default shared preference file. Whenever the user updates the account details and taps the save button on the UI, the account details will be stored locally and a `OneoffTask` task is built and registered on GCM NM to publish the changes on our network servers.

Let's see what the save button `OnClickListener` looks like:

```java
public class AccountSettingsActivity extends Activity {

  public static final String TASK_BACKUP = "backup";

  public static long FOUR_HOUR = 3600*4L;

  // Executed when the user taps on save button
  OnClickListener listener = new OnClickListener() {

    @Override
    public void onClick(View v) {
      // Store the details on the default shared preferences file
      ...
      // Obtain a GCM NM Instance
      GcmNetworkManager gcmNM = GcmNetworkManager.
        getInstance(AccountSettingsActivity.this);
      OneoffTask task = new OneoffTask.Builder()
        // Sets the Service to start
        .setService(MyBackupService.class)
        // Task Identifier
        .setTag(TASK_BACKUP)
          // Will run in the next 4 hours
        .setExecutionWindow(0L, FOUR_HOUR)
        // Requires WIFI Network
        .setRequiredNetwork(Task.NETWORK_STATE_UNMETERED)
        // Requires Charging
        .setRequiresCharging(true)
          .build();

      gcmNM.schedule(task);
    }
  };
}
```

To register tasks from your `Activity`, we obtained an instance of `GcmNetworkManager` using the `Activity` context. Next, we created a `OneoffTask.Builder` object and set the task to start the `MyBackupService` service to complete the task and to run the task at least 4 hours after the scheduling.

Notice that the framework will start your job as soon as all the criteria are met and taking into account other jobs scheduled to run. As explained before, the GCM NM will delay the job execution and batch jobs to reduce the number of CPU wakeups from idle state.

Now, we will create the `MyBackupService` that extends from `GcmTaskService` and implements the following method:

```
int onRunTask(TaskParams args);
```

Our `OnRunTask` method will publish our account detail updates to our XMPP server:

```java
public class MyBackupService extends GcmTaskService {

  @Override
  public int onRunTask(TaskParams taskParams) {
    Log.i(TAG, "Backing up the account settings");
    try {

      // Obtain the default Shared preference object
      SharedPreferences sp =PreferenceManager.
        getDefaultSharedPreferences(this);

      // Builds the upstream data bundle
      Bundle data = new Bundle();
      data.putString(FIRST_NAME, sp.getString(FIRST_NAME, ""));
      data.putString(LAST_NAME,sp.getString(LAST_NAME, ""));
      data.putString(AGE, sp.getString(AGE, ""));

      // Specify the resource to update (Optional)
      data.putString("resource","/account");
      data.putString("operation","update");

      String msgId = Integer.toString(new Random().nextInt());
      GoogleCloudMessaging gcm = GoogleCloudMessaging.
        getInstance(MyBackupService.this);
      gcm.send( SENDER_ID + "@gcm.googleapis.com", msgId, data);
    } catch (IOException e) {
      Log.e(TAG, "Failed to backup account", e);
      return GcmNetworkManager.RESULT_RESCHEDULE;
    }
    return GcmNetworkManager.RESULT_SUCCESS;
  }
}
```

To execute the `onRunTask` method, the `GcmTaskService` started by GCM NM will spawn a background thread with `THREAD_PRIORITY_BACKGROUND` priority and will keep the device awake holding CPU `Wakelock` for at most 3 minutes. After 3 minutes of execution, if your task has not returned, GCM NM considers that your task has timed out, and will release the CPU `Wakelock`.

If your service receives more than one request at once, you should serialize the job execution with a synchronized section to avoid thread safety issues.

The result code returned by onRunTask will determine the task execution success (RESULT_SUCCESS), failure (RESULT_FAILURE) or failure with reschedule (RESULT_RESCHEDULE). In our particular example, if an exception is thrown during the upstream message submission the result code RESULT_RESCHEDULE returned will force the task to be re-executed again after a back-off period (exponential).

Summary

In this chapter we learned how to send and receive data using a battery-efficient communication channel provide by GCM Platform.

First, we learned the differences between polling and push/pull communication techniques to interact with network servers. The push and pull messaging used by GCM is able to reduce the battery efficiency of your application by avoiding redundant server queries to keep the user's data up to date.

In the meantime, we learned how to setup and configure the GCM library on our application. To interact with Google Services, our device obtained a instanceID and registration token to authenticate and identify our device on the GCM service.

Next, we learned how handle notification messages and topic messages on our application and we interacted with a custom XMPP server using GCM upstream messages. At the same time, we built group chat system that is able to aggregate messages from different users in a unified stream of messages displayed on the screen.

Finally, we learned how to use GCM Network Manager to schedule network tasks that run when certain criteria are meet on the device such as the device is connected to the WIFI network.

In the next chapter, we will introduce the reader to the RXJava, a library used to compose asynchronous and event-based tasks on Java by using observable data streams.

11
Exploring Bus-based Communications

In previous chapters, we have been using different techniques to disseminate data/events/notifications between several Android application components (`Activity, Fragment, Service, BroadcastReceiver,` …):

- Intents were sent through the system carrying communication messages or notifications to notify a `Service` or `Activity` to start
- Broadcast Intents were used to report a result back from background processes
- Handlers were used to communicate between different processes and thread executions

These techniques usually involved a tight coupling between the component that sends the message and the component that receives it. Typically, the sender dispatches a message to a certain receiver and deals with the receiver lifecycle in order to detect any receiver unavailability.

In this chapter, we are going to present to the reader a new construct and pattern, delivered by the `EventBus` library, that most of the time simplifies communication between the different application components by decoupling the event producer and event consumer component.

In this chapter, we will cover the following topics:

- Introducing bus-based communication
- Setting up an `EventBus` library in your project
- Defining and dispatching events in the Bus

- Registering subscribers
- Processing events asynchronously with `threadMode`
- Posting and removing sticking events

Introduction to bus-based communication

The Bus based communication software pattern, also known as Publish/Subscribe, is a pattern that allows sender and receiver entities to communicate without requiring them to explicitly know each other. This communication model suppresses the tight coupling between components and allows the delivery of messages from one receiver to more than one final recipient. There are five different entities involved in the communication pattern: publisher, subscriber, event, bus, and broker.

The **publisher** submits events to a shared messaging pipeline, named **bus**, controlled by an entity called **broker**, that governs the stream of events submitted and forwards them to a list of interested entities, called **subscribers**, that previously registered in the broker to receive certain kinds of event.

In order to receive certain kinds of event, the subscriber should express interest in these events by creating a subscription in the broker and the broker should keep a list of enabled subscriptions and forward the events to all of the subscribers.

If a consumer loses interest in one kind of event, it terminates the subscription, and as a consequence, the broker will stop forwarding the unsubscribed events related to the subscriber.

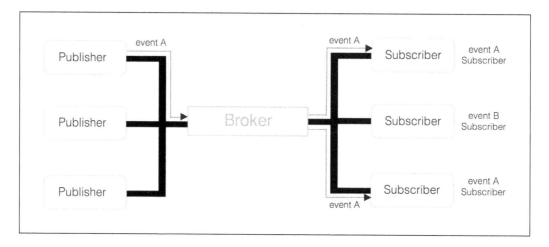

In this loosely coupled communication model, the publisher submits event A in the shared bus without knowing the exact subscriber that will consume the event. In the same way, the subscriber does not know about the sender entity that submitted the event unless something is sent in event A to identify the event's origin.

On Android specifically, it could simplify the communication between `Fragments`, `Activities`, `Services`, or any other business logic object, such as persistence service, that manages your application or UI state. In our examples, we will use the library to send notifications between activies and fragments. However, the same kind of construct could be applied to communicate between services and broadcast receivers.

EventBus library

Although there are several open source libraries that are able to deliver this kind of pattern in Android, we will base our code examples on the popular event bus library (`http://greenrobot.org/eventbus/`) since it offers advanced features and high performance.

The high performance library is optimized for the Android OS and it has been used by many popular applications on Google Play.

These are the advanced features delivered by the `EventBus` library that you should be aware of:

- Annotation-based subscription – You can define an subscription method by annotating an Android `Activity`, `Service`, or `Fragment` instance method

- Background and main thread event delivery – The subscriber could define in which thread the event will be delivered regardless of whether it was generated in a background or main thread

- Event and subscriber inheritance – We can construct events or subscribers by extending (Java subclass) other events or subscribers:

  ```
  class OtherEvent extends MyEvent
  ```

- No configuration required – The library, by default, allows us to use a ready-to-use default `Bus` that does not require explicit instantiation, and can be used to submit events from anywhere in the application:

  ```
  EventBus.getDefault().post(new MyEvent());
  ```

Before we start using it, we will add the GreenRobot `Eventbus` dependency to our module or application `build.gradle` file:

```
dependencies {
    compile 'org.greenrobot:eventbus:3.0.0'
}
```

Before we go deeper, we will present a simple example in which we use the library to publish a simple event from a `BroadcastReceiver` to an `Activity`. Thus, the `Activity` receiver method will deliver a notification on the screen.

First, we will create a `BroadcastListener` that listens for network changes and submits an event in the `Bus` when the mobile network is not available and an event with a detailed network state when the device mobile network is available. The events will be propagated in the `Bus` and delivered to all the subscribers interested in them, which in our case, will be an `Activity` that will display a message on the screen that shows the mobile network state.

Defining events

First, we will define the POJO classes that would be submitted in the `Bus` by the publisher to notify the interested entities whether the mobile network connectivity is available or not:

```
public class MobileNetConnectedEvent{
  public final String detailedState;
  public MobileAvailableEvent(String detailedState) {
    this.detailedState = detailedState;
  }
}
public class MobileNetDisconnectedEvent {}
```

The `MobileNetConnectedEvent` event is a POJO class that will be sent when the mobile network is available and will carry a string message with the detailed network state.

The `MobileNetDisconnectedEvent` is an event that does not carry any information but it will notify the event subscriber that connection with the network was lost.

Submitting events

Now with events defined, we will create the BroadcastListener that is going to receive Intents from the Android OS when any network connectivity changes (Wi-Fi, Mobile, ...) occur on the device, and submits the events in the Bus when the mobile connectivity has changed:

```java
public class MobileNetworkListener extends BroadcastReceiver {

    @Override
    public void onReceive(Context context, Intent intent) {
        // Retrieve the NetworkInfo from the received Intent
        NetworkInfo info = (NetworkInfo)intent.
            getExtras().get(ConnectivityManager.EXTRA_NETWORK_INFO);
        if ( isMobileNetwork(context, info) && !info.isConnected()) {
            // Publish an mobile network disconnected Event
            EventBus.getDefault().post(
                new MobileNetDisconnectedEvent());
        } else if ( isMobileNetwork(context, info) &&
                    info.isConnected()) {
            // Publish an mobile network connected Event
            EventBus.getDefault().post(
                new MobileNetConnectedEvent(info.getState().toString()));
        }
    }
    public boolean isMobileNetwork(Context context,
                              NetworkInfo info) {
        return info != null &&
            (info.getType() == ConnectivityManager.TYPE_MOBILE);
    }
}
```

As we described before, the default and ready-to-use EventBus could be retrieved from anywhere in our application, so, when a network change event is received regarding the mobile network, we just get the default Bus by invoking EventBus.getDefault() and we submit an event to it by calling the Bus.post(Object event) function.

Note that we will identify a network based on the NetworkInfo received in the ConnectivityManager.EXTRA_NETWORK_INFO Intent extra.

When a network change related to the mobile network is detected, we submit either MobileNetConnectedEvent or a MobileNetDisconnectedEvent in the default Bus.

Registering sbscribers

With the `Publisher`/`Sender` class and event class already specified, all that remains is to register our `Activity` class to receive both events and print the event sent on the screen.

Like we stated before, to receive any event from the `Bus`, the `Subscriber` entity, which could be any Java class on your code, will have to register on the Bus and subscribe to the event that it is interested in.

Any object will have to register on the Bus by calling the register function and provide a single on<EventName>(EventType) method annotated with `org.greenrobot.eventbus.Subscribe` for all the kind of event that it is interested in:

```
@Subscribe
void on<EventClassname>(EventClassname event) {
    ...
}
```

Let's implement the functions that are going to handle the `MobileNetDisconnectedEvent` and the `MobileNetConnectedEvent` event in our Activity:

```
@Subscribe
public void
onMobileNetDisconnectedEvent(MobileNetDisconnectedEvent event){

    String message = String.format(
      "Mobile connection is not available \n");
    appendToConsole(message);
}

@Subscribe
public void
onMobileNetConnectedEvent(MobileNetConnectedEvent event){

    String message = String.format(
      "Mobile connection is available State - %s\n",
      event.getDetailedState());
    appendToConsole(message);
}
```

Both public callbacks have the @Subscribe annotation and an `MobileNetDisconnectedEvent/MobileNetConnectedEvent` object as the only method argument. Hence, whenever any of these events are posted on the Bus by our `BroadcastReceiver` sender and the `Activity` has already subscribed to them, our callbacks are notified, appending a new message on the UI console screen.

Finally, to register our `Activity` on the default Bus, we will override the `onStart` and `onStop` `Activity` functions to register and unregister, respectively:

```
@Override
public void onStart() {
    super.onStart();
    EventBus.getDefault().register(this);
}

@Override
protected void onStop() {
    EventBus.getDefault().unregister(this);
    super.onStop();
}
```

Once we register our class object, the Bus will transverse the `Activity` methods using the reflection API and check for any methods that are annotated with the `Subscribe` annotation. Once it finds any @Subscribe annotated methods with a POJO Event as an argument, it will register the instance method to be invoked when the event is published on the `Bus`.

As soon as our `Activity` is destroyed, we terminate the bus subscription and the `Bus` will stop sending the events. In any Android component, such as `Activity`, Fragment, and `Service`, we should register and unregister on the Bus according to the component lifecycle. It is really important to unregister the components from the Bus, otherwise the Bus will maintain a reference to the registered component and prevent it from being garbage collected. As a result, it will generate a memory leak in the application.

Thread mode

`EventBus`, by default, delivers the event in the subscriber in the same thread where the sender posted the event. Although this delivery scheme might work for most use cases, such as events that perform Android UI changes, when a long operation is executed in the event callback, the subscriber might block the main thread and prevent the system from running the UI rendering in time and drop some UI frames as a result.

To cope with time-consuming operations that might happen during the event delivery, the EventBus library allows us to define the Thread in which the Bus will call to deliver the event to the subscriber (ThreadMode).

There are four modes supported by EventBus that we can use to control the event delivering behavior:

- ThreadMode.POSTING – The subscribers callback will be invoked in the same thread where the sender posted the event. This is default behavior and the events will be delivery synchronously to all the entities that subscribed to the dispatched event.

- ThreadMode.MAIN - The Bus will invoke the subscriber's callback in the main UI thread. Thus, if the sender is running in the background thread when it posts the event to the Bus, the bus will queue the message in the main Looper and the event will get delivered in the main thread. For more details about how Looper and Handlers work, see *Chapter 2, Performing Work with Looper, Handler, and HandlerThread*. When the event is produced in the main thread it behaves as the ThreadMode.POSTING mode.

- ThreadMode.BACKGROUND – The bus will invoke the subscriber's callback in a background thread that prevents the event handling from blocking the UI thread. Notice that EventBus uses only one background thread to invoke all the callbacks, so, any long-running component could defer the delivery of subsequent events. When the event is produced in the background thread it is in the ThreadMode.POSTING mode.

- ThreadMode.ASYNC- The Bus will invoke the subscriber's callback using a group of threads managed by the Bus. The thread pool of worker threads, created from Executors.newCachedThreadPool, is going to be recycled and might be used to execute blocking operations, such as network or long computing operations.

You should set the thread mode required for your example based on the kind of processing required to consume the Event. For example, when the consumer updates the UI a ThreadMode.MAIN should be explicitly specified if the producer could post an event from the background thread. In other use cases, if the consumer does blocking or intensive operations you should use the ThreadMode.ASYNC mode to span the events over a group of threads.

To explicitly determine in which thread the method is to be called by EventBus, we must specify the threadMode property in the Subscribe annotation:

```
// Execute the callback on a  Background Thread
// managed by EventBus
@Subscribe(threadMode = ThreadMode.BACKGROUND )
public void onMyEvent(MyEvent event) {...}
```

Typically, an Android application requires tasks to run background work to obtain dynamic data from the network service or from a content service. The data retrieved is then dispatched to the main thread to be presented in the UI main thread. In previous chapters, we used different techniques (AsyncTask, Loader, and HTTP Async client) to accomplish this. In our next example, we are going to use `ThreadMode.BACKGROUND` mode to perform an IO blocking operation that retrieves product information using an `EventBus` asynchronous background thread pool.

With the results from the previous operation, we will build an event with product details that will be reported back to the main UI thread to update the product on the screen.

Our `Activity` will present a `Fragment` with the product details and **Next** and **Previous** buttons to browse between the product list. As explained before, we will use the `EventBus` to dispatch an event details request to a background thread and we will use an event to publish the results back from the Activity background method to the `DetailsFragment` fragment.

First, we will define the `RetrieveProductEvent` and `ProductDetailEvent` POJOs used to model a product details request and to model the product details:

```
public class RetrieveProductEvent {

    // Product Identifier
    final long identifier;
    ...
}

public class ProductDetailEvent {

    final long identifier;
    final String brand;
    final String name;
    final float price;

    ...
}
```

Then, we will create the Fragment that is going to register on the Bus and subscribe to receive the ProductDetailEvent events with the product data. As you know, it's essential to register and unregister the Fragment on the bus in order to prevent leaked memory resources, so, we will use the Fragement onResume and the onPause lifecycle callbacks to accomplish that:

```java
public static class DetailFragment extends Fragment {

  @Override
  public void onResume() {
    EventBus.getDefault().register(this);
    super.onResume();
  }

  @Override
  public void onPause() {
    EventBus.getDefault().unregister(this);
    super.onPause();
  }
  . . .
}
```

Given that we want to update the UI when we receive the ProductDetailEvent, we will create a subscriber that runs on ThreadMode.MAIN thread mode, and therefore, receives the event callback in the main Thread:

```java
public static class DetailFragment extends Fragment {
  . . .
  @Subscribe(threadMode = ThreadMode.MAIN)
  public void onProductDetailEvent(ProductDetailEvent event) {
    Log.i(TAG, "Product details received for identifier"
                +event.identifier+" on" +
                Thread.currentThread().getName());
    // Update the Product Details on the UI
    brandTv.setText(event.brand);
    nameTv.setText(event.name);
    priceTv.setText(Float.toString(event.price));
  }

  @Override
  public View onCreateView(LayoutInflater inflater,
                           ViewGroup container,
                           Bundle savedInstanceState) {
```

```
    // Inflate the layout for this fragment
    return inflater.inflate(R.layout.detail_fragment,
                                container, false);
  }


  @Override
  public void onViewCreated(View view,
    Bundle savedInstanceState) {
    // Initialize the UI widgets
    ...
  }
}
```

Following that, we will create the Activity that loads the `DetailsFragment` and will request to load the first product (`productId=0`) from the product catalogue:

```
public class PaginatedActivity extends FragmentActivity {

  int productId = 0;

  @Override
  public void onCreate(Bundle savedInstanceState) {
    super.onCreate(savedInstanceState);
    setContentView(R.layout.paginated_layout);

    // Loads the Details Fragment
    FragmentManager fragmentManager = getSupportFragmentManager();
    FragmentTransaction fragmentTransaction = fragmentManager.
                                        beginTransaction();
    DetailFragment fragment = new DetailFragment();
    fragmentTransaction.add(R.id.detail_fragment, fragment);
    fragmentTransaction.commit();

    // Request to load the first product
    EventBus.getDefault().post(
       new RetrieveProductEvent(productId));
    ...
  }
  @Override
  public void onStart() {
    super.onStart();
    EventBus.getDefault().register(this);
  }
```

```
    @Override
    protected void onStop() {
      EventBus.getDefault().unregister(this);
      super.onStop();
    }
  }
```

The `Activity` will create a `FragmentTransaction` to the `DetailsFragment` and commit it to the `FragmentManager`. To conclude, it will post an event on the bus to load the first new product `RetrieveProductEvent(productId)`.

Next, we are going to implement the subscriber method that is going to process the `RetrieveProductEvent`, obtain the product details for the specified identifier in the background, and dispatch the new product details event to all the interested entities:

```
  @Subscribe(threadMode = ThreadMode.ASYNC)
  public void onRetrieveProductEvent(RetrieveProductEvent event) {
    Log.i(TAG, "Retrieving the product " + event.identifier
              + " on " + Thread.currentThread().getName());

    // Retrieve on background the product details
    // for the product with the event.identifier id
    ProductDetailEvent pde = ...;

    // Post an EventDetailsEvent on the Bus to
    // publish the event details for the product requested
    EventBus.getDefault().post(pde);
  }
```

Using `ThreadMode.ASYNC`, we will force the `EventBus` to invoke the callback on one of the Threads available in the `EventBus` asynchronous thread pool. This thread mode is used to perform asynchronous operations that might block for some time or take some time to execute, such as long computation calculations or network operations.

Based on the thread mode defined by you, `EventBus` will manage all the thread switching required to deliver to events in the right group of threads or thread, regardless of whether the event is dispatched from the main thread or a background thread.

When the details of the product requested are loaded, the returned `ProductDetailEvent` object is posted on the Bus for further processing.

Given that the `DetailsFragment` has the function onProductDetailEvent subscribed to receive the `ProductDetailEvent` in the main thread, the bus broker will call the function in the UI thread updating the `brandTv`, `nameTv`, `priceTv`, and `TextView` widgets with the product details.

With the `EventBus threadMode` feature, we could submit events to the main thread from any thread in the application and we can even hand over work to background lines of execution using a clean and simple interface.

Just to conclude the example, we will add two buttons to browse between the product list sequence. The **Next** button will submit a `RetrieveProductEvent` request to get the next product on the list and the **Previous** button will submit a `RetrieveProductEvent` to get the previous product on the list:

```
@Override
public void onCreate(Bundle savedInstanceState) {
  super.onCreate(savedInstanceState);
  setContentView(R.layout.paginated_layout);
  ...
  // Submit an event to load the next Product
  Button next = (Button)findViewById(R.id.next);
  next.setOnClickListener(new View.OnClickListener() {
    @Override
    public void onClick(View v) {
      EventBus.getDefault().post(
        new RetrieveProductEvent(++productId));
    }
  });
  // Submit an event to load the previous Product
  Button prev = (Button)findViewById(R.id.previous);
  prev.setOnClickListener(new View.OnClickListener() {
    @Override
    public void onClick(View v) {
      if ( productId > 0 ) {
        EventBus.getDefault().post(
        new RetrieveProductEvent( --productId ));
      }
    }
  });
}
```

Using the `Publish/Subscribe` pattern delivered by EventBus, we were able to update the `DetailFragment` without sharing a strict interface with the `Activity`. Moreover, the event might have come from any other Android component and the result would have been dispatched in the main thread by Event Bus.

Posting sticking events

Whenever we publish an event on the bus, the EventBus broker automatically delivers the event to all the current subscribers, and by default, will immediately clear the transient event. The new subscribers that register after the event is delivered to the current subscribers will not get the event.

There are situations when a new subscriber registers on the bus and no new event is produced or submitted on the Bus for a long period of time. As such, the subscriber will wait until the next event appears on the bus to produce any output from it.

Furthermore, when the new subscriber is responsible for updating an Android UI component like an `Activity` or a `Fragment`, the subscribers have to wait for a new event to occur, hence, it might delay the UI update for a significant amount of time.

To solve this problem, the `EventBus` allows us to create `Sticky` events that are kept in the memory and delivered to subscribers once they register on the Bus. `EventBus` will keep the latest event of certain types in the memory and deliver it during the registration whenever the subscriber creates a subscription with sticky delivered on.

To deliver a sticky event on the bus, the only thing that we need to do is invoke the `Bus.postSticky` function rather than the post function:

```
void postSticky(new MyEvent())
```

And create a `Subscriber` method with the `sticky` property enabled:

```
@Subscribe(sticky = true)
public void onMyEvent(MyEvent event)
```

As an example, the `LocationManager` service allows us to create a `LocationListener` that receives the current geographical location when the device's location changes by a certain `minDistance`:

```
LocationManager.
requestLocationUpdates(String provider,   // GPS or NETWORK
                       long minTime, float minDistance,
                       LocationListener listener)
```

If we use `LocationListener` to publish non-sticky `LocationEvent`s on the Bus and the device's location does not change for a long period of time, new subscribers will have to wait until the device position changes to receive the current position from the Bus:

```
public class LocationEvent {

    final double latitude; // location latitude in degrees.
    final double longitude; // location longitude in degrees.

    LocationEvent(double latitude, double longitude) {
        this.latitude = latitude;
        this.longitude = longitude;
    }
}
```

Moreover, to reduce the device's energy consumption, the minimum time between location updates (`minTime`) should be significant enough to be noticeable by the application user in order to remove the waiting time for the next event the will have the sticky event technique.

If we register our `Subscriber` method with sticky delivery enabled, the new sticky registration will immediately get the latest position from the bus, stopping the subscriber from waiting for the next location update posted by the `LocationListener`.

To demonstrate this, first we will create an `Activity` that manages its own `LocationListener`, receives location updates, and posts sticky `LocationEvent` events on the Bus:

```
public class LocationActivity extends Activity {

  @Override
  public void onResume() {
    super.onResume();

    LocationManager manager = (LocationManager)
      getSystemService(Context.LOCATION_SERVICE);
    Location location = manager.getLastKnownLocation(
      LocationManager.GPS_PROVIDER);

    // Post the latest known position if available
    if ( location != null ){
      EventBus.getDefault().postSticky(
            new LocationEvent(location.getLatitude(),
```

```
                               location.getLongitude()));
    }
    // Request a location update only if device location changed
    // Minimum time between updates: 5000ms
    // Minimum distance between location updates: 100 meters
    manager.requestLocationUpdates(
LocationManager.GPS_PROVIDER, 5000, 100, listener);
  }

  @Override
  public void onPause() {
    super.onPause();
    LocationManager manager= (LocationManager)
      getSystemService(Context.LOCATION_SERVICE);
    manager.removeUpdates(listener);
  }

  //Handle location callback events
  private LocationListener listener = new LocationListener() {
    @Override
    public void onLocationChanged(Location location) {
      EventBus.getDefault().postSticky(
        new LocationEvent(location.getLatitude(),
                          location.getLongitude()));
    }
    @Override
    public void onProviderDisabled(String provider) { }
    @Override
    public void onProviderEnabled(String provider) { }
    @Override
    public void onStatusChanged(String provider,
                                int status, Bundle extras) {}
  };
}
```

In the preceding code, we register our anonymous listener to receive location updates when the `Activity` enters the foreground and we unregister the listener when the `Activity` is paused, to either be destroyed or moved away from the foreground. We register our listener to receive updates almost every five seconds and when the position changes by 100 meters.

In the meantime, when the last known position is available from the GPS Location Provider, we post a sticky event on the Bus to deliver the last known position for future subscribers.

Our `LocationListener`, once again, will convert a Location object received by an `onLocationChanged` callback to a `LocationEvent` object and submit a sticky event on the bus with the callback. This sticky event will update the `EventBus` cached `LocationEvent` and all sticky `Subscriber` methods will immediately get this event once they subscribe.

Note that we start from the assumption that the GPS Provider is enabled on the device. For a more complete example, before you try to use the `LocationManager`, verify whether the GPS Location is available or not and ask the user to enable it on the device settings when the provider is not available.

Beyond that, in order to receive location updates, the `android.permission.ACCESS_COARSE_LOCATION` or `android.permission.ACCESS_FINE_LOCATION` permissions must be declared in the application permissions or requested at the runtime for API Levels greater than 23 (Marshmallow). The full source code is available from the Packt Publishing website. Take a look at the complete source code to appreciate how to request the required Android OS permissions.

Next, we will create a button that launches new `LocationEvent` subscribers that register and unregister on the `Bus` immediately:

```
Button newSubs = (Button) findViewById(R.id.launch);
newSubs.setOnClickListener(new View.OnClickListener() {
  @Override
  public void onClick(View v) {

    new Runnable() {
      @Subscribe(sticky = true)
      public void onLocationEvent(LocationEvent event) {
        String locTxt = String.format(
            "Lat[%f] Long[%f]", event.latitude, event.longitude);
        Log.i(TAG, "Last known Location is "+ locTxt);
        // Update the UI with the last position
        // retrieved from the new Subscriber
        TextView locationTv = (TextView)
                          findViewById(R.id.location);
        locationTv.setText(locTxt);
    }

      @Override
      public void run() {
        EventBus.getDefault().register(this);
        //...
        EventBus.getDefault().unregister(this);
      }
    }.run();
  }
});
```

The code in the button's OnClickListener will register a new Runnable object instance on the Bus and unregister after that. During registration, the sticky Subscriber method, onLocationEvent, will immediately get invoked with the previously posted Location sticky object dispatched on the bus by our LocationListener.

As soon as it receives a LocationEvent, the onLocationEvent method will update the UI with the last position longitute and latitude and print the position on the Android Log. With this approach, a sticky Subscriber method will not have to wait until the position changes to receive a device position and update the UI.

Removing sticky events

In some use cases, it could be convienient to invalidate a sticky event from the Bus and prevent a cached event from getting delivered to the following Subscribers. EventBus allows us to clear the sticky events by calling the following functions:

- removeStickyEvent(<MyEventClass>) – Removes and gets the recent sticky event for the given event type

- removeStickyEvent(Object event) - Removes the sticky event if it equals the passed event

- removeAllStickyEvents() - Removes the sticky events for all types

Let's use one removeStickyEvent function to remove the latest sticky LocationEvent from the bus:

```
// Check if the sticky event exist on the Bus
LocationEvent evt = EventBus.getDefault().
                        getStickyEvent(LocationEvent.class);
// Check if the event is null
if ( evt != null) {
   EventBus.getDefault().removeStickyEvent(stickyEvent);
}
```

After we remove the sticky event from the bus, the latest LocationEvent will be removed from the bus and no event is delivered during the registration to new LocationEvent subscribers.

Summary

In this chapter, we learned about the publish/subscribe messaging pattern used to communicate between decoupled entities on an Android application. This pattern must be applied to send event notifications or data to one or more Android component recipients.

Next, we introduced to the reader the `EventBus`, an optimized open source library that delivers the publish-subscribe pattern for the Android platform and provides advanced features such as sticky events and asynchronous event delivery.

Following that, we learned how set up the library, how to model events, and how to dispatch events on the default `Bus`. The Bus, a shared entity that receives the events, will act as a broker and proxy for the events to the final recipients that previously subscribed to them.

We took a detailed look at `Eventbus threadMode` feature of EventBus that allows us to define the thread in which the `Bus` delivers the event to the subscriber. Hence, we were able to consume events in different threads (background, main thread, and asynchronous threads) from the posting thread.

To finish our journey, we learned about sticky events, events that are cached on the Bus and delivered to new sticky subscribers during the registration and prevent such methods from waiting for the next event, in case of the absence of new data.

12
Asynchronous Programing with RxJava

In previous chapters, we have been using Android-based constructs such as `Loader` and `AsyncTask` to offload work from the main thread to low priority background threads.

Although these straightforward constructs are able to deliver results that require intensive IO operations or network data, they don't provide out-of-the-box solutions for exception handling, task composition, and asynchronous event processing.

Beyond that, the popular `AsyncTask` construct is not able to deal with `Activity` or fragment configuration changes or cache results between configuration changes. Therefore, to cope with these kinds of problem, most of time the developer ends up creating a lot of extra code and complicated flows to handle the traits of these simple constructs.

To simplify the development of composable asynchronous work, we will introduce you to `RxJava`, a functional framework that allow us to observe, transform, filter, and react to streams of events (click, touch, network, I/O events, and so on) in order to compose complex lines of execution that are able to react to errors and chain asynchronous computations.

In this chapter, we will cover the following topics:

- Introduction to RxJava
- Creating Observables
- Transforming Observables
- Understanding Schedulers
- Performing Asynchronous IO with Schedulers

- Composing Tasks with RxJava
- Observing UI events with RxJava
- Combining Tasks with RxJava
- Working with Subjects

Introduction to RxJava

RxJava is an implementation of Reactive Extensions (ReactiveX) on JVM, which was developed by Netflix and is used to compose asynchronous event processing that reacts to an observable source of events.

The framework extends the Observer pattern by allowing us to create a stream of events that could be intercepted by operator (input/output) functions that modify the original stream of events and deliver the result or an error to a final Observer. This framework abstracts away concerns about things such as low-level threading, synchronization, thread safety, concurrent data structures, and non-blocking I/O.

There are three main basic building blocks that interact with each other in RxJava processing, the Observable, the Observer, and the Subscriber.

An Observable is an entity that emits a sequence of events (zero or more events) of the generic type T (such as String or any Java type) at any point in time, or emits a Throwable when a failure occurs during the event processing. Beyond that, it provides methods to subscribe to its event stream and manage Observer subscriptions.

A Single is a special kind of Observable that can only emit either a single success event value or an error event.

An Observer, after registering as a subscriber, consumes the events of type T generated by the Observable<T>. An Observer must implement Observer<T>:

```
public interface Observer<T> {

    void onCompleted();
    void onError(Throwable e);
    void onNext(T t);
}
```

Any Observer will receive a callback to onNext whenever a new event is emitted by the Observable it's subscribed to until it receives onCompleted or onError to close the event stream.

A Subscriber is a helper abstract class you can use as your Observer's base if you want subscription support. The Subscriber class provides methods to cancel the Observable subscription:

```
abstract class Subscriber<T>
    implements Observer<T>, Subscription


public interface Subscription {

    void unsubscribe();
    boolean isUnsubscribed();
}
```

unsubscribe is the function used to cancel the Observer subscription. Therefore, once the Observer subscription is terminated, the Subscriber will no longer receive the events generated by the Observable.

Here is a simple graph displaying the common interactions between an Observable and a Subscriber:

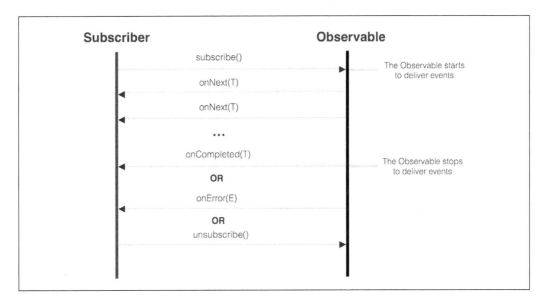

The onNext(T) Observer's callback is invoked when a new item is emitted by the Observable.

The onError(Throwable) Observer's callback is invoked to notify that an error condition was found and the stream will be terminated.

The `onCompleted()` Observer's callback is invoked to indicate that the stream has completed successfully and all the events were delivered with success.

Cold versus Hot Observable

An Observable can be classified as hot or cold based on the time that it starts emitting events. A cold Observable only starts emitting events to the Observers when an Observer subscribes to it. In this case, it is expected that the Observer will receive the stream from the beginning.

A hot Observable will begin emitting events as soon as it gets created, so the Observer will only receive the events emitted after the subscription is created. The events emitted before the subscription will not be received by the Observer.

RxJava setup

Before we move further, let's add the required libraries to your project. If you're using Android Studio, just add the following dependencies to the module `build.gradle` script:

```
dependencies {
    ...
    compile 'io.reactivex:rxandroid:1.1.0'
    compile 'io.reactivex:rxjava:1.1.0'
}
```

rxjava is a library that implements the Reactive Extensions (http://reactivex.io/) on Java , and rxandroid is a library that adds classes to help write reactive components with RxJava in Android applications.

Creating Observables

To create an `Observable`, we can either create an `Observable` from scratch using the `create` function and calling Observer methods explicitly, or we can use built-in `Observable` creation methods that convert common data types to `Observable` streams.

Let's start with a simple example and create an observable that emits a `String` using the creating `Observable.from` operator:

```
Observable<String> myObservable =
    Observable.from(Arrays.asList("Hello from RxJava",
                                  "Welcome...",
                                  "Goodbye"));
```

The `Observable.from` static function creates `Observable` from an array that will synchronously emit `String` items to any Observer. The Observable created will be a cold Observable and will only start emitting events after an Observer subscribes to it.

Now, let's create a `Subscriber` that consumes the data and prints each `String` to the Android Log until `Observable` invokes the `onComplete` callback:

```
Subscriber<String> mySubscriber = new Subscriber<String>() {

  @Override
  public void onCompleted() {
    Log.i(TAG, "Rx Java events completed");
  }

  @Override
  public void onError(Throwable e) {
    Log.e(TAG, "Error found processing stream", e);
  }

  @Override
  public void onNext(String s) {
    Log.i(TAG, "New event -" + s);
  }
};
```

Next, with `Observable` and the subscriber class just defined, once we subscribe our `Subscriber` class on `Observable`, the `onNext()` function will be called three times passing each `String` in the Array, defined previously.

Subsequently, after all the `Strings` are consumed by the `Subscriber`, the `onCompleted` function is called to close the stream:

```
myObservable.subscribe(mySubscriber);
```

The `Observable` instance is responsible for managing all subscriptions, notifying all its `Subscribers`, and it won't begin emitting items until we subscribe to them.

Apart from using `Observable.from` or another creation operator, we can create Observables by calling the `create` method and implementing `Observable.OnSubscribe<T>` that explicitly calls `onNext`, `onError`, and `onCompleted`.

Let's create our own `Observable` that emits integer numbers using the `create` function:

```
Observable<Integer> myObservable = Observable.create(
    new Observable.OnSubscribe<Integer>() {
```

```
        @Override
        public void call(Subscriber<? super Integer> sub) {
            // Emitting Numbers
            sub.onNext(10);
            sub.onNext(3);
            sub.onNext(9);
            // Stream completed with success
            sub.onCompleted();
        }
    }
);
```

Remember that a well-behaved `Observable` must attempt to call either the observer's `onCompleted` or `onError` exactly once after emitting all the items by calling the subscriber's `onNext` function.

Notice that the previous Observable is also classified as a cold Observable because it will only start emitting when a Subscriber entity subscribes to it.

Alternatively, we can subscribe to `Observable` using `Action` functions to handle the items dispatched in different separated functions. All that you need to do is pass an `Action1<T>` function for event processing, an `Action1<Throwable>` for the error emission, and `Action0` to receive the stream completion notification.

Let's write the required action functions that react to our `Observable<String>` emissions:

```
Action1<Integer> onNextAction = new Action1<Integer>() {
  @Override
  public void call(Integer s) { Log.i(TAG, "New number :" + s); }
};
Action1<Throwable> onError = new Action1<Throwable>() {
  @Override
  public void call(Throwable t) {
      Log.e(TAG, "Error: " + t.getMessage(), t);
  }
};
Action0 onComplete = new Action0() {
  @Override
  public void call() { Log.i(TAG, "Rx number stream completed") }
};

myObservable.subscribe(onNextAction, onError, onComplete);
```

Beyond the `from` operator and the `create` operator functions there are other simple `Observable` functions that can be used to build `Observable`:

- `Observable.just`: Creates an `Observable` from a short number of objects (Max 10 Objects):

  `Observable<Integer>.just(1,2,3)`

- `Observable.range`: Emits a range of numbers:

  `Observable.range(1,10);`

Transforming Observables

Apart from the ability to widely implement the `Observable-Subscribe` software pattern, the `RxJava` framework allows us to transform, filter, convert, aggregate, manipulate, and work with the stream of items emitted by `Observable` by using `Observable` operators. These entities are able to completely transform the event stream before the events are delivered to the final `Subscriber`.

`RxJava` comes with a handy collection of operators that are able to transform the event's content and control the time that the event is delivered.

Let's describe the most common operators available on `RxJava`:

- `map`: Applies a function to each item emitted and emits the result of the function as a new item.
- `flatMap`: Applies a function to each item emitted by the source `Observable` where the function returns an `Observable` that could emit a different number of items or a different type of event.
- `filter`: A transformation operator that uses a function that verifies if each item emitted by the source `Observable` satisfies a condition. If the condition passes the item, it is forwarded to the following `Subscriber`.
- `first`: Emits only the first item emitted by the source `Observable`.
- `count`: Emits the number of items received from the original `Observable`.
- `zip`: Combines the emissions of two `Observables` using a function that receives the `N` item of each original `Observable` as an argument.
- `contains`: Emits a `Boolean` event that indicates whether the source `Observable` has a specified `Object`.
- `merge`: Merges the events of multiple `Observers` into one event stream.
- `delay`: Delays the emission of an item by a specified amount of time.

For a more complete, detailed, and up-to-date list of operators supported by RxJava, check the RxJava Wiki on GitHub (https://github.com/ReactiveX/RxJava/wiki/Alphabetical-List-of-Observable-Operators).

The RxJava operators generally process an Observable and return an Observable. This design feature allows us to chain the operators and create a composed sequence of operators that transform the event stream. The last operator is responsible for delivering the items to the Subscriber, or deliver an error when something goes wrong.

Now, let's create our first operator example that transforms a multiline text emitted by the source Observable and delivers a new deliver an Integer with the number of lines that contain the word RxJava:

```
String content = "This is an example \n " +
                 "Looking for lines with the word RxJava\n" +
                 "We are finished.";
Observable
  .just(content)
  .flatMap(new Func1<String, Observable<String>>() {
    @Override
    public Observable<String> call(final String content) {
      return Observable.from(content.split("\n"));
    }})
  .filter(new Func1<String, Boolean>() {
      @Override
    public Boolean call(final String line) {
      return line.contains("RxJava");
    }
})
  .count()
  .subscribe(new Subscriber<Integer>() {
    ...
    @Override
    public void onNext(Integer s) {
      Log.i(TAG, "Number of Lines " + s);
    }
});
```

To start, we create an Observable from the original using the Observable.just creation operator passing the text source as the unique object.

Next, to split the original text in to lines, we use the flatMap operator, which receives the original text emitted by the first Observable and returns a new Observable created from the sliced lines array.

The new `Observable` coming from the `flatMap` operator will emit a single `String` for each line available on the original content, therefore, in order to count the lines with the word `RxJava`, we will discard the lines that don't have the word using the filter operator.

To finish, we will count the number of events emitted and publish the results to a Subscriber that is expecting an integer as a result.

Here is a graphical presentation of the previous functional pipeline:

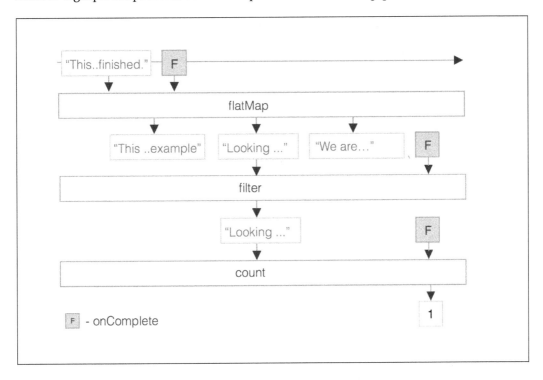

Yes. The extensive set of transformation operators allows us to create a complex functional processing chain that is able to transform the data on the way and deliver results to any `Subscriber` object in a readable and functional way.

Understanding Schedulers

There is an incorrect misconception and belief that `RxJava` processing is multithreaded by default. An `Observable` and the list of transformations applied by the specified operators occur on the same thread that the subscription is made.

Hence, on Android, if the subscription is carried out on the main thread, the operators chain processing will run on the main thread, blocking the UI until the work is done.

While this behavior might work for lightweight processing tasks, when the operation requires IO interaction or CPU-intensive computing, the task execution might block the main `Thread` and crash the application with an ANR.

To simplify the asynchronous and concurrent executions, the `RxJava` framework allows us to define a `Scheduler` entity that defines the thread where a unit of work is executed.

The `subscribeOn(Scheduler)` operator allows us to set the Scheduler that defines the thread on which the subscription has been made and the Observable will start to operate.

When no Scheduler is specified, the Observable and operations will run on the thread that invoked the `subscribe` function.

On Android, a `subscribe` function is typically invoked from an Android Activity or Fragment that runs on the main Thread, then if any operation takes a substantial amount of time to finish it will block the UI Thread and degrade the UI responsiveness.

By controlling the thread where the subscription is made, we are controlling the thread where the Observable and its operators are going to execute and even the thread where the subscriber will receive the callbacks.

The `observeOn(Scheduler)` allows us to set the Scheduler that defines the thread in which the Observer callbacks (`onNext`, `onError`, `onCompleted`) are invoked.

During the Observable and operator chain, we can use `ObserveOn` several times to change the thread where the computation will run.

To simplify `Scheduler` use, the `RxJava` and the `RxAndroid` library compiled a list of predefined `Schedulers` ready to be used to create multithreaded asynchronous chains:

- `Schedulers.immediate()`: Default `Scheduler` that returns a `Scheduler` that executes the work immediately in the current thread.

- `Schedulers.trampoline()`: Returns a `Scheduler` that queues work in the current thread to be executed after the current work completes.

- `Schedulers.newThread()`: Returns a `Scheduler`, spawns a new thread, and executes the work on the new `Thread`.

- `Schedulers.computation()`: Returns a `Scheduler` intended for computational intensive work. This can be used for event loops, processing callbacks, and other computational work. Do not perform blocking IO work on this `Scheduler`. This Scheduler uses a fixed thread pool size where the size is dependent on the CPUs to optimize CPU usage and minimize CPU switching.

- `Schedulers.io()`: Creates and returns a `Scheduler` that executes the work of a cached pool of threads that grows and shrinks as needed, reusing already created threads that are idle to execute the require work. This `Scheduler` is intended for asynchronously performing blocking IO tasks, such as network or file system read and write.

- `Scheduler.from(Executor)`: Creates a Scheduler that will execute the unit of work on the `java.util.concurrent.Executor` passed as argument.

- `AndroidSchedulers.mainThread()`: Creates a `Scheduler` that executes the required work on the Android application main thread. This Android `Scheduler`, provided by the `RxAndroid` library, is based on the `HandlerThread` that runs the unit of work serially.

- `HandlerScheduler.from(Handler)`: Creates a Scheduler that executes work on a specified `Handler`. The `AndroidSchedulers.mainThread()` is of specialization of this `Scheduler` that runs on a `Handler` attached to the Android UI thread.

> By default, `Rxjava` uses `Schedulers.immediate()`, which subscribes to the Observer on the current thread and delivers the events in the current thread.

RxJava allows us to define our own Scheduler, but for the scope of this book, we will only use the built-in Schedulers to cover our concurrency needs.

Performing IO operations with Schedulers

In the next example, we will use `Schedulers` to mirror the behavior of `AsyncTask` and retrieve text from the network on the background thread. Subsequently, the result will be published to a `Subscriber` that runs on the main `Thread`.

First of all, we will create a function that creates an Observable that emits the String retrieved from the network:

```
Observable<String> getTextFromNetwork(final String url) {

  return Observable.create(
    new Observable.OnSubscribe<String>() {
      @Override
      public void call(Subscriber<? super String> sub) {
        try {
          String text = downloadText(url);
          sub.onNext(text);
          sub.onCompleted();

        } catch (Throwable t) {
          sub.onError(t);
        }
      }
    }
  );
}
```

Before we specify the Scheduler used to run our asynchronous call, we need to state two assumptions:

- Since the code that runs on Observable performs a network operation we must run Observable on the background thread
- To publish the result and update the UI, we must execute our Subscriber callbacks on the main Thread

Now, let's build up the asynchronous RxJava execution that retrieves the text and update the UI following the previous assumptions and using the Scheduler entities described earlier:

```
class MySubscriber extends Subscriber<String> {

  @Override
  public void onCompleted() {}

  @Override
  public void onError(Throwable e) {
    // Shows a Toast on Error
    Toast.makeText(RxSchedulerActivity.this,
                   e.getMessage(),
                   Toast.LENGTH_LONG).show();
```

```
    Log.e(TAG, "Error retrieving ", e);
  }

  @Override
  public void onNext(String text) {
    // Updates the UI on Success
    EditText textFrame = (EditText)findViewById(R.id.text);
    textFrame.setText(text);
  }
};


  . . .


getTextFromNetwork("http://demo1472539.mockable.io/mytext")
  .subscribeOn(Schedulers.io())
  .observeOn(AndroidSchedulers.mainThread())
  .subscribe(new MySubscriber())
);
```

subscribeOn(Schedulers.io()) will make the Observable created by the getTextFromNetwork function run on the Scheduler.io thread pool intended for blocking IO operations.

Once we call the subscribe function, downloadText will be queued to run on a thread managed by the Scheduler created by Schedulers.io(), emitting the results as a String in the onNext() function.

The observeOn(AndroidSchedulers.mainThread()) ensures that the Subscriber callbacks onNext, onCompleted, and onError will run on the Android main Thread. Therefore, if the network operation completes with success, OnNext is invoked updating EditText with the result obtained.

If any exception is thrown during the network execution, a Throwable object is delivered to the Subscriber.onError callback, which executes on the UI Thread, and a Toast that shows an error is displayed on the UI.

This example shows how simple and concise an asynchronous call can be on RxJava. Moreover, it abstracts you from the thread management as AsyncTask does and provides you exception handling facilities to deal with exceptional errors.

Canceling subscriptions

When an Activity or a Fragment gets destroyed, our chain could continue to run in the background, preventing the Activity from being disposed if the chain has references to the Activity or Fragment. When you no longer need the result of the chain, it could make sense to cancel the subscription and terminate the chain execution.

When we call the `Observable.subscribe()` function, it returns a Subscription object that can be used to terminate the chain immediately:

```
Subscription subscription = getTextFromNetwork(
            "http://demo1472539.mockable.io/mytet")
            ...
            .subscribe(new MySubscriber());
```

Again, the most appropriate Activity lifecycle method for this is `onPause`, which is guaranteed to be called before the Activity finishes:

```
protected void onPause() {
  super.onPause();
  if ((subscription != null) && (isFinishing()))
    subscription.unsubscribe();
}
```

Composing Observables

As we explained earlier, an `Observable` interface is defined in a way that allows us to chain and combine different `Observables` to create complex tasks in a functional and declarative way.

Starting from our previous work, in our next example, we will make use of the `RxJava` composing feature and execute a second network call that depends on the previous `Observable` that will translate the text downloaded using a web service before we emit the translated text to the `Subscriber`.

To execute the translation on the network on a logically separate unit, we will create a new `Observable` that receives the text to translate, executes the task on the network, and emits the translated text as a String to the following `Observable`:

```
Observable<String> translateOnNetwork(final String url,
                                    final String toTranslate) {
  return Observable.create(
    new Observable.OnSubscribe<String>() {
      @Override
```

```
      public void call(Subscriber<? super String> ts){
        try {
          String text = translateText(
            "http://demo1472539.mockable.io/translate",
            toTranslate);

          sub.onNext(text);
          sub.onCompleted();
        } catch (Throwable t) {
          sub.onError(t);
        }
      }
    }
  );
}
```

Next, we are ready to chain the network executions and display the results on the UI using the same `Subscriber` used previously:

```
getTextFromNetwork(RETRIEVE_TEXT_URL)
  .flatMap(new Func1<String, Observable<String>>() {
    @Override
    public Observable<String> call(String toTranslate) {
      return translateOnNetwork(TRANSLATE_URL, toTranslate);
    }
  })
  .subscribeOn(Schedulers.io())
  .observeOn(AndroidSchedulers.mainThread())
  .subscribe(new MySubscriber());
```

The network IO operation defined on the `translateOnNetwork`, which depends on `getTextFromNetwork`, will only run if the previous operation finished with success, and takes the result from `getTextFromNetwork` as an argument.

After `translateOnNetwork` `Observable` receives the text content from the previous network operation, it will use it as input for its operation and will perform the translation of the previous content on the network, invoking the function `translateText(url, content)`.

Given that `translateText()` finishes with success, the translated content is delivered to the next Observable. Since the next Observable is the Subscriber, the result is delivered transparently on the main Thread to update the UI.

Besides that, since we override the Subscriber is onError function, if something goes wrong during the execution of either network requests, the error is propagated to our callback to be handled properly. Hence, with a few lines of code, we are able to inform the user that an asynchronous task has failed and we were not able to deliver the expected data to them.

Great, with a few lines of code we created a complex task that performs a chain of asynchronous network operations in the background, delivering the results on the main thread, or delivering an error when something goes wrong.

Monitoring the event stream

Although so far we have been using the Observable operators to manipulate stream events, there are operators that allow us to monitor the events without changing them. These operators, known sometimes as utility operators, are able to react to the events or errors emitted on the Observable chain created between the source Observable and the final Subscriber without creating any side effects.

Let's enumerate them and explain the more common utility operators used to observe the event stream:

- doOnSubscribe(Action0): Registers an Action0 function to get called when a Subscriber subscribes to the Observable.

- doOnUnsubscribe(Action0): Registers an Action0 function to get called when a Subscriber unsubscribes from the Observable.

- doOnNext(Action1): Registers an Action1 to be called when a new event is emitted from the source Observable. The Event <T> object is also passed as an argument to the Action1 function.

- doOnCompleted(Action0): Registers an Action0 function to be called when the source Observable emits the onComplete event.

- doOnError(Action1): Registers an Action1 function to be called when an error is emitted from the source Observable. The Throwable emitted on the OnError is also passed to the Action1.call function.

- doOnTerminate(Action0): Registers an Action0 function to be invoked when an error or onComplete is emitted by the source Observable. This callback function also means that the previous Observable will emit no more items.

These multipurpose operators will allow us to observe and debug complex chains that usually involve several transformations, create progress dialogs to show progress, cache results, and even generate processing analytics.

In our next example, we will make use of these operators to log the progress of our previous multi network operation in the Android Log, and to present a progress dialog on screen as long as the operation is progressing:

```
Observable.just(RETRIEVE_TEXT_URL)
  .doOnNext(new Action1<String>() { // Runing on the main Thread
    @Override
    public void call(String url) {
      progress = ProgressDialog.show(RxSchedulerActivity.this,
                  "Loading",
                  "Performing async operation", true);
      Log.i(TAG, "Network IO Operation will start "+ tmark());
    }
  })
  .observeOn(Schedulers.io()) // Running on a background Thread
  .flatMap(new Func1<String, Observable<String>>() {
    @Override
    public Observable<String> call(String url) {
      return getTextFromNetwork(url);
    }
  })
  .doOnNext(new Action1<String>() {
    @Override
    public void call(String text) {
      Log.i(TAG, "Text retrieved w/ success " + tMark());
      Log.i(TAG, "Translating the text " + tMark());
    }
  })
  .flatMap(new Func1<String, Observable<String>>() {
    @Override
    public Observable<String> call(String toTranslate) {
      return translateOnNetwork(TRANSLATE_URL, toTranslate);
    }
  })
  .doOnNext(new Action1<String>() {
    @Override
    public void call(String translatedText) {
      Log.i(TAG, "Translation finished " + tMark());
    }
  })
  .observeOn(
    AndroidSchedulers.mainThread() // Executing on main Thread
  )
  .doOnTerminate(new Action0() {
```

```
    @Override
    public void call() {
      if (progress != null)
        progress.dismiss();
      Log.i(TAG, "Dismissing dialog " + tMark());
    }
  })
  // Starts the execution on the main Thread
  .subscribeOn(AndroidSchedulers.mainThread())
  .subscribe(new MySubscriber());
```

As you know, to make changes in the Android UI, it is imperative to run your code on the main Thread. Hence, in order to receive doOnNext from the first Observable in the main thread, we invoke subscribeOn() with AndroidSchedulers. mainThread() forcing the first Observable, the one created with the just operator, to emit notifications to doOnNext in the main Thread.

As soon as doOnNext() receives the notification with the String carrying the URL to retrieve the text, we display ProgressDialog in the UI and we log a message in the Android Log.

Next, since we want to perform network operations off the main thread, using the observeOn operator, we force following Observables to send notifications to the threads managed by the IO Scheduler. This means that the following operators and Observables will execute and emit events in the IO Scheduler threads.

In the meantime, between each network operation, we intercept the start of the second network operation to print the message in Android with a doOnNext between getTextFromNetwork and translateOnNetwork Observables.

When the network operations finish, and before we update the UI with the results and we dismiss the progress dialog, we switch the execution to the main thread by again invoking the operator observeOn() with the main Thread Scheduler.

Before we display the results on the screen, with the doOnTerminate operator we register an Action function to be called to dismiss the progress dialog previously started. As described before, the function will be invoked, whether the chain terminates with success or with an error.

At the end, the Subscriber callbacks will be invoked to update the UI with the results returned or to show an error message.

If the network operation terminates with success you should see a similar logging stream in the Android Log:

```
...54.390 I Network IO Operation will start T[main]
...54.850 I Text retrieved w/ success T[RxCachedThreadScheduler-1]
...54.850 I Translating the text T[RxCachedThreadScheduler-1]
...55.160 I Translation finished T[RxCachedThreadScheduler-1]
...55.200 I Dismissing dialog on T[main]
```

For debugging purposes, [<Thread_Name>] shows the name of the thread that logged the message.

Combining Observables

In the previous example, we used two Observable to create a simple sequence of network operations. The second asynchronous operation operated with the result of the first operation and the two operations that executed serially produced a String result that updates the UI.

In our next example, we will run two tasks in parallel and combine the results of both operations using a combining RxJava operator. Each operation will retrieve asynchronously a JSON Object from the network and combine both results in the JSON Object to produce the JSON String passed to the UI main Thread.

Since we only want to emit one Event or an error from the operation, we are going to use, for the first time, a special kind of Observer, Single.

While an Observable is able to invoke onNext, onError, and onCompleted Observer functions, a Single entity will only invoke either onSuccess or onError to a SingleSubscriber:

```
// Success callback invoked on success
void onSuccess(T value);

// Callback to notify that an unrecoverable error has occurred
void onError(Throwable error);
```

After one of the callback functions is called, the Single finishes and the subscription to it ends. Like a regular Observable, the Single object emitted event can be processed with operators before it reaches the final SingleSubscriber.

Now, let's define the two `Single` operations that retrieve a single `JSONObject` from the network:

```
Single<JSONObject> postSingle = Single.create(
  new Single.OnSubscribe<JSONObject>() {
    @Override
    public void call(SingleSubscriber<? super JSONObject> sub) {
      try {
        // Retrieve the Post content JSON Object
        sub.onSuccess(
         getJson("http://demo1472539.mockable.io/post"));
      } catch (Throwable t) {
        sub.onError(t);
      }
    }
  }
).subscribeOn(Schedulers.newThread());

Single<JSONObject> authorSingle = Single.create(
  new Single.OnSubscribe<JSONObject>() {
    @Override
    public void call(SingleSubscriber<? super JSONObject> sub) {
      try {
        // Retrieve the Author content JSON Object
        sub.onSuccess(
          getJson("http://demo1472539.mockable.io/author"));
      } catch (Throwable t) {
        sub.onError(t);
      }
    }
  }
).subscribeOn(Schedulers.newThread());
```

Like we did for the previous `Observable`, we used the `Single.create` static function to build a custom `Single` entity that either explicitly calls the `SingleSubscriber.onSuccess` function when the network operation finishes with success, or calls the `SingleSubscriber.onError` function when an error is thrown on the `getJson` IO operation.

The `getJSON` function will basically retrieve a JSON Object by connecting to the HTTP URL provided as an argument and return a `JSONObject`.

By forcing the Single to `subscribeOn` the `newThread` `Sheduler`, we are allowing each custom `Single` entity to run their operation concurrently on a new thread.

Since the two operations will run in parallel, we need to use the combining operator to combine the `Single` results together in a single `JSONObject` and emit the resulting JSON `String` to the final `SingleSubscriber`. The appropriate combining operator for our example is zip, because it is able to wait for the result of two or more `Single/Observable` and apply a function to each `Single` output object.

The function that receives the emitted objects as an argument can produce a result of the same type or of a different type.

This is the `zip` operator function definition for combining two Singles into a `Single<R>`:

```
Single<R> zip(Single<T1> o1, // First Single
              Single<T2> o2, // Second Single
              final Func2<T1,T2,R> zipFunction)
```

In our example, R is a String, T1 and T2 are a `JSONObject`, and `zipFunction` receives the `JSONObjects` arguments to generate a `String` as the result.

Now we are ready to use the `zip` operator and combine the result of each independent asynchronous operation into a `String`. The resulting string will update a `Widget`, so the final `Subscriber` should be invoked in the main Thread.

Let's write the functional code that fetches the `JSONObject` parts and dispatches the resulting `String` to the UI:

```
Single.zip(postSingle, authorSingle,
           new Func2<JSONObject, JSONObject, String>() {
  @Override
  public String call(JSONObject post, JSONObject author) {
    String result = null;

    // Create the Root JSON Object
    JSONObject rootObj = new JSONObject();
    try {
      // Add the post object to root JSON Object
      rootObj.put("post", post);
      // Add the author object to root JSON Object
      rootObj.put("author", author);
      // Save the JSON Object, Encode the JSON Object
      // into a String
      result = rootObj.toString(2);
    } catch (Exception e) {
      Exceptions.propagate(e);
    }
```

```
      return result;
    }
  })
  .observeOn(AndroidSchedulers.mainThread())
  .subscribe(subscriber);
```

Using the zip operator, we combined the result of the two operations, `postSingle` and `authorSingle`, that ran on a new thread created by the `newThread` Scheduler, on the `Func2` that received the two `JSONObjects` as arguments and produced a `String`.

Since we subscribed the `Single` to work on its own Thread, the `zip` function will combine the result of both `Singles` on the thread built by the last defined Single (`authorSingle`) resulting in a log similar to the following output:

```
.040 I ...: Getting the Post Object on RxNewThreadScheduler-1
.050 I ...: Getting the Author Object on RxNewThreadScheduler-2
.660 I ...: Combining objects on RxNewThreadScheduler-2
```

After combining the objects, the `String` produced by `Func2` is delivered to the final `Subscriber` in the main `Thread`.

All that remains is to implement the trivial `SingleSubscriber` that updates the UI:

```
SingleSubscriber<String> subscriber =
  new SingleSubscriber<String>() {
  ...
  @Override
  public void onSuccess(String result) { // Updates the UI }
};
```

Observing UI Events with RxJava

So far, we have been using `RxJava` to process and manipulate data streams, which simplified the development of asynchronous that require IO blocking operations that will hang the application for a while.

In this section, we want to explain how to use `RxJava` and reactive streams to simplify the handling of UI events generated from Android Widgets.

In our next example, we will present a list of Soccer Teams with an instant search result input field. As you type in the input field, the names available in the list will be filtered if the text that you typed matches the beginning of any soccer team on the list.

To achieve the result required, we will create a custom `Observable` that attaches a `TextWatcher` to the searching input field, listens for `onTextChanged` events, and emits a String event when the text changes.

The Observer will feed a reactive functional stream that will filter our list of teams in a Recycler View.

First, we will write a Custom Observable that registers `TextWatcher` to `EditField` when an `Observer` subscribes, and deregisters `TextWatcher` when the subscription finishes:

```
public class TextChangeOnSubscribe
  implements OnSubscribe<String> {
  // Don't Prevent the GC from recycling the Activity
  WeakReference<EditText> editText;

  // Receive the EditText View to verify Changes
  public TextChangeOnSubscribe(EditText editText) {
    this.editText = new WeakReference<EditText>(editText);
  }

  @Override
  public void call(final Subscriber<? super String> subscriber) {
    final TextWatcher watcher = new TextWatcher() {

      @Override
      public void onTextChanged(
        CharSequence s, int start, int before, int count) {

        // Emit a new String when the text changes
        if (!subscriber.isUnsubscribed()) {
          subscriber.onNext(s.toString());
        }
      }
    };
    // Remove the Text change Watcher when the subscription ends
    subscriber.add(new MainThreadSubscription() {
      @Override
      protected void onUnsubscribe() {
        editText.get().removeTextChangedListener(watcher);
      }
    });
    // Sets the Watcher on the EditField
    editText.get().addTextChangedListener(watcher);
```

```
        subscriber.onNext("");
    }
};


...
EditText search = (EditText) findViewById(R.id.searchTv);
Observable<String> textChangeObs = Observable.
    create(new TextChangeOnSubscribe(search))
                                            .debounce(400,
TimeUnit.MILLISECONDS);
```

The `TextChangeOnSubscribe` class, which implements the `OnSubscribe<String>`
and receives a subscription callback, will set a `TextWatcher` in the received
`EditField` once the subscription is performed by the `Subscriber`.

When `TextWatcher.onTextChanged` is invoked to notify a text change in `EditField`,
a new String event with the new content should be emitted in the Subscriber.

To unregister the `TextWatcher` in the `EditField`, we add a
`MainThreadSubscription` anonymous class to the subscriber list that removes our
`TextChangeListener` in the `EditField`.

To prevent the text change event from generating too many updates in the UI, we
used the `debounce` operator to only emit a new search term if there's been a 400
millisecond delay since the last text change event.

Next, we will use the search Events generated by our `Observable` to filter the teams
available in the `ReciclerView` list:

```
List<String> soccerTeams = Arrays.asList(
    "Real Madrid","Barcelona","Sporting CP",...,"Chelsea");


subcription = Observable.combineLatest(
    // Observables
    Observable.just(soccerTeams), textChangeObs,
    // Combine Function
    new Func2<List<String>, String, List<String>>() {

        // Filter the list with the filter String and sort the list
        @Override
        public List<String> call(List<String> fullList,
                                    String filter){
            List<String> result = new ArrayList<String>();
            for (String team : fullList) {
```

```
            if (team.startsWith(filter)) {
              result.add(team);
            }
          }
          // Sort the Collection
          Collections.sort(result);
          return result;
        }
    })
  .observeOn(AndroidSchedulers.mainThread())
    .subscribe(new Action1<List<String>>() {
      @Override
      public void call(List<String> teams) {
        // Update the Recycler View with a filtered list of Teams
        mAdapter = new MyAdapter(teams);
        mRecyclerView.setAdapter(mAdapter);
      }
    });
```

To filter the soccer team list with the search term emitted by the `textChangeEvent` we applied the operator `combineLatest` to `textChangeObs` Observable and to the `Observable` created from the soccer team list with the operator just.

The `combineLatest` will combine the latest item emitted by each `Observable` using a specified function and emit items based on the results of this function invocation.

The function that combines both `Observables` will simply filter the soccer list with the last text content emitted by the `onTextChanged` and sort the resulting list.

To finalize, a new `RecyclerView.Adapter` is created with the resulting `List<String>` and the filtered list of teams will be displayed to the user.

Notice that to update our `RecyclerView` with the resulting filtered list, we explicitly set the `Observer` to run on the main Thread by passing the Android main Thread `Scheduler` to the `observeOn` operator.

 Don't forget to terminate the subscription before the Activity is destroyed by calling `subcription.unsubscribe()`;

Although, for educational purposes, we built our own Observables from the Android EditField Widget text change events, there is an easy-to-use, open source library named RxBinding (`https://github.com/JakeWharton/RxBinding`) that is able to create Observables for most Android Widgets available on the Android SDK.

If you don't want to implement your own Observables, or process UI events in a traditional way, you can make use of it to process Android UI events using a functional RxJava reactive paradigm.

Working with Subjects

So far, we have been working with `Observables`, `Subscriber`, `Observer`, and `Scheduler` entities to create our `RxJava` functional processing lines. In this section, we will introduce the reader to a new kind of entity in the `RxJava` framework, the `Subject`. The `Subject` is a sort of adapter or bridge entity that acts as an `Observable` and `Observer`:

```
public abstract class    Subject<T,R>
                extends     Observable<R>
                implements Observer<T>
```

Since it can act as a `Subscriber`, it can subscribe to one or more `Observables` that emit `Objects` of the generic type `T`, and since it acts as an `Observable`, it can emit events of the generic type `R` and receive subscriptions from other `Subscriber`. Hence, it can emit events of the same type as received or emit a different type of event.

For example, the `Subject<String, Integer>` will receive events of type `String` and emit events of the type `Integer`.

The `Subject` could receive the events from the `Observable` and generate a new event stream with different timings, proxy the events, convert to a new kind of event, queue the events, transform the events, or even generate new events.

A `Subject` is always considered a hot `Observable` and will begin emitting events as soon as it is created. This is a very important `Subject` feature and you should consider it when you want to process the full event stream sequence.

RxJava comes with some standard **Subject** classes designed to be used in distinctive use cases. The list below will enumerate the most common ones:

- `AsyncSubject`: Subjects that will only emit the last item emitted by the source `Observable` when the source `Observer` completes the stream by calling `onComplete()`
- `PublishSubject`: The Subject only delivers to the Observers the events emitted after their subscription

- `ReplaySubject`: Emits all the events emitted by the source `Observable`, even those that were emitted before the subscription is made
- `BehaviorSubject`: Emits the last emitted item by the source `Observable` when the subscription is done, then continues to any other items emitted by the source observable

In the following example, we will show you how to use `PublishSubject` and demonstrate how the events are propagated to a final `Observer` that subscribes and later unsubscribes to the `Subject`. Moreover, we will submit events to `Subject` before and after the subscription is made:

```
PublishSubject<Integer> pubSubject = PublishSubject.create();
pubSubject.onNext(1);
pubSubject.onNext(2);
Subscription subscription = pubSubject.doOnSubscribe(new Action0() {
  @Override
  public void call() {
    Log.i(TAG, "Observer subscribed to PublishSubject");
  }
}).doOnUnsubscribe(new Action0() {
  @Override
  public void call() {
    Log.i(TAG, "Observer unsubscribed to PublishSubject");
  }
}).subscribe(new Action1<Integer>() {
  @Override
  public void call(Integer integer) {
    Log.i(TAG, "New Event received from PublishSubject: " + integer);
  }
});
pubSubject.onNext(3);
pubSubject.onNext(4);
subscription.unsubscribe();
pubSubject.onNext(5);
pubSubject.onCompleted();
```

First, we created the `PublishSubject` by calling the `PublishSubject.create` static function, and then we started delivering integers to it and calling the `onNext` function.

In the meantime, we subscribed to the `Subject` with an `Action1` function in order to consume the events.

To print the exact time when the subscription and unsubscription is made, we provided an `Action0` function to the `doOnUnsubscribe` and `doOnSubscribe` that prints a message to the Android Log.

As a result, the code above should output the following output:

```
...  43.230 I Observer subscribed to PublishSubject
...  43.230 I New Event received from PublishSubject: 3
...  43.230 I New Event received from PublishSubject: 4
...  43.230 I Observer unsubscribed to PublishSubject
```

As described before, only the events dispatched while the final `Observer` is subscribed are emitted to the `Action` callback. Therefore, the events submitted before the subscriptions and after the unsubscription are not received by our Subscriber.

Now, for comparison, let's try to compare the event stream emitted by a `ReplaySubject`, with the exact sequence of events submitted to the Subject.

Again, the `ReplaySubject` class was built by calling the create static function, and as a result, you should see the following output:

```
.600 I Observer subscribed to ReplaySubject
.600 I New Event received from ReplaySubject: 1
.600 I New Event received from ReplaySubject: 2
.600 I New Event received from ReplaySubject: 3
.600 I New Event received from ReplaySubject: 4
.600 I Observer unsubscribed to ReplaySubject
```

On the `http://reactivex.io/documentation/subject.html` website, there are diagrams to help you understand graphically the interactions between Subjects, Subscribers, and source Observables.

As expected, `ReplaySubject` will receive all the events submitted to the `Subject`, even the ones delivered before the subscription was made are received by the `Observer`. After the `Observer` unsubscribes, it stops receiving the events from the `Subject`.

As an exercise, you can try to create the same for the `AsyncSubject` and `BehaviorSubject`.

Summary

In this final chapter, we learned how to use RxJava, an open source library that helps to process our Android application data or event streams using functional and reactive processing pipelines.

In the first sections, we learned in detail some of RxJava basic building blocks— Observable, Observer, and Subscriber.

Next, we introduced some of RxJava most common operators that are able to manipulate, transform, and combine event streams generated by an Observable.

In order to perform operations asynchronously and concurrently, we learned about the Scheduler, a magic RxJava entity that controls the concurrency, and is able to schedule RxJava units of work to run in background threads and feed the results back to the main Android Thread.

Next, using custom Observables and combining operators, we learned how to associate and compose interdependent complex blocking or long computing operations, such as REST API network operation.

In the meantime, we also learned how to react to a custom Observable that emits Android Widget UI events using a RxJava event functional pipeline.

Finally, we learned about the Subject RxJava entity, an entity that can act as an Observer and Observable and can act as a proxy between our source Observable and the final Observer.

Over the course of this book, we've armed ourselves with a powerful array of tools for building responsive Android applications. We discovered that it is incredibly important to move as much work as possible off the main thread, and explored a number of constructs and asynchronous techniques to make the smoothest and most awesome experience for your users.

Remember that to keep your application responsive and avoid any UI lost frames, an Android callback (Service, Activity, and so on) that runs on the main UI Thread should terminate in under 16 ms.

Index

setting up, for application 296, 297
Google GSON library
  reference link 228
Greenwich Mean Time (GMT) 168

H

HTTP requests
  interacting, with JSON web APIs 227, 228
  performing, asynchronously 218-224
  reference link 238
  text response, retrieving 225-227
  XML web APIs, interacting with 234, 235
HTTP timeouts
  customizing 241, 243
HTTP uploads
  with IntentService 144
Hybrid Service 130

I

indeterministic progress feedback
  providing 69-71
inheritance 53
input/output (I/O) 7
IntentService
  applications 143
  HTTP uploads 144-146
  progress, reporting 146-149
  used, for building responsive apps 136-138
Internal Remote Service (IRS) 131
Internet Engineering Task Force (IETF) 216
inter-process communication (IPC)
      technique 27, 150
IO operations
  performing, Schedulers used 351-353

J

Java code
  C functions, calling 256-259
Java exceptions
  handling, in native layer 280
Java monitor
  interacting with, from native code 283-286
  native data objects, wrapping 287-291
Java Native Interface (JNI) 254

Java objects
  accessing, from native code 262-264
Java threads
  native background work, executing 265-269
job
  cancelling 211
  pending jobs, listing 208-210
  periodic job, scheduling 211, 212
  scheduling 200-202
JobScheduler
  about 196
  applications 212
  features 196, 197
  job, scheduling 200-202
  running criteria, setting 197-200
JobService
  implementing 203-207
JSONPlaceHolder
  reference link 231, 232
JSON web APIs
  interacting with 227, 228
  Java objects, converting to JSON 228-233
Just-In-Time (JIT) compilation 3

L

Least-Recently-Used (LRU) 5
Linux user ID (UID) 6
Loader API
  about 96
  Loader 97
  Loader Manager 98
  LoaderManager.LoaderCallbacks 99
Loaders
  about 96
  applications 125
  combining 119-124
  Lifecycle 100
  used, for loading data 101-107
Local Service (LS) 131
Looper
  about 32, 33
  composition, versus inheritance 52, 53
  explicit references, leaking 43, 44
  Handler, applications 59
  Handler class 34-37

applications 163
bound service 130
hybrid service 130
started service 130-135
SimpleXML
reference link 235
Software as a Service (SaaS) 241
SSL sessions
setting up 244
used for secure communications 243-251
started service
about 131-135
IntentService, applications 143
issues 25, 26
responsive apps building, IntentService
used 136-138
results, handling 139
results, posting as system
notifications 142, 143
results posting, PendingIntent
used 139-141
sticking events
posting 334-338
removing 338
Subjects
working with 366-368
subscribers
about 322
registering 326, 327
Subscriptions
cancelling 354

T

tasks
executing, GCM Network Manager
used 315, 316

thread ID (TID) 7
thread mode 327-333

U

UI Events
observing, RxJava used 362-366
UI/Main thread 8
unhandled broadcasts
detecting 160
upstream messages
setting up 310-313
user identifier (UID) 6

W

WakeLocks
used, for staying awake 188-190
Window Alarm
setting 173
World Wide Web Consortium (W3C) 216

X

XML web APIs
interacting with 234, 235
Java objects, converting to XML 235, 236
XML, converting to Java objects 237-241

Z

Zygote 4

www.ingramcontent.com/pod-product-compliance
Lightning Source LLC
LaVergne TN
LVHW081330050326
832903LV00024B/1101